The N~~on-Thera~~pist

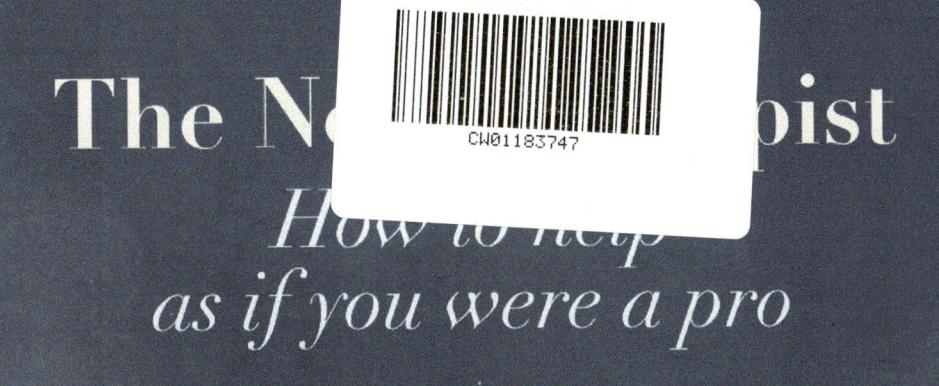

How to help as if you were a pro

Kate Tompkins
MEd RCT

with significant contributions from

Chaplain Christina Baxter MTS BCC

© 2024 Kate Tompkins

All rights reserved. No part of this book may be reproduced or transmitted in any form or by any means, electronic or mechanical, including photocopying, or by any information storage or retrieval system, without permission in writing from the publisher.

Cover design: Rebekah Wetmore, using art by Gianna Pellerin

Editor: Andrew Wetmore

ISBN: 978-1-998149-68-1
First edition November, 2024

MOOSE HOUSE PUBLICATIONS

Moose House Publicatons
2475 Perotte Road
Annapolis County, NS B0S 1A0
moosehousepress.com
info@moosehousepress.com

Moose House Publications recognizes the support of the Province of Nova Scotia. We are pleased to work in partnership with the Department of Communities, Culture and Heritage to develop and promote our cultural resources for all Nova Scotians.

We live and work in Mi'kma'ki, the ancestral and unceded territory of the Mi'kmaw people. This territory is covered by the "Treaties of Peace and Friendship" which Mi'kmaw and Wolastoqiyik (Maliseet) people first signed with the British Crown in 1725. The treaties did not deal with surrender of lands and resources but in fact recognized Mi'kmaq and Wolastoqiyik (Maliseet) title and established the rules for what was to be an ongoing relationship between nations. We are all Treaty people.

For whom the bell tolls

No man is an island,
Entire of itself.
Each is a piece of the continent,
A part of the main.
If a clod be washed away by the sea,
Europe is the less.
As well as if a promontory were.
As well as if a manor of thine own
Or of thine friend's were.
Each man's death diminishes me,
For I am involved in mankind.
Therefore, send not to know
For whom the bell tolls,
It tolls for thee.

John Donne

Dedications

Kate:
This book is dedicated to a young man named Brian, whom I failed when I was still a wet-behind-the ears helper, 50 years ago. May there never be another helper who does not know how to respond to suicidal crisis. May there never be another young man who feels he has no options. You taught me a great deal, Brian.

Christina:
To ACPE Certified Educator, Chaplain Gerald Jones MA, BCC; Chaplain Lynne Gilbertson BCC; Chaplain David Faudree BCC; and Chaplain Ben Curry BCC in appreciation for who you are, what you do every day, and what you taught me. Thank you!

This material is as comprehensive as the authors could make it,
and is accurate to the best wisdom available at the time of writing.

The Non-Therapist

1: What is this book about?..11
    What do informal helpers do?...12
    Why do we need this book now?...12
    Who is this book for?...14
    What is in this book?...16
    Terms and assumptions...18
    Key take-away points..18
2: What on earth should we do?...19
    What is my role as a lay counsellor?...19
    Your agenda...23
    What are the risks for frontline workers and lay counsellors?..................................24
    Key take-away points..27
    Exercises and activities...27
3: Effective listening fundamentals..28
    Just be there, with your empathy hat on...28
    Authenticity: A matter of balance...31
    It's not about me..35
    Have faith in people..36
    Use plain language..37
    Don't touch me!...37
    Start from where the client is today..38
    Everyone is an onion...40
    Confidentiality and anonymity are key...49
    Super(wo)man does not live here..50
    A happy ending? Not always!...51
    Separate the person from the problem..52
    When should I call in the big guns?..53
    Where can I refer my client for more help?..56
    Rapid self care...57
    Key take-away points..58
    Activities to consolidate your learning...58
4: What on earth should I say?...59
    Key Skill 1: Listen actively...59
    Key Skill 2: The body cannot lie..64
    Key Skill 3: Ask helpful questions..70
    Key Skill 4: Be a mirror for your client..78
    Key Skill 5: Avoid giving advice..87
    Key Skill 6: Avoid self-disclosure..88
    Key Skill 7: Probe, summarize, reframe and confront helpfully..............................89
    Rapid creation of trust, connection and cooperation..95

- Key take-away points ... 96
- Activities to consolidate your learning ... 96

5: Freebies to swipe ... 100
- Tools for exploring the past ... 101
- Tools for exploring relationships ... 105
- Tools for creating a better future ... 133
- Tools for improving mental health and awareness ... 138
- Self-regulation tools ... 145
- Triage and response tools ... 152
- Key take-away points ... 158
- Activities to consolidate your learning ... 158

6: What should I expect? ... 159
- Suicidal thinking ... 159
- Self-harm ... 168
- Trauma and past trauma ... 169
- Emotional crisis ... 174
- Intimate partner violence ... 180
- Depression ... 185
- Grief ... 190
- Anxiety ... 196
- Loneliness ... 199
- Sexual assault ... 203
- Substance abuse ... 208
- Child protection concerns ... 215
- Social justice issues ... 215
- Multiple issues ... 218
- Key take-away points ... 220
- Activities to consolidate your learning ... 220

7: Plan and structure for a helping encounter ... 222
- Key take-away points ... 233
- Activities to consolidate your learning ... 233

8: Wrap-up ... 234
- How can I assess my skills? ... 234
- Self-Assessment Quiz ... 235
- Self-Assessment Quiz discussion ... 237
- How can I learn new skills? ... 241
- Key take-away points ... 244
- The final words ... 244
- Acknowledgements ... 247
- About the authors ... 249

The Non-Therapist

Kate Tompkins

1: What is this book about?

My buddy Duncan (that's not his real name) attached his vacuum cleaner hose to his car exhaust, taped up the windows, pushed play on his favourite music, turned on the car, and fell asleep. Permanently.

Duncan's suicide made big waves in our small Arctic town of 300 souls. His widow was shocked and devastated. His friends were bereft. There were many conversations that started more or less like this: "He seemed okay, getting by, as well as any of us do. So if this could happen to him, what about me...?"

There was nobody "official" to help. We had a nursing station, staffed by some pretty dedicated, overworked nurses, but no mental health team. We were on our own. I was the closest thing to a counsellor in town in those days, and I was impacted by Duncan's death, too.

So we helped each other. One family opened their home to the widow, who sheltered quietly for several days until she got her feet back under her again. I provided some counselling support for the widow and for the supporting family and some friends.

> I was able to help when Duncan killed himself. His wife stayed with me for a while after and I kept her company while she got her feet back under her.

A year or so later, some of the town residents decided they wanted some training in how to respond appropriately to their friends and neighbours. I was contracted, via a government grant, to train them, and from that training, a community-driven volunteer support group emerged.

In my more than fifty years as a therapist and adult educator, I have encountered more than one Duncan, more than one small community in crisis, and helped create community support groups, peer counselling groups, local shelters and crisis support phone lines. I have taught counselling skills to frontline workers, including nurses, social workers, addiction counsellors, supervisors and union shop stewards; and on-line in-service courses for therapists.

Throughout, one inescapable fact shone through consistently: the best supporters, the folks that others seek out to talk about their troubles are often just folks. Not pros with several degrees behind their names (when there happen to be some about and available), but friends and neighbours who listen and who care.

There are many titles for these compassionate individuals: informal helpers, lay counsellors, peer counsellors, supportive listeners, frontline workers, and paraprofessionals. And the movement is growing. Empathetic listeners may not be able to solve every problem. But they can help to improve the lives of many people.

What do informal helpers do?

They listen, mostly. They offer companionship, a hand to hold, human support, help with common-sense problem solving and decision making. They educate and guide people through challenging life events. If more help is needed, they refer to a pro who can help in specialized ways. For all you informal helpers out there, this book is for you!

Now I don't want you paraprofessionals to feel left out. Nurses, social workers, clergy and EMTs; chaplains and doctors and physio and occupational therapists; supervisors, union shop stewards, and HR people. You are all pros in your own field. You may also offer counselling, but not necessarily as your main gig. All of you perform the same exceptionally important and valuable service, without being professional therapists. I salute you all. This book is for you, too!

There are countless legions of people looking for support, and lay counsellors and paraprofessionals can be that trusted resource.

Recent studies show that advanced education and professional designations are not very good predictors of who will be able to connect deeply with a client and inspire them to want to come back for more. What matters is the ability to be compassionate, to understand what a client is feeling and respond in an authentic and human way.

The American Counseling Association (ACA) defines counseling as "a professional relationship that empowers diverse individuals, families, and groups to accomplish mental health, wellness, education, and career goals." So what exactly is lay counseling, and how does it differ from professional cousnelling? Lay counsellors do not need to be licensed by a governing body or the government. They have a desire to help others, and may be trained and supervised by a professional therapist, such as a psychologist or psychotherapist. Their goal may be to assist someone with getting through a tough time in their life, improve a relationship, access local resources, make a change in their life, make an important decision, or perhaps to find ways to cope with life in a healthy way. The questions or issues a lay counsellor might help with are as numerous as pebbles on a beach. If it is a human concern about life, lay counsellors may choose to help. Often, lay counsellors work together with NGOs, police, churches, professional therapists and others to provide a broad support net for people in need of assistance to lighten their burdens.

Why do we need this book now?

There are several reasons why this book is needed right now. Let's take a look at the circumstances that point to the need for informal compassionate helpers.

In Canada and the US, and perhaps in similar countries, the mental health system is in disarray. There are simply not enough professional therapists and government funded services to help all of the people that need to be helped. Non- government organizations (NGOs) are trying valiantly to fill some of the gaps, but with precarious funding being suspended or eliminated, many of these agencies are either closing or are stretched so thin that responding to people in need at the local level is more difficult every day. For therapists, that means that some of the community resources we might have sent people to in the past, are either no longer available, or they are unable to keep up to the demand for their services.

The issue is complicated, and it has been going on for some time. Many people with mental health issues and everyday life issues feel lost and abandoned because they don't know how or where to access help.

Mental health concerns are escalating in North America. Anxiety has always been a popular issue, and seems to be on the rise, partly due to COVID 19. Roughly 1 in 5 people suffer from anxiety. The overall suicide rate in the U.S. has increased by 31% since 2001. In Canada, 90% of suicides are by people who are already suffering from a mental health issue, and for every suicide death, there are 25 to 30 attempts. In 2019, approximately 4.4 million Canadians (14%) reported having a diagnosed mood or anxiety disorder.

There are frequently competing demands dumped on frontline workers. For example, how can a busy nurse take the time to engage with a noisy demanding family while trying to support a dying patient? Right now, health practitioners are feeling overwhelmed with the task of caring for physically ill patients, so looking out for the emotional needs of those who can breathe safely are less critical.

> Once a woman I did not recognize stopped me on the street and made my day with these words: "Kate, you may not remember me, I was in one of your courses about 10 years ago. What you said changed my life. I just wanted you to know. Thank you."
>
> I had no idea what I had said years earlier that had impacted her, but clearly it was significant for her. Then she moved on and I glowed for some time afterwards.
>
> That is why I do what I do.

How can police support victims of spousal assault while also managing the abuser, if NGO services such as a victims' support group are unavailable? How does a union shop steward support a stressed out employee while trying to uphold a workplace policy such as drug or alcohol use affecting work performance? It can be a balancing act.

One more issue to look at: professional therapy can be quite expensive, placing it out of the reach of many people. Too often, employment benefit plans and extended health care insurance plans are fairly limited, making it tough to access ongoing counselling. So where can people turn?

It seems that helpers of all types and at all levels are being called on to do more with less.

Some frontline workers are being asked to step into counselling roles that they may be unfamiliar with or don't have the time to do. Or maybe their training was ages ago, and lacking current practice, their skills are rusty. Counselling may be added on top of their usual responsibilities, so how do folks in that situation do a good job of supporting while also trying to look after their usual tasks?

Some people just don't feel comfortable going to see a professional therapist. Perhaps there is discomfort with the idea of appearing weak or of wasting time or money and yet feeling like they are getting nowhere. There have been conversations for decades in the psychotherapy community about how helpful professional help actually is. There are many people to whom therapy seems like nothing short of voodoo or charlatan nonsense. As a therapist, I am not about to knock therapy. I think that an experienced well-informed therapist can be extremely helpful. But does it always take someone with several degrees behind their name to be helpful? In my opinion, no.

This all means that others are being called on to pick up the slack. There is a gap crying out to be filled. And it can be filled by warm, compassionate people who are not professional therapists. The fact is, **it does not require a boat load of fancy skills and degrees to be helpful. It takes compassion, common sense, authenticity, empathy and a few key skills.**

Who is this book for?

This book is for helpers who are not professionally trained therapists, but find themselves counselling anyway. People like you, ordinary folks, who want to create an informal, community-based peer counselling service. It is also for people in helping roles and professions who have not received comprehensive, or recent training in counselling skills, but find themselves counselling folks anyway.

Some of you will be volunteers. Some will be working on their own, but most volunteers will be working with others in an informal community group, a not-for-profit organization or agency, such as a mental health service, or a shelter, or an institution, such as a hospital, a rehab clinic or a school.

Some of you will be salaried (or otherwise supported financially), working in jobs that help or support people in some way, either as the main task in your job description, an occasional requirement, or as an "extra" or unanticipated task in your day.

You will find useful information in this book if your job or volunteer title is something like the examples on the next page:

- Addiction worker
- Career coach
- Chaplain
- Childcare/ protection worker
- Chiropractor
- Church worker, volunteer, elder
- Clergy
- Coach
- Community workers
- Corrections officer
- Crisis intervention worker
- Elder
- Elected official
- EMTs
- Family services worker
- Frontline worker
- Funeral director
- Group leader
- Hairdresser
- Housing support worker
- HR officer
- Informal helper
- Instructor
- Lay counsellor
- Lawyer
- Listener
- Mental health worker
- Mentor
- Nurse/LPN
- Orderly
- Paraprofessional
- Parent, foster parent
- Parole/probation officer
- Peer counsellor
- Personal care assistant
- Personal trainer
- Physio/occupational/ speech therapist
- Physician
- Police officer
- Problem solver
- Recreation worker
- Rehab counsellor
- Shelter worker
- Social Worker
- Spiritual guide
- Street Worker
- Supervisor
- Supporter
- Teacher, trainer, tutor
- Union shop steward
- Victim services worker
- Youth worker

You may be in a role that would not normally be considered a helping role, but you find yourself wanting to offer some support to a customer, client, patient, neighbour, or friend.

Professional helpers will find useful tips, too. Maybe your professional training was ages ago and a refresher is needed, or maybe your preparation did not include counselling skills in any depth.

If you are a professional therapist, with a regular practice, you already have the skills in this book in your toolbox.

In summary, if you are not a professional therapist and you want to help—then this book is for you.

What does it take to be an effective helper? This book will give you the basics to get started. When you have finished this book, you should know how to support friends, loved ones, neighbours, colleagues, employees, clients, patients or parishioners effectively when professional therapy help is unavailable, by doing the following:

- Reach different types of people, draw them out and help them explore their issues with easy-to-use listening techniques that can be helpful immediately and can be used quickly, and tips on what not to do.
- Stop worrying about whether or not they might say the wrong thing and make things worse.
- Feel confident that they know how to choose the best regional resources to refer

someone who needs more help than they can give.
- Feel confident that they can respond appropriately to common issues that frequently pop up in a counsellor's office, with user-friendly tools that readers can use with their clients.
- Supervisors or HR people or union reps can feel satisfied that their support of an employee, or colleague in their issues can result in enhanced work performance and work relationships.
- Professional helpers can feel satisfied that their new (or renewed) skills complement and contribute to the other services that they offer.
- Lay helpers can feel confident that they can assist their community by filling a service gap effectively.
- Find it easy to seamlessly incorporate their new skills into their current job or volunteer position.

What is in this book?

This book covers basic skills including how to get started, what skills you will need, some pointers on dealing with common issues, and when to refer a client onwards when more help is needed. You will discover:
- Simple, easy to use listening techniques that can be helpful immediately and can be used quickly.
- Specific strategies for responding to the most common issues you are likely to face as a helper.
- Tips about what not to do.
- A framework for planning a helping encounter.
- User-friendly tools that you can use with your clients.
- Case studies, examples, exercises, chapter summaries and key take-away points.
- Suggested resources.

Here is a summary of the chapters:

1: What is this book about?
The opening chapter (you are in it now!) describes who the book is for, what you will find in it, terms and assumptions.

2: What on earth should we do?
This chapter helps readers to think through what their role will be, and what it will not be. For lay helpers, it also offers some thoughts about how to get started organizing a community peer counselling group.

3: Effective listening fundamentals
This chapter provides some of the most important foundations for effective counselling, including empathy, authenticity, confidentiality, immediacy, cultural contributions, and recognizing when it is time to call in the "big guns".

4: What on earth should I say?
You will learn the seven key skills:

- listening well
- interpreting body language
- asking questions that draw out your client
- being a mirror for your client
- avoiding giving advice
- avoiding self-disclosure;
- how to clarify, reframe, and confront in a helpful way.

5: Freebies to swipe
Here are helpful tools you are welcome to swipe and use.

6: What should I expect?
This chapter outlines some of the most common complaints that tend to walk through a helper's door, and offers some guidelines for responding effectively. Depression, anxiety, loneliness, suicidal thoughts, substance abuse, sexual assault, domestic violence, and trauma are covered.

7: Plan and structure a helping encounter
Not sure how to start? This chapter gives you a road map for what a helping encounter might look like and ideas for how to navigate the journey.

8: Wrap up
Useful articles, lists of resources, suggestions for enhancing knowledge and skills and links complete the book.

Terms and assumptions

- "Client" – You may be speaking with patients, parishioners, employees, union members or mentees. For the sake of simplicity, in this book, I have referred to anyone you work with as being a "client".
- "Helping" – is any exchange that is intended to be therapeutic. In other words, the encounter helps people face a human issue, solve a problem, survive a crisis, feel better about themselves, or feel supported to take some action that would improve their lives.
- "Lay counsellor" and "helper" – the terms I use most frequently in this book for any volunteer or salaried helper who is not a professionally trained therapist.

All the stories in this book are real. Some of them are from my own personal experience helping others, some are contributed by other helpers, and some stories and some characters are composites. But all of the stories are real life examples of counselling skills in action.

Key take-away points

The key messages of this chapter:

- There is a gap crying out to be filled. It can be filled by warm, compassionate people who are not professional therapists.
- "Help" is anything that contributes to someone coping with a human issue.
- Anyone can be helpful with compassion and a few key skills under their belt.
- Regardless of your job or volunteer title, if you find yourself counselling, but you are not a professionally trained therapist, you should find this book useful.

For more information, check out the resources here:
      seawinds-education.mykajabi.com/o-pt-in-to-resources-for-the-non-therapist

2: What on earth should we do?

This chapter will have the most relevance to readers who are interested in establishing a community-based service. For example:

- A mental health information and referral service
- A peer counselling group
- A shelter for the homeless or for women escaping intimate partner assault
- An outreach service for the unhoused
- An addiction counselling service as part of some organization with a broader mandate
- A victims' support group
- A drop-in centre for teens

If you are already working or volunteering for a similar type of service, you may find the sections on mandate and roles useful to fine tune your service protocols. If you are working for a government department or agency, seeing clients or patients, or perhaps supporting Non Government Organizations who do, you may find some ideas to assist community-based services to be as effective as possible.

What is my role as a lay counsellor?

Know your organizational mandate and policies
The first place to start when determining your role is to check out the mandate of your organization. It may seem a bit obvious, but these questions are critical to make certain that you are able to provide the best service you can, in keeping with your organization's mandate, making the most of your support from the community, and the resources available to you.

If you are just organizing your own community-based counselling group, you will need to think about these questions to ensure that your group operates in a way that will be useful to your community.

I will not address organizational structure in depth here, since there are many possible variations and conditions, and since resources and regulations differ from place to place. Here are some general thoughts:

- Some groups will be quite informal, simply ad-hoc gatherings of concerned citizens who wish to offer a useful service to neighbours and friends. This type of loose structure has the advantage of easy flexibility, intimacy, and little or no overhead costs, such as salaries, rent or phone lines. One disadvantage is that such a service would likely be ineligible for most funding programs. There may also be some leadership or management issues in an informal group. Who is responsible for accomplishing which tasks will need to be an important focus of planning.
- Some groups will want to align themselves with an existing agency or service for support and possibly for leadership and funding. For example, lay counsellors might align themselves with organizations such as a shelter, a mental health service, a crisis line, a government department, a hospital, an advocacy agency, or any other service. Freed from leadership, management and funding concerns, your service can focus on what it does best.
- Some groups will want to create a formal organization, which may be called a registered society or something similar where you live. One major advantage of this option is the eligibility to receive funding. Others include recognizability, and thus legitimacy, and perhaps easier promotion of the service as a result. The organization may have a board of directors, a hierarchy of employees, and formalized policies and procedures to help guide the service.

Your group will need to address questions about the expectations, assumptions, policies and protocols that will guide your service. For example:

- Who will be your clients? How will they find you?
- What is the overall purpose of the service?
- Are you there to provide information only?
- Are you expected to respond to emotional challenges?
- Are you required to do crisis intervention, such as pulling a hopped-up suicidal dude off a bridge at 3 in the morning? If so, are you required to take along a second worker? Or maybe police back-up?
- Who or what agency will provide back up when needed?
- Are you expected to refer people with especially challenging situations to someone else, such as a professional therapist or a specialist?
- Are you there to do phone or text response only, with someone else tasked with in-person outreach?
- Will you be seeing people in an office only? Or will be there be "street work"? Will you see people in their own homes, or in institutions?
- If office space will be required, what is available locally? Is the space safe, secure, private, accessible, affordable and not too grotty?

- Will you be expected to report on potential risks, such as suicide or homicide threats? To whom? Then take what actions?
- How will you be expected to keep notes and report? To whom? How often? Using what forms or format?
- How much room is there for individuals to make their own determinations about what to do or not to do? What types of decisions need to be discussed with a supervisor or board member before taking action?
- What are the possible consequences if you overstep your mandate?
- How will you promote your service? Where, when, how and how often?
- How big a budget will you require for your service? Where will operating funds come from? What must your service do to obtain funding?
- Will your service require staff? If so, what positions need to be filled? What qualifications will staff need to demonstrate? How will you recruit staff candidates?
- What will your service require in the way of office space? Furniture? Equipment?
- Will your service need a vehicle to travel to see clients? If yes, will it be a "company car" or will individual staff use their own vehicles? If so, what compensation is in place for use of a private vehicle? Insurance requirements? Special licensing?

Different types of "help"

Let's take a look at some different ways in which helpers "help". You will need to be clear on what your role is, and what it is not.

First there is *compassionate support*. When you simply sit with a friend and listen to their story, without trying to change anything, or to wave your magic wand to fix anything, you are offering compassionate support. Anyone can provide compassionate support, with a few pointers on how to listen well. Here are some examples of compassionate support:

- Walking with a friend in distress and just listening.
- Sitting with someone while they wait in a hospital waiting room for news of a loved one who is sick or hurt.
- Driving your neighbour to the drugstore when her car is not working and listening to her vent her frustrations.
- Visiting a lonely person and drinking tea while offering friendly companionship.
- Volunteering to visit with elderly folks in a nursing home.
- Providing information on regional mental health services at a walk-in clinic.
- Babysitting your neighbour's kids while she sorts out a big problem.
- Being "at home" or "open" to neighbours with a coffee pot always ready.
- An elder providing advice to a troubled youth in the form of a story with a message.

Next is crisis intervention. This is a more specific type of compassionate support which responds to people in crisis, such as suicide or an accident. It is often a quick response provided under stressful conditions and almost always involves a lot of emotion. There may be some considerable emotional drama around a crisis response. Crisis intervention is about getting past an immediate Big Problem and is usually time limited, in other words, it will probably be over soon. Effective immediate intervention is a very important key to future happiness for a person whose life is in crisis.

Crisis intervention may evolve later to become therapy. It usually involves not only compassionate support, and having lots of information on regional resources handy, it may also involve some action to help sort out the crisis, such as calling the police to halt a suicide attempt, or sending out a support team to pick up a person in distress and take them to the hospital.

Crisis intervention may be carried out by someone with related professional training, such as a social worker, or a chaplain, or it may be provided by lay volunteers with some intermediate level training. Usually, crisis intervention is the mandate of an organization such as a mental health centre, a rape crisis centre, a suicide prevention service, or a hospital outreach program. There may be a mix of salaried employees and volunteers helping out with crisis intervention, and there may be more than one agency or organization involved in the crisis response.

Here are some examples of crisis intervention:

- Answering a telephone crisis helpline and responding to whatever the caller brings to you.
- Picking up your neighbour, whose husband has just suicided, and taking her someplace safe, warm, nurturing, and private, where she can recover from her shock and distress. Sitting with her quietly, and listening if she needs to talk.
- Bringing food to your neighbour who has lost her husband in an accident and listening while she cries on your shoulder.
- Taking a teenaged woman to a rape clinic after she has been attacked, and being there for her throughout the ordeal of reporting, medical testing, and police statements.
- Helping a woman who is leaving an abusive relationship to pack up and retreat to a safe shelter.
- Picking up children from an unsafe environment and delivering them to a child protection worker.
- Comforting the family of a dying patient.
- Sitting in a hospital with an elderly woman who is slipping away and offering spiritual comfort for her final moments of life.
- Accompanying police as they deliver the news of the death of a loved one, to offer support and tissues and a shoulder to cry on afterwards.

And then there is *therapy*. Therapy may be short term or long term, but it is often aimed at long term solutions to an issue or a pattern that is a problem. It always involves high level skills training, such as a masters' degree or a doctorate in a helping field, such as psychiatry, psychology, psychotherapy, or clinical social work.

Most people providing therapy need to be licensed by a governing body, which requires demonstrating proof of training and proof of competency. Therapy usually involves some specific technique or approach designed to help the client heal.

Here are some examples of therapy:

- An alcoholic attends a rehab center for therapy to help beat an addiction.
- A trauma specialist offers a course of EMDR (Eye Movement Desensitization and Reprocessing), a special therapy for relieving the impact of traumatic memories, to a veteran who has PTSD.
- A person who has attempted suicide is offered CBT (Cognitive Behavioural Therapy), a technique which is used to treat depression and anxiety.
- A woman with bipolar disorder is offered therapy to learn to manage her condition.
- A child psychologist uses play therapy to help a child who has been abandoned by a parent.
- A chaplain working in a rehab center provides grief therapy including healing rituals for a man who has lost a leg.

What role will you be playing? What role do you *want* to play? Did any of the descriptions above make you cringe with discomfort? Or can you see yourself playing any of these roles comfortably? Do any of them trigger your own history and cause you fear just to contemplate providing that type of service?

Is there some type of help that is beyond your current level of skill training? Is there something that you refuse to do or think you cannot ever do? What type of service does your community need right now? What type of service could you offer soonest, with the least amount of challenge?

Your agenda

Why do you want to be a lay counsellor or a frontline worker? Ask yourself these questions:

- What do I want to accomplish for my community? If the goal is some way of bettering life for your family, friends and neighbours then you are on the right track. Be as specific as possible about your own goals and check to see if they match the goals of the organization you will be working for, your community leadership's goals, or the goals of the people of your community.
- What do I want to accomplish for the people who become my clients?
- What vision do I have of how helping contacts with people will go, and what benefits it should have for those who seek help? Again, check with the mandate of your group or organization to be sure your vision meshes with the visions of others involved.
- What do I want to accomplish for myself? No one is 100% altruistic. Whenever we volunteer to help others in some way, there is also some idea of ways in which it might benefit ourselves as well, and that is fair game. Why would you want to engage in an activity that leaves you feeling dissatisfied or unappreciated or incompetent? It's good to

think that you can expand your skills and learn new stuff through being a lay counsellor, and maybe also achieve long term career goals. It's good to want to meet new people or feel more connected to your community by serving as a lay counsellor. It's good to feel useful. It's good to feel accomplishment for achieving your personal goals.

But if your answer is something like these: "I want to be important" or "I want to increase my chances of being elected to Council by appearing to be generous with my time" or "I want for people to take me more seriously" then it is likely that waiting for some other time to get involved might be the best choice for you. These are short term goals that are unlikely to help sustain your engagement, and of what benefit is someone who starts things but does not follow through or quits after a short time? They are also self-serving goals that are probably incompatible with volunteering or working as a lay counsellor.

- Am I relatively stable emotionally? Have I addressed my own personal issues, or are there any quirks that might get in the way of my being an effective helper? For example, if you have PTSD and find your emotions easily triggered by witnessing other people's emotions, then you might want to engage in therapy yourself before putting yourself out there as a lay counsellor to help others.
- Are my family situation and my working commitments stable enough to allow me to respond when I am needed? Or do I need to make some changes first before I dive in? Do I have reliable child-care or doggie day care? Do my spouse/partner and children support the idea of my getting involved with counselling? Do my job demands and volunteer commitments allow me the time to do what is needed? Do I have reliable transportation?

What are the risks for frontline workers and lay counsellors?

It is important to realize that there are some risks involved in this type of work and volunteer activity. It would be helpful to consider whether these, and other possible risks you may encounter are manageable and allow the work to be worth the risk.

Consider these possible risks:

Fuzzy boundaries. It is very common for lay counsellors to become over-involved. This might take the form of trying to solve all of the client's problems for them, or giving advice that is unwanted in an effort to be useful. Or it might be that a volunteer puts in much more time than is good for themselves, in an effort to try to solve all the world's problems (or perhaps to avoid their own?). Or it might be that you become "friends" and find it harder to be objective about the other's issues. Or there may even be a familiarity that slides across a line of appropriateness to sexual energy that makes the relationship confusing for both the client and the helper.

While there is an argument to be made for helpers to be totally relaxed and authentic, it is likely that fuzzy boundaries will make it very difficult for the helper to actually be helpful, and for the client to accept that help.

"Dependency" and "Transference" are terms that therapists learn about in Counselling 101, but they apply to lay counsellors and helpers as well. Sometimes a client is so relieved that someone is listening, they relax so much that they would rather hand any problem over to the counsellor to solve rather than taking steps themselves. They become dependent on the helper.

Perhaps in the midst of an emotional crisis, if the client is in too much shock to do whatever needs to be done, a helper can (and should) take charge. But when things have calmed down, the person needs to take hold of their own reins again. The client needs to learn how to solve their own issues, and deserves the satisfaction and strengthening that comes with knowing they have solved an issue on their own. If the relationship between helper and client develops fuzzy boundaries, or if it exists for some time, transference may occur. The client transfers to the helper the affection and love that should be given to a partner or other family member. This is not healthy for the therapeutic relationship nor is it helpful to anyone, most especially to the client. Getting out of that type of relationship can be emotionally messy, and may make it impossible for future useful help for that client.

Be wary of any suggestion of sexual energy between client and helper. There have been lots of cases of clients suing a counsellor or helper for supposedly taking advantage of them in a "helping" relationship. A licensed worker can lose their license and thus lose their ability to work after such an event.

Litigation. North America, especially the USA, has become a "litigious" society. In other words, the legal community is making lots of money helping people sue each other. "Sexual misconduct" is just one possible legal issue. Others might include accusations of drug abuse or other personal problems that someone else thinks would make the helper unsuitable to advise others. A family might sue if they think a helper did not do enough to prevent the suicide of a family member.

Fortunately, volunteers and individual employees are normally protected from litigation by their organization's structure and insurance policies. In Canada, litigation is a much less worrisome risk, thanks to a "Good Samaritan" law that protects those who attempt to help another in distress.

Street work. Those helpers who meet their clients on the street need to be aware of the potential dangers posed by mixing with street people and the dark alleys where they may be found. People who are desperate for the necessities of life or perhaps needing cash for a drug purchase may have standards for behaviour that do not include being gentle with a well- meaning helper. It is important to carefully plan an excursion into the dangerous streets of a city, making sure to pin-point specific threats and to ensure that back up is available quickly. Choose a location that is well lit at night, and **never** go out alone in a dangerous neighbourhood.

Overstepping your authority. Once your organization has thought out its mandate and roles, its protocols and policies, it will also likely have sanctions available for a staff member or volunteer who over-steps the authority given to them. For example, are you expected to contact a supervisor in the event that a home visit is needed? Are you expected to refer a client to some other resource if they have specific issues you are not trained to respond to?

Keep in mind that protocols such as these have been developed to protect workers, and also to ensure that your service can be as effective as possible. Yes, sometimes decisions need to be made on the fly, and there may not be time to contact your supervisor, or she may not be available, and you may need to take your own best guess as to what would be most appropriate. But avoid deliberately side stepping a protocol for other reasons or you may find yourself being let go for inappropriate behaviour.

Unstable clients. Sometimes, lay counsellors and volunteers find themselves asked to work with clients that pose a risk to the helper. For example, someone is violent, the police think it is a mental health issue and you are asked to go deal with it. Or a friend is "out of his mind" with grief, throwing things and threatening anyone who tries to help. In this circumstance, it is best to leave managing unstable clients to the local police or to some other professional service trained to deal with unstable or violent people.

> Sometimes I was asked to do things that were out of my control, because I had the training. At one point, someone from the Council approached me, saying, 'You've had the training, will you go talk to him?' A man was trying to cut his girlfriend's house in half with a chainsaw.
>
> I said, 'No way will I do that, that it is beyond my scope, call the police'. Thankfully I knew enough not to touch that one.

It is important to identify the risks that your service may encounter and to take appropriate actions to reduce the risks. For example, develop service policies and protocols that can be reviewed frequently and made accessible to all; plan out how back-up will be provided; consult with a lawyer about legal vulnerabilities for your service; train staff and volunteers how to reduce their vulnerability; create an atmosphere of trust and collegial support for staff and volunteers so that they can feel safe to admit mistakes and learn from them and support each other.

But should being aware of possible dangers stop you from giving your time to help others? No. Just be aware and take whatever steps you need to take to stay safe.

Key take-away points

- Make sure your organization or group is clear on its mandate, and that individual staff and volunteers are clear on their roles and the type of help they will offer.
- Decide what expectations, assumptions, protocols and policies you need to develop, and how they will be provided to volunteers and staff.
- Make sure your service explores the potential risks to the service, to the organization, and to staff and volunteers, and that it puts plans into place to reduce vulnerability and keep everyone safe.

Exercises and activities

- Consult with other service providers in your region to learn about how they have set up their services.
- Consider borrowing whatever resources other organizations may have to share, such as a policy and protocol manual.
- Organize a brainstorming session with anyone who is involved (for example, staff, key volunteers, board of directors, local council, staff from other organizations your service might work in partnership with) to create your group's own service guidelines.

For more information, check out the resources here:

    seawinds-education.mykajabi.com/o-pt-in-to-resources-for-the-non-therapist

3: Effective listening fundamentals

This chapter contains important fundamentals for all helpers.

Just be there, with your empathy hat on

It's not uncommon for lay helpers to panic when their listening skills are called for, while secretly despairing that they don't have any fancy techniques in their tool boxes to be of any real use. Or else they pretend they actually *do* know what's up and have all the answers so that they can wave their magic wand and—poof! "Problem gone."

> The #1 thing to do: Just be there, with your empathy hat on…relax and respect the client's ability to solve problems on their own.

It's understandable. We just want to help make things better for someone. Some people may avoid trying to help soothe a troubled soul because they can't imagine where to start or what to say. Some may dive into complex situations that are over their heads. Some may feel the desire to take over and solve everything for the client.

The main key to success? Just relax and respect the client's ability to solve problems on their own, with some information and support from you.

It's amazing how much help we can be by simply being there, with our empathy hats on. One human heart to another, maybe just in companionable silence. It's all about the bond between two human beings.

We all have a drive to be seen and heard, to have someone else "know" us and our pain. It's elemental, one of the most compelling human motivations. It can transcend all other considerations. And often, just being there, even if only for a moment or two, is simply all that is required.

> We need to adopt a philosophy of "walk alongside me". We must realize that we cannot change anyone. Change is scary, what is known and familiar is easier than what is new and unknown. So don't think about changing your client's life. Think about walking beside her for the journey.
> - Christina Baxter, Chaplain

Maybe there will come a time later when conversation will help, but don't be afraid to offer simple, unvarnished companionship. It might be just what the client needs at that moment to survive.

My empathy hat, huh. So, ahem, what exactly is empathy? Well, here are some definitions:

- "*Sympathy*, constructed from the Greek *sym*, meaning "together", and *pathos*, referring to feelings or emotion, happens when one person shares the feelings of another, as when one experiences sadness when someone close is experiencing grief or loss. *Empathy* is a newer word also related to "pathos." It differs from sympathy in carrying an implication of greater emotional distance. With empathy, you can imagine or understand how someone might feel, without necessarily having those feelings yourself. In general, sympathy is when you share the feelings of another; empathy is when you understand the feelings of another but do not necessarily share them."[1]
- "Feeling yourself into, or participating in, the inner world of another, while remaining yourself."[2]
- "To care for another person, I must be able to understand him and his world as if I were inside it. I must be able to see, as it were, with his eyes what his world is like to him and how he sees himself. Instead of merely looking at him in a detached way from outside, as if he were a specimen, I must be able to be with him in his world, going into his world in order to sense from inside what life is like for him, what he is striving to be and what he requires to grow."[3]
- "Helpers communicate to clients an understanding of what clients say indirectly and what they merely imply, hint at and say non-verbally...they base their understanding on cues clients present."[4]

So, if sympathy is sharing and empathy is understanding, what is compassion?

- "*Compassion*...refers to both an understanding of another's pain and the desire to somehow mitigate that pain". [5]

Compassion has received some attention and study. It turns out, compassion is pretty darn valuable[6]. For example, did you know that compassion:

> Human compassion involves the motivation to learn how to be helpful.

- blocks fear and activates courage in our brains?
- can dial down threat responses in the brain?
- improves heart rate variability and improves the functioning of the vagus nerve? (More about the vagus nerve and its job in relaxation later.)
- affects the development of the brain and various human organs and systems, self confidence, and the expression of some genes?

---

1 Merriam Webster Online Dictionary, 2021.
2 Alfred Benjamin, *The Helping Interview*, NY: Houghton Mifflin, 1981, p. 49.
3 M. Mayeroff. *On Caring*, NY: Perennial Library (Harper and Row), 1971.
4 Gerard Egan, *The Skilled Helper*, Pacific Grove, CA: Brooks/Cole Publishing Company, 1982, p.40.
5 Merriam Webster Online Dictionary
6 Paul Gilbert, *Current Opinion in Psychology*, "Explorations Into the Nature and Function of Compassion." Derby, UK: Centre for Compassionate Research and Training, University of Derby, 2020, pp. 104-114.

Kate Tompkins

As helpers, we are shooting for empathy and compassion. Sympathy is not the goal: a client needs a helper to be her anchor, her rock. If the helper is crying along with her, the helper loses the ability to be objective and thus to actually be helpful.

So how do we "do" empathy and compassion?

- First of all, pay attention. Notice body language and vocal cues. (More on this skill in the next chapter.) Watch and listen especially for what is not said but is implied or hinted or maybe even conspicuously left out. If there is a discrepancy between the body language and the words, which do we believe? Keep in mind that body-language cues are almost all unconscious. They appear without us willing them to. Thus, body language speaks for the innermost thoughts which are often not voiced and the client may not even be aware of them. The body cannot lie!

  > The body cannot lie!

- Listen for cues and messages that tell us what the client's oldest, most basic and private thoughts and fears may be.
- Acknowledge what you have seen and heard, using the skills detailed in the following chapter, especially "reflection of feeling".
- After you have responded to the client, watch for further cues to tell you how the client feels about what you said. Does the client agree or disagree with you? Does the client have deep feelings that need to be explored further?
- Be respectful, caring and gentle. Don't try to push the client too quickly in any direction, but especially not towards the direction you think she should take. More on this thought later in this chapter.
- Refocus the client on important issues if he wanders, or avoids talking about the key points in his story. If the topic is sensitive or contains a lot of emotion, take your hints from the client's body language about how quickly to move into them.
- Pay attention to cues of resistance from the client. Perhaps you are moving too quickly, or misunderstood something and need to clarify. Perhaps your observations were correct, and lead the client to emotions or thoughts she is not ready to tackle yet. Mention what you have observed and let the client say more about that, if she chooses to.[7]

> Try not to hand a tissue to someone who is crying. It can be misinterpreted as a signal to stop crying—which is what we don't want. We want the client to be able to freely express the sadness, grief, anger, whatever in tears. Our job is to just hold the time and space for them to feel safe to do that. Studies have found that the chemical make up is different between sad tears and happy tears—seems that not just an emotional release is taking place, but a physical one, too.
>
> Best practice is to make sure tissues are available on tables and in plain site and easy reach before meeting with a client.
>
> \- Christina Baxter, Chaplain

---

[7] Egan, *The Skilled Helper*, pp. 294-301.

- Be authentic, focus on the client, start from where the client is today, approach the client and their issues from a problem-solving approach, and separate the person from their problem. (More follows about all these.)

If we practice empathy and compassion, and listen rather than blabbing, it's pretty hard to say something that will be harmful.

Authenticity: A matter of balance

At one point, I owned and was the principal of a private school. I was also the official school counsellor, since I had the letters behind my name and I had the experience.

But it did not take too long before I noticed that it was not me that our students came to talk to about their every-day troubles. It was another teacher, Joanne. I watched her to learn why.

This is what it came down to: Joanne was real with the students and I was not. I was too taken up with my officialness and my exalted position, too worried about the school's finances and the local politics. I tended to be more formal and somewhat distant, where Joanne was more relaxed, more personal, more informal, and more immediate. So she was able to be much more help with her warm chatter than I was with my fancy degrees.

I'm not saying that skills training and education are a hindrance. Clearly there are lots of very capable therapists out there with a boatload of training that save the lives of their clients every day. I am saying that being authentic is a huge factor contributing to our ability to connect with our clients.

What makes one person more effective than another? Training is important, of course. But all the training in the world with a false countenance will get us nowhere. People can easily suss out whether or not we are being authentic.

What is authenticity?

- "Don't merely know thyself—be thyself."[8]
- "Being true to one's own personality, spirit, or character"[9]
- "The degree to which a person's actions are congruent with their beliefs and desires, despite external pressures to conformity."[10]
- "A person [acting] in accordance with desires, motives, ideals or beliefs that are not only hers (as opposed to someone else's), but that also express who she really is."[11]

Does authenticity require that we share all of our thoughts and emotions with the client? No! It requires that we know what we think and feel, and relax about it. To do that, we need to release

---
8   The Oracle of Delphi, ancient Greece
9   Merriam Webster Online Dictionary
10 Wikipedia article on authenticity, 2021
11 *Stanford Encyclopedia of Philosophy* article on authenticity, 2021

our own most volatile emotions privately and fully, so that we can respond calmly and honestly to the client.

The trick here is to understand that many of our most volatile emotions are in fact not the truth, but artifacts created by some warped thought.

Imagine that we each have a recording in our heads, containing our thoughts about all of the significant events in our lives up to this moment. Some of what is recorded in our heads makes sense and some is downright off the wall. Messages we give ourselves in childhood are often inaccurate, because as children we frequently do not understand the context of what we see and hear around us.

That recording, including all of our warped thoughts, plays over and over again until we don't notice it. It becomes the soundtrack to our lives, through which we filter all we see and hear to understand what it is supposed to mean.

And this is the important part: by filtering our observations through that soundtrack, our understanding of what we see and hear changes.

Try an experiment: while watching TV, turn off the volume and see if you can follow the action. It is usually tough to do, because we have become so used to having a musical soundtrack tell us what to think and feel, and how to interpret the visual action. The music creates anticipation of pleasure, of fear, or of humour.

In much the same way, our mental soundtrack tells us how to interpret the meaning of what we perceive around us.

For example, a five-year-old child witnesses her parents fighting. Maybe daddy hits mommy, which would be pretty frightening for that child. At five, we think the world revolves around us because it pretty much has done so for our entire short lives. Then she thinks, "It must be my fault. They must be fighting about me. I must have been a bad girl. I must be useless if I cannot protect my mother and stop the fighting."

When we look back with adult eyes, we know that this is nonsense: the girl does not need to think that of herself. But this thought is now recorded in the child's brain. The more often she travels down that thought pathway in her memory, the more it becomes a four-lane highway, drawing her towards its warped emotional conclusions.

As an adult, that woman is at work, and her boss shouts at her. What if those warped thoughts about being inadequate happen to be playing on

> We all are triggered at some point in dealing with clients because we are all human with our own baggage. As a helper, our job is to cultivate awareness of being triggered, recognize it is taking place, and mindfully set it aside with a promise to ourself to deal with it later. And, all while paying attention to our client! Not easy to do, but can be done over time by cultivating awareness of the dynamic.
>
> It's also helpful to have someone (a professional if possible) to accompany one in processing these triggers. To the extent we deal with our own history and baggage, we will be less prone to triggering. That said, no matter how much therapy and processing we do, we need to always be mindful that we can be triggered. It seems there is always one more pesky issue out there just waiting to trip us up the moment we let down our guard.
>
> - Christina Baxter, Chaplain

her tape at the moment the boss has a meltdown? Her mind may go to, "it's my fault, I'm no good, I'll never do this job right," or something similar.

Soon she is in the washroom, crying her eyes out and maybe raging. Her emotional reaction seems off the wall, too big, inappropriate and inauthentic, because it does not belong to the present moment. It belongs to people and events in her past.

In order to be authentic, she needs to pull up her big girl pants, grab a tissue, dry her eyes and have a good honk, then think rationally about the situation to uncover her true emotions. Maybe her boss is having a bad day and overreacted to something that had nothing to do with her.

Now that she has reframed her thinking, she feels entirely differently. Now she can relax and act with honest compassion for her boss and authentically care for his issues and the work at hand, rather than being swamped by her own inauthentic emotions of anger.

What the five-year-old child was incapable of doing, the adult helper must do. We must understand our past and its contributions to our present. We must understand that we all have struggles with past scripts in our heads that don't fit our lives in the present.

Authenticity is about getting down to the true core of oneself, without being sidetracked by historical issues or warped thoughts, and thus by warped emotions. Then we can allow our clients to see who we really are under our inauthentic masks.

Modelling authenticity for our clients can be very helpful. When we can be authentically human, then our clients may see that they can be, also.

Can anybody practice authenticity? There is not a specific type of person, no specific personality type that lends itself to authenticity. Folks who are naturally soft-spoken and gentle may find it easier to reach out and touch another's shoulder in support; however, people who are natural loners and task-oriented doers, or logical, data-oriented, researcher types, can also learn to relax and allow clients to see their humanity, within boundaries.

Keep in mind that there are limits to authenticity for a helper. We must be aware of our boundaries to protect both our clients and ourselves. For example, if I am feeling authentically sad because of a death in my family, should I allow my client to see this grief? Perhaps. Should I allow the client to comfort me? Probably not.

> Keep the focus on the client, regardless of your own thoughts, values or emotions.

The focus needs to stay on the client. So I may need to shift my own emotional focus for a while so that my attention can remain on my client. That requires that I know my own history and the emotions I carry about my past and what might trigger them, and that I have processed them enough that I can set my own emotions aside temporarily when I am working with a client.

How do we do this? It takes some practice. Here are a few ideas to add to your tool box.

The first is to learn how to **relax** your entire body quickly. There is a section in Chapter 5 about self-regulation skills, and here is a trick anyone can use right away:

> Breathe as if you were breathing right down to the bottom of your toes and make your exhales longer than your inhales. Now try to drop your jaw. Just relax and let your jaw,

your mouth, and especially the roof of your mouth, drop down towards your chest.

You can do this without looking too weird, and it immediately engages your parasympathetic nervous system (the "calm down" system—more about this later). That should make it easier for you to focus on what your client is saying, even when emotions are running high or you are frightened by what you are hearing.

Body relaxation accomplishes a few things:

- If you can stay relaxed, then you are being a model for your client, who is likely to calm down right along with you. If you model deep breathing, dropping your shoulders, and maybe also your jaw, then your client will be better able to do the same.
- You can be an anchor for your client when they are becoming overwhelmed. If you fall apart and get emotional in response to your client's emotions, you lose any ability to help them. The client may evaporate if they do not feel confident that you can be an emotional anchor for them.
- You can more easily let go of any distancing formality you are keeping pasted onto your face and body language for your own emotional protection, making it easier for you to be real and easier for your client to relax and trust you. You can build a shared sense of connection. Remember, effective helping is ALL about relationship. It's a lot easier to be open to developing a relationship if the helper unconsciously gives off an aura of relaxed, calm, solid confidence along with accessibility and genuine emotional expression.
- If you understand your history, you will be less easily triggered and less likely to revert to any of your habitual or automatic thoughts and emotional states. Being authentic does not require us to blubber about our own troubles. It asks us to relax and respond to our clients from a deep and authentically calm place within ourselves. This keeps the focus on the client and their issues, not on us.
- You will hear and see more of your client's message if you are not worrying about what you will say next or what your own emotions might be doing under the surface.
- You will be able to let more of your real self show on the outside, because you will feel emotionally safe, and your client will sense that you

> I was taught, "Listen with your third ear" which basically means listening with your heart, as if it were a third ear. This has helped me a lot.
>
> I am also glad you talked about triggers—it took me a while to realize when I was being triggered and in the moment to set it aside with the promise to my self that I would deal with it later. I saw a therapist twice monthly to deal with this and to be able to unpack difficult cases in a confidential setting.
>
> Learning to notice triggering and to set it aside with compassionate intention is so important. We need to stay one step back from the client's emotions. Our genuineness can shine through while we keep our boundaries in place.
>
> - Christina Baxter, Chaplain

are showing them something personal which they are privileged to share in, leading to more trust and openness.

Another tool of authenticity is to **admit** when we don't know the answer to a question. There is more to be gained by saying, "I'm not sure about that, but I can do some research and get back to you with that information," than there is in bluffing or stringing a line of B.S. to look knowledgeable.

A **sense of humour** helps, too. Laughing full-heartedly is not only great medicine in itself; laughter also quickly builds a sense of sharing and connection. If you can laugh with your client, you may win her trust a lot faster.

> I'm learning to care and not to care. To be responsive but not responsible. I'm learning how to be still. To be present. To practice sacred listening with all my heart.
> - David Treadway PhD, in *Psychotherapy Networker Magazine*, Sept/Oct 2021

So how much authenticity is too much? The general guideline is to remember that a helping interview is all about the client and his needs, not about the helper and her needs. It may be tempting to reveal things about ourselves and our current issues, or to cry on our client's shoulder for a moment. The problem with this type of confiding is obvious. The conversation becomes a mutual crying fest, not a helping encounter.

If you wish to engage in therapeutic, helping exchanges, you need to wear a somewhat different hat than when you are being a close friend. If it happens to be your friend who comes to you for therapeutic support, then take a moment or two to put on your "helper" hat.

It might be tempting to tell a story about our own experience that is supposed to show a point or suggest a course of action. Doing so takes away from the client their ability to learn on their own and gain confidence in their ability to solve their own problems. Best to save your story for some other time.

> It's a bit of a balancing act. Authenticity for a helper is honesty, with discretion and boundaries.

So it's a bit of a balancing act: be real but be careful. Be yourself, but keep your boundaries well-defined so that you can continue to be a model of calmness. Be relaxed and authentic, but also be aware of keeping the focus on the client, not on yourself.

Authenticity for a helper is honesty, with discretion. It's openness, without sharing stuff that will make the client feel uncomfortable or damage the therapeutic nature of the relationship.

It's not about me

What comes into your mind when you hear something like the following?

> "How can I listen to someone talk about how they want to die when I know that Jesus can save them? It is my Christian duty to bring this poor soul into the light."

> "Of course you should go back to your husband. A wife should be there to support him

and look after him."

"Well, what did you expect? A young woman walking alone in that neighbourhood, and dressed like that?"

If you thought something like, "Of course my beliefs matter, they form the foundation of who I am, so I will always speak from my values," then you may have a problem being an effective helper. If your client does not share your particular values, it is likely that espousing them will cause your client to avoid being with you or to withdraw altogether, discarding your version of help as being offensive.

The basic concept here is that "it is not about me. It is about my client." We need to learn to set our own values aside in order to give the client what she needs in the moment. Rather than tell the client what you think about a situation, try asking the client what she thinks.

If you think, "Well, that does not fit with what I would do. I would not make that choice, but I wonder what the client's choice will be and why," then you are on the right track. If you think, "I don't agree with that idea, but I don't need to convince my client that I am correct," then you are the right track. Thinking this way, and speaking from this stance, will allow the client to trust you more, and make it easier for you to be a better helper.

It's about respect for the client, which does not leave much room for judgment. If you find yourself judging silently, bite your lip and listen more. We can support without agreeing.

Arguing with your client, or trying to force him to see things your way, is not helping. It is just you exercising power games. It is most likely not your client's values that you need to focus on anyway, but rather his emotional state. If a client comes to you it is because he is in distress about something. Helping him get through that distress to arrive at a more peaceful place is the goal.

There may be times when the client's thinking is faulty, creating warped emotions. Helping him see the situation from a different viewpoint ("reframing") can be just what the doctor ordered. But if you encounter resistance from your client, back off. Let them gently come to see reality some other way, maybe at some other time. If you find yourself pushing, you are on the wrong track.

> If you find yourself pushing, you are on the wrong track. Back off.

Have faith in people

Do you believe that most people are resilient and a lot stronger than they think? Especially when things get rough? Or do you believe that most people are weak, likely to buckle under pressure, and need a firm hand to guide them down the right path?

Think about it. If you assume that your client is strong and resilient, what is the outcome likely to be? If you assume the client would be lost without you, what is the outcome likely to be?

Try offering hope that your client's current distress can be behind them in no time. "This too shall pass." Offer hope without the promise of any specific result. Making promises about the outcome can be risky, since we do not control all the factors that might come into play. "I will support you, whatever happens. We will get through this together. I don't know where our path might lead, but I will walk by your side."

A little positive reinforcement and diplomacy help, too, even if the outcome may not turn out as the client wanted.

- "You are really handling this well."
- "You have worked really hard at this, I admire your determination."
- "Let's look for the rewards of your hard work. Even though we may not manage to turn things around as you want, you have made other gains."

Use plain language

Have you ever met a trained helper who talks as though he were reading from a Psych 101 textbook? Not only is the academic jargon incomprehensible to lots of people, it sets up a barrier between the helper and those he may want to help. The helper may sound like he is an expert and knows a lot about the topic, so he can bask in the glory of being celebrated as an expert, but in fact his golden words will fail to reach a lot of people who will tune him out.

Speak as if you were having an informal, ordinary conversation with your buddy or your neighbour. Use ordinary vocabulary, what literacy folks call "plain language". In other words, free from "academic-speak", free from technical jargon, free from long-winded BS. If you do an online search for "Plain Language", you will find numerous examples and resources to simplify writing and speech.

Don't touch me!

Once I was working with a group of prospective leaders on a learning tour in the Arctic. They had with them a man billed as being an "elder" and a "healer", although by northern standards, he was neither. This man seemed fond of hugs. He dispensed them liberally to the group, and an expectation grew that everyone should hug everyone else as a matter of course, and "warm up" exercises were planned to encourage this contact.

The group facilitator failed to notice that not all of the students were comfortable with this activity. A few women hung back and avoided the hugs every time. I spoke quietly with one of those reluctant huggers and learned that she had a history of sexual assault, so of course she was not interested in forced hugs from near-strangers.

So is hugging a suitable way for a helper to show support? No, not without permission. Even with permission to touch, physical contact can cross safety boundaries and damage the therapeutic relationship. I suggest that all helpers make a point to never initiate touch contact with a client, and to be very careful about your boundaries when a client requests a hug. Men, of course, need to guard against even the possible perception of impropriety; even a stray glance can be misconstrued and cause a lot of trouble. So, men, just be wary.

Start from where the client is today

This approach is important for success as a helper. There is not much point in the helper having an agenda when going into a helping interview. Unless it happens to also be the client's agenda, you won't get very far. If you are seeing the client more than once, it's OK to plan. For example, "OK next week, let's talk about XX or YY". If something has happened in their life since that plan was made, that will be where the client wants to start. Immediate engagement with your agenda will be reluctant. Save your agenda for after the client has a chance to talk about their immediate concerns.

If it is the first time you are meeting with the client, you could try an opening such as one of these:

> "What brings you to seek help?"
> "What can I help you with today?"
> "What is going on in your life today?"
> "What would you like to talk about first?"

An open-ended question such as these allows the client to determine what to talk about, giving them a sense of control, and making it far more likely they will open up with the important stuff.

If you saw the client last week, you might open with something like this:

> "How was your week?"
> "How did XXX work out this week?"
> "What is on your mind today?"
> "How is life today?"

See the section in Chapter 4, "What on earth should I say?", for more on useful questions.

Allowing the client to determine the agenda is helpful in almost every circumstance. Here are some examples:

- You are supporting a woman who is living in an abusive situation. Abuse is a very complex matter. There are many reasons why women choose to stay or to return to an abuser. (Please see the section in Chapter 6 for more on abusive relationships). If you are determined that she should leave her abuser when she is not ready to do so, she may deny the reality of her life, defend her abuser, and fall back a few steps in her progress towards happiness. Who can she go to if she does not have the strength yet to end the abuse? Who will she go to when she decides she is ready? Not to you, if you have pres-

sured her to leave her relationship when she is not ready to. You will have lost the opportunity to help. If you go with her unique flow, and treat every day as a new day with its own challenges and opportunities, then she is more likely to come to you when she is ready to make a change. If you try to push her, she will probably be gone.
- You are visiting with a man who is a heavy drinker. You know that because you live in the same community and his excesses are legendary. He comes to you to talk about his relationship with his mother. If you insist that he talk about his drinking because you see that as being his main issue, then he will be likely to evaporate. What if he realizes that his childhood relationships are what is driving his drinking and he knows he needs to deal with them before he can tackle his addiction? It is important to allow people to take their time coming to their own conclusions about making changes in their lives that will be lasting.
- You meet with a youth who tells you his girlfriend is pregnant. You want to discuss their options and how you think he should support her. However, by doing so, you might miss the fact that he is suicidal, feeling desperate and helpless. The pregnancy questions can wait for a bit. The suicidal thoughts cannot.
- A teenage girl opens up to you, saying that she is lonely. You can see that she is anxious and fidgety, so you suspect there is something else on her mind. If you allow her to start with the topic of loneliness, then, after she feels comfortable with you and trusts that she can say anything to you, maybe she will open up about what else is on her mind. You could create a window of opportunity by describing what you see in her body language. ("I notice that your hands are busy and your foot is tapping. It looks like you are feeling a bit anxious today. Is there anything else you'd like to talk about?") But if you push her to talk about whatever else is on her mind first, she may balk and you will have lost the opportunity.

When would you **not** wait for the client to determine the agenda? Here are some thoughts:

- In an emergency, when fast action is needed to save a life or prevent injury or some other disaster.
- When the client has already said he is suicidal, and is avoiding the issue by trying to direct the conversation away from that reality.
- When the client is clearly in considerable distress (you might still ask, "What do you need from me right now?" or something similar) or so zoned out (the pros call it "dissociating") that she cannot think or act safely on her own behalf.

Here is an example of the last point: A man I know witnessed a serious car accident and stopped to help. He could see that the entire front end of the car was smashed in and that there were people inside. When he looked in, he could see that the driver was dead. A woman, sitting in the passenger seat, was conscious and appeared unhurt, but was clearly in shock. She was sitting very still and looking like she was on some other planet. There was no way that the car doors could be opened.

The rescuer, after calling 911, crawled onto the hood of the damaged car and spoke directly to the woman inside. He calmly directed her where to place each hand and foot and to look only at his face until she had scrambled out of the car through the shattered windshield. He then helped her to the grass to wait for the ambulance.

She could never have managed to do that on her own at the time, so the rescuer needed to take calm and gentle control of the situation.

That is a pretty dramatic example. Usually the situations you encounter will be much less dramatic and stressful. The point is that sometimes the helper *does* need to take control.

Everyone is an onion

Each of us has many parts. Think of our components like layers of an onion. Take a look at the diagram below. While researchers are still investigating how we become who we are, this diagram illustrates the components of a whole human in a simplified way that is easy to grasp. (Feel free to share this diagram with your clients.)

The innermost layers that are genetic, the human characteristics that we are born with, are in darker blue. The characteristics we learn are in light blue. Those that can be both genetic and learned are medium blue.

We are all like an onion

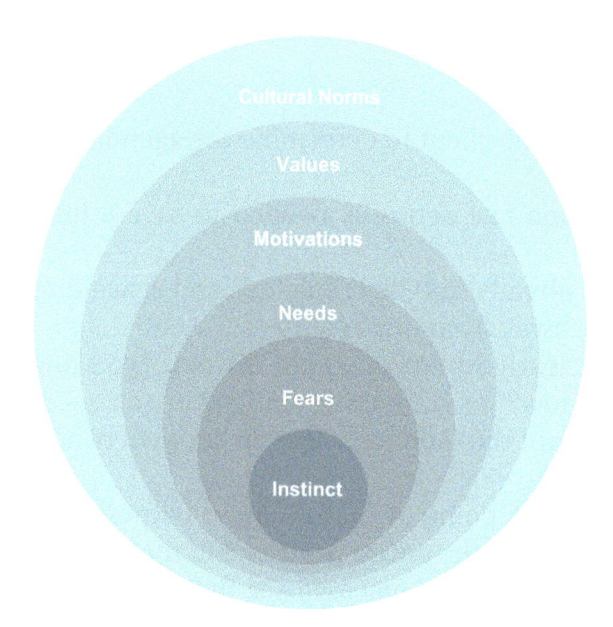

- Cultural Norms
- Values
- Motivations
- Needs
- Fears
- Instinct

Instincts

Our instincts, at the centre of the onion, are in charge of finding what we need in order to survive. Babies seem to experience a few emotional states, based on the overriding imperatives of survival. "Am I warm enough? Is my tummy full?" If my tummy is full, and if there are no loud noises around me, I probably feel safe. If I cry in the night when it is dark, I feel fear. But if Mommy or Daddy comes to rescue me and rocks me and speaks soothingly to me, I am probably safe.

"Am I being touched and held?" If I am held and touched, I probably feel loved. Built-in factors assist with that: the irresistible large baby eyes, my soft baby skin with that distinctive baby smell, and my ability to focus my eyes on my parents' faces at an early stage, all work to help baby get the care needed from mom and dad.

Survival fears, such as "Am I safe?", "Am I fed?", "Am I loved?" and "Am I held securely?" are innate to all living creatures.

More complex emotions develop over time. Later on, my parents, my schoolmates, and media all teach me whom I am supposed to hate, and whom I should trust.

Fears

The next layer out in our onion is fears that seem to be partly genetic and partly learned. As babies grow, the effects of their genes begin to surface. Our genetics are responsible to a large degree for what we fear; each person will have a different mix of fears.

Those fears are affected by our early childhood experiences, and new fears can be added onto our instinctual drives. The fears and the behaviours they create help to form our personality. Parents routinely notice that their children are quite different from each other, even though they were raised by the same parents, in the same home, with more or less the same circumstances. That's genetic variation at work.

Our genes provide us with natural strengths, limitations, styles and preferences, and our early experiences modify those natural tendencies and determine how they are expressed.

Personality is the unique mixture of how we think, how we feel and how we interact with others.

> One of the best sources of information are our clients. Invite the client to share what their cultural/spiritual needs might be by asking open ended questions. Further the conversation with, "Tell me more…". Often clients are relieved to know someone cares enough to ask, to cultivate understanding of these needs.
>
> If a helper shows genuine interest, most folks are willing to share. Possible exceptions to this are Wicca (long memories about "The Burning Times") and Roma (use this term in-stead of "Gypsy"—lots of mis-conceptions about them and their culture which have led to centuries of persecution, in-cluding being sent to Hitler's concentration camps in WW II). With the rise of Islamaphobia, some Muslims may be hesitant to share. Again, showing genuine interest can go a long way.
>
> If you work or volunteer with folks from other cultures, faiths, talk with them. Let clients know you want to approach them in a respectful way and can they share any tips with you to help educate you. That goes a long way to fostering an open, welcoming work environment.
>
> -Christina Baxter, Chaplain

Kate Tompkins

Needs and Motivations

Our needs arise from that which we fear. If I fear loss of social contact, I probably need lots of social interaction and will act in such a way that I can have that social interaction whenever I need it. On the other hand, if I fear not being perfect, I will need lots of time to research and get my arguments complete and correct. If I fear chaos, risk and change, I will need to manage my environment to keep things familiar and stable. If I fear being taken advantage of, I will need to have control over the work of my colleagues to focus on the important bottom line for our team.

We are motivated then to search for or create conditions which can meet our needs. Our motivations determine what we do, and how we do it, especially when it comes to relationships.

Values

How we express those motivations and how we act on them are strongly affected by our values about how we should treat other people, and those values are created largely by our cultural norms. Both values and cultural norms are completely learned, from family, school, media.

These middle layers that contribute the most to our sense of identity are open to growth and change. Within limits, we can learn to express our selves in new ways, we can make a choice to honour some of our perceived needs and ignore others, and we can modify our choices to make others feel comfortable.

Cultural norms

The outer layer of our personal onion is entirely learned. Our values and what we share with our families and communities is culture. "Culture is an umbrella term which encompasses the social behaviour and norms found in human societies, as well as the knowledge, beliefs, arts, laws, customs, capabilities, and habits of the individuals in these groups." [12] These shared values and the rituals, ceremonies, comforts and expectations associated with them become extremely important to many people.

But while it is a powerful influence, culture is not destiny. In order to have a healthy outer skin to one's personal onion, it is not necessary to embrace all the facets of one's culture. Anyone can pick and choose which aspects to embrace and which to ignore. That is a lot easier to do in some cultural systems than in others. In a conservative culture or a close-knit community, stepping away from what is expected will be much tougher than it would be in an open society.

The word "culture" can mean different things to different people. Here, I use the word to mean:

- that which provides a sense of "we-ness".
- group wisdom
- learning in a social context

---

12 Wikipedia article, 2021

Here are some thoughts about how to describe culture:

- Culture is dynamic, not static; culture shifts as environmental circumstances shift (e.g.: food availability, climatic or geographic changes, predators, illness or disease affecting the survival of the group, changes in technology, contact with other cultures having different social organization or technology, competition for economic survival).
- Culture must adapt to changing circumstances or die out. Cultures that isolate themselves or refuse to adapt in the face of changing circumstances rapidly become redundant.
- Culture identities are flexible; we are all members of sub-groups, each with its own cultural identities and expectations; we move between different cultural expectations and act differently while interacting in each. None of us is solely a member of just one "culture".
- Cultural norms and expectations are flexible. There are variations among members of a culture in how cultural expectations are lived and experienced due to individual, personal differences. Cultures vary in their degree of tolerance for individual differences, but viable cultures allow at least some degree of variation.
- Culture is often not as important as individual personality in determining how we interact with others and how we behave in groups. This is true both among members of the same culture, and in cross-cultural situations. There are personality traits that seem to be deep rooted, universal, and consistent with peoples from other cultures. Personality structure may be largely determined by genetic factors, and only refined by environmental factors, including cultural expectations.
- People from different cultures are more alike than they are different. We all share things that are of the deepest significance: a desire to belong and be social, love and caring for our children, a need to learn, a desire to be happy and healthy, a need to find a viable way to make a living, a concept of dying and birth as part of a cycle, a concept of some higher power or larger existence, a need for spiritual beliefs.
- We are all related genetically, we are just more closely related to some people than to others. Genetic research indicates that all homo sapiens sapiens, all human peoples, of all races and cultures, may have descended from the same individual mother.
- Politics is often mistaken for culture. People often do and say things in an effort to score political points or advance a political or personal agenda and call it "culture". Apparent differences in culture are often used as an excuse for intolerant and aggressive behaviours intended to advance personal or political agendas.

Our job as helpers is to learn which cultural traditions are important to our clients and to respect and honour them to the best of our ability. Some of those cultural traditions will impact how we help. For example:

- Roma believe that items that contact the top and bottom halves of the body should not touch, so in a residential or hospital setting, provide 2 sets of towels, and wash cloths,

and soaps, one for each body half. Romani are normally very animated, often shout and are argumentative, but that does not necessarily indicate disagreement. It is best for a helper to not overreact.
- Most aboriginal groups in North America rose from hunting cultures, and those adhering to traditional ways view the spirit world as a collection of powerful entities with whom a hunter needs to communicate in order for a hunt to be successful. An animal gives himself to a hunter if he has been pure of spirit and has not wasted animals he has in the past killed for food. Christianity was embraced much later. Even while attendance in church on a Sunday is common, private spiritual practices still respect belief in an actively engaged spirit world, so prayer will not always be to a Christian God. As helpers, we need to respect any spiritual beliefs that our clients wish to honour. Doing so is not an insult to our own beliefs, which are not important in that moment, when we are in a helping role. Park your beliefs outside the door. When you enter a client's world, your job is to find out what he needs, not to impose what you think is right.
- In Philipino culture, head nodding does not always mean agreement, and silence during a conversation is accepted and may be welcomed. Handshakes are welcomed. Any older male family member is seen as the main decision maker for the family, although ideas may be discussed with the family ahead of time. Discussion about risks or bad outcomes may provoke anxiety and to an elder, such conversation may be seen as a lack of caring from a service provider. Use an indirect approach when discussing events such as death or terminal illness. A person may believe that if faith is strong enough, a person in trouble will survive but if a person dies, the family may believe that the longer the grief, the better.
- Indonesian culture values indirect communication. "Saving face" is an important concept. Indonesians may smile even when disagreeing and nod when they do not understand. Paying attention to non-verbal language is important. Eye contact can be viewed as aggressive behaviour, so make direct eye contact only intermittently. Avoid using a loud voice. Society is patriarchal, with the eldest male being the spokesman or decision maker.

For some thoughts on helping African American clients, go to

seawinds-education.mykajabi.com/o-pt-in-to-resources-for-the-non-therapist

Then navigate to the Resources page. Under the section for Chapter 3, look for "Interview with Mary Desmond". Mary was a nurse in the Canadian correctional system and is now a community activist in Nova Scotia.

For more specific examples, consult "Handbook Patients' Spiritual and Cultural Values for Health Care Professionals" at spiritualcareassociation.org/resources.html

When considering your own onion, ask yourself these questions:

- What are some cultural traditions that influence how I act?

- - What parts of my culture do I embrace?
  - What parts of my culture do I reject?
- What are some of my most important values?
  - How do I think other people should be treated?
  - How do I want to be treated?
  - What is the most important thing to me in my life?
- What drives me to make the choices I make?
- What do I most need from other people?
- If I am really honest, I most fear….
- I recall a time when I acted from pure instinct. This is what happened….

When considering a client's onion, start looking from the outside inwards towards the centre of the onion. Ask:

- What cultural norms do I see influencing my client? What do my client's friends, family and community expect of my client? What cultural norms affect how I can best help my client?
- What has my client said about what she values? What is most important to my client?
- What can I see of my client's motivations? What seems to be driving her choices?
- Given what I can see of her motivations, what can I conclude she needs to feel okay and safe? Can I give my client some of what she needs in an appropriate way? Is she getting what she needs from the relationships around her? If not, what can be done about that?
- What can I learn about my client's fears? What can I do to ensure that I do not accidentally activate her fears?
- Is my client reacting from some instinctive drive for survival? What does she need to feel safe, and what can I do to see that she gets it?
- How can I adapt my own communication style, and my helping style, to make my client feel comfortable?

Not sure how to learn about another culture? The following chart may help. There are several different elements to culture. If you can learn about how each of these elements is expressed, then you are well on your way to understanding your clients.

Kate Tompkins

Cultural elements

Cultural element	What it concerns	My observations
Family belonging, individualism	Who is important? Who is most valued? How are children treated? How are elders treated? What are the roles for each sex within the family? What is considered masculine? Feminine? What is taboo? Who is considered to be immediate family? What is shared, what is private within a family? How are conformity, "differentness", individualism, independence and belonging viewed in the society?	
Spirituality and religion	What is the role of spirituality or religion in every day life? What place do spiritual leaders have in the society?	
Work	How are food, water and other essentials for survival obtained? Which occupations are most valued? What rules govern who may do what types of work? What value is placed on work? How is work recognized or rewarded? How are community re-	

The Non-Therapist

Cultural element	What it concerns	My observations
	sources shared?	
Relationships and communication	Who may approach and speak to whom? What rules exist for conversation in formal situations? Who may marry whom? Is there freedom to choose a mate, or is an arranged marriage the norm? What importance is placed on marriage? How is divorce viewed? Who has the highest status and respect and why?	
Health	What is considered normal mental and physical health? What factors are thought to contribute to physical and mental well being? What is the role of healers in the society?	
Leadership and governance	Who makes what types of decisions? What rules are in place for group decision making? Whose authority is ultimate? What rules are in place for resolving disagreements in the community?	
Time	How is time measured? What is the basic unit of	

Kate Tompkins

Cultural element	What it concerns	My observations
	time? In general, what is the tempo of life?	
Ownership of land	What space is used for what purposes? Who controls what space in a community? What is considered private space, and what is public space? How is space defended? Who owns land? Can land be owned? Or is it shared and cared for?	
Interpersonal communication	What are the customs about what may be talked about, and how thoughts and emotions are expressed? What are the speech and body language patterns?	
Teaching and learning, knowledge	Who teaches? What qualifies a person to be a teacher? How do young people learn? What types of knowledge are the most highly valued?	
Patterns of interaction and association	Who may speak directly to whom? Who may associate with whom? Who are leaders and why? What rules exist for association?	

Cultural element	What it concerns	My observations

Confidentiality and anonymity are key

Confidentiality is a key factor for all helpers. No client is likely to return to talk to you if they hear about their issue on the street or in the local watering hole. How you manage confidentiality depends on how your group functions. Following are some ideas to consider.

If your organization keeps records of contacts in order to meet the requirements of the law, you will need to have policies and procedures in place to be compliant with the legislation. These might include:

- Store records in locked filing cabinets.
- Use only initials or file numbers on written notes and records.
- Summarize contacts in the form of statistics to maintain confidentiality. Stats will also help when it's time to justify your job or the service, and for an annual performance review, or a report to funders.
- Don't keep written records on a computer that others can access.

The most important thing to remember is to ensure that no one talks about clients or their issues, at any time, to anybody, including spouses or partners. If an occasion arises when you need to share information with someone else for the sake of the client, perhaps a doctor or another helping agency, first get the client to agree (in writing if possible) to your sharing information. Without that written agreement, use only initials when talking to another helper.

Beware of the small-town gossip factor. Spilling even the smallest detail can identify a client in a community where everyone knows everyone else and most of their business. Make it a policy to **never** say a word to anyone other than another helper in your organization about your clients or the conversations you have with them (and even then, use only initials or descriptions such as "the teen pregnancy case I am working on").

When is it okay to break confidentiality?
There are times when breaking confidentiality is not only acceptable, but required. In Canada, provincial law requires that anyone in a regulated profession who suspects or hears about child neglect, child assault, or child abuse must report it to the local child protection service, usually a branch of whatever provincial department handles social welfare. There is no leeway in this requirement. That applies to most informal helpers as well.

If a person is suicidal, whether or not and to whom a helper is required to report that vulnerability depends on the policies of your organization. If there are no policies in place or you are not attached to an organization, then common sense prevails.

If you are a volunteer listener at a crisis line and someone reveals that they are suicidal, then how you respond will depend on a number of factors. For example, if your suicide assessment (See Chapters 5 and 6) suggests that the person has a plan and the means to carry it out, they are in immediate danger, so getting help to them immediately will be a priority, likely regardless of whether the caller wants a big response or not. In this case breaking confidentiality is acceptable. Will you call in someone to help? Probably. Who you call will depend on how your organization has set up its crisis response team.

If the caller has occasional passing suicidal thoughts but no plan, then the danger is not imminent, so there is time to refer the caller to a therapist for counselling help. In this case, you probably will elect to maintain confidentiality to protect the client.

If the client is homicidal, has a gun and says he will use it to kill someone, then a call to the police is called for; confidentiality is not even considered.

Working with a child has its own unique challenges. I usually tell children and teens that I will not tell their parents about everyday stuff they talk about but I will tell them anything I think they need to know to keep the child safe. Teens over 16 in most jurisdictions (the age is different in each province) are considered adults for the purpose of making decisions such as what to reveal, so you probably will maintain confidentiality with older teens.

Sometimes with kids I tell them I will not reveal their secrets if they don't want me to, and if the issue is not serious, but I encourage them to tell their parents themselves. I offer to help them tell their parents whatever the secret is, and that usually works out well.

You may find yourself in grey areas where you are uncertain what to do. If you are not sure whether or not to break confidentiality, you could ask the client for their permission to do so. Provide the rationale and explain what will happen when you do so the client can make an informed decision.

Super(wo)man does not live here

One of the toughest realities for a helper to embrace—even a pro—is that there is only so much we can do. Helpers want to help. It's what we do, and most of us who choose helping professions or volunteer activities feel like we were made to help, that there is rarely any real choice other than to help.

For our own mental health, we need to accept that we are not Superman or Superwoman. In spite of lots of well-meant help, we still often feel that we have failed a client. We might lose a client or a friend to suicide, to drugs or alcohol, to abuse or to depression.

A professional woman who worked in a social services type of job came to see me. She told me a story of having, in her perception, utterly failed a friend. She felt overwhelmed with guilt. He had trusted her, and talked with her often about his life and his woes, because he found her easy to talk to. These conversations continued over a few years. One evening, they talked late into the night, when he told her about something distressing in his life.

The next afternoon, he texted her and asked her to call him. She chose not to because she was working, and because she was concerned that the friend's wife might feel threatened, and she did not want to cause trouble for him.

The following day she got the news that he had shot himself that night, the evening she did not call him back.

The woman was distraught. She blamed herself for her friend's death. Logically, she knew that he had made his own choice and that she probably could not have done much to help, but she still felt enough guilt to sink a battleship. She spiralled down into depression, and she was in pretty bad shape.

As we talked, a few things came to light. The loss of her friend was bad enough in itself, but because she worked a job as a professional helper, she thought that she should have been able to do more for her friend. Her image of herself as a competent professional was shredded, and she had to take leave from her work. As she reflected, she recalled a time in her childhood when her father had threatened suicide by shotgun. Her memories of that earlier traumatic time were triggered by her friend's successful suicide and she fell apart.

I treated her for PTSD and for depression. The most critical change in her spirits came when she realized that in fact, there was very little she could have done to change the outcome. Her friend had been depressed and likely suicidal, for quite some time. She had, with her supportive listening, probably kept him alive for a year or longer than he would have managed without her help. He made his own choice and it is unlikely that kind words would have changed anything in the long run. If he had not killed himself that day, he probably would have found some other opportunity to do so later. She was responsible for an important part of his living, somewhat happier than may have been otherwise, but she was not responsible for his death. Once she was able to accept that reality her emotions changed a lot. In the end, she was able to go back to work, and felt calm and contented.

The bottom line here is that even the most well-trained professional helper is limited in what they can actually do. Our impact on the lives of others is important but we are not magic. We have no superhuman properties. We need to keep a bit of emotional distance from our helping relationships, as protection for ourselves, in case it all goes south.

Imagine you are wearing a Teflon cape. It's invisible and partly permeable. Through your protective cape, you can see and hear, you can identify and acknowledge your client's feelings, but they run off your Teflon cape like water off a duck's back. You don't need to take those feelings in or take them on. But you can still be there, an emotional anchor for your client, without losing your own cool. It's not always easy to do that, but developing that image is very helpful.

A happy ending? Not always!

Helpers want to help. We want to see happy endings. So it can be tough when we cannot successfully help our client reach the outcome they want to achieve.

Suppose you are a shop steward in your union trying to help a union member who is dealing with an illness that is disabling him. The employer wants to retire the worker because he cannot do the job well any more but the employee is looking for accommodations. The employee has worked very hard to get to where he is today and is adamant that he wants to continue working longer. As his shop steward, you want to help your union member in any way you can.

You feel for him, and care about his situation. But what if the best thing for him is to retire?

Your job may become less about advocating for change and more being a sounding board as the worker vents about how he feels about having to retire before his time.

Things don't always go the way we would like. So we need to be able to "pivot", to change direction in what we are trying to achieve. We may need to let go of our plans and schemes and focus on simple respectful listening instead.

Another situation in which a helper may feel impotent to actually help is when a victim experiencing intimate partner violence returns to the abuser. It is natural to feel frustrated, frightened for her. You might even think about cutting off help if she does not leave her abuser, even though you may know deep down that unconditional support will be more effective.

Sometimes we just have to let go of our expectations about the outcomes of our help and our role in creating change, and let go of the need for closure if we don't receive news of what happens after a client leaves us. If you have done your best to listen, and to help create the conditions the client needs to make good decisions, then you have done your job and need to step back. Look after your left-over feelings by talking with your colleagues or your supervisor.

Separate the person from the problem

Which of the following statements do you think would do the best job of encouraging your client to look at themselves and consider some changes in their lives?

"What's wrong with you?"
or
"What brings you to seek help today?"

If I think there is something wrong with me, I might think, "I might just as well pack it in. It's too much to change me, I'm too messed up". But if I think that there is some discreet issue, some single problem getting in my way, then it's just a matter of solving that one issue, which will probably sound much more doable. "I'm not a hopeless case, I just have this one wee thing I want to change…"

Here are some suggestions for how to separate the person from the problem:

"If you could talk to your anxiety right now, what would you say?"
"Tell your sadness what you want it to do."
"What needs to get talked about today?"
"Once you clear this up, what great plans do you have for the future?"
"What has worked for you in the past to reduce this issue?"

Simple changes in phrasing can have a big impact! If the client's focus can be shifted away from thinking what a mess he is, then there is room for problem solving. Focus on having the client brainstorm ways he can try to solve his problem, and suddenly he will have more hope. It becomes possible then for his life to change.

Another principle of ethical listening in action, to separate the person from the problem, is to remember that the client is their own best resource, and, deep down, knows better than anyone else what needs to happen to make constructive change successful. If you adhere to the philosophy that healing comes from within, given the right circumstances are present for healthy growth, then your job is to provide support, knowledge and encouragement. When the client has managed to solve her own problem herself, and she learns from the experience, then she is less likely to repeat the problem behaviour. She gets to feel proud that she did it herself. She can be proud of the new coping skills she has learned.

> The client is their own best resource and knows better than anyone else what needs to happen...Healing comes from within.

If you assume that the helper knows best (a risky idea at best, and arrogant at its worst) then who gets the credit for success? The helper, not the client. The growth and change are more modest. The relationship between helper and client may shift towards an uncomfortable balance where the helper holds more power than the client, which is not conducive to healthy growth and change.

When should I call in the big guns?

Call in an expert any time you feel uncomfortable or out of your depth. Here are common situations in which you will probably want to ask for professional assistance.

Trauma
Simply being there and offering supportive companionship in the early stages following a trauma has a huge value, but there is no point in attempting to do therapeutic listening with someone who has just experienced something dreadful and is likely in some degree of shock. Taking the person to the hospital is probably the best move after a traumatic event, even if they seem unhurt or denying they need to go. Often, we don't think straight after a trauma and cannot see what we actually need for ourselves.

If you can get the person to visit a hospital, sitting with them until they can be seen, then driving them home afterwards can feel like a life saver to the client. Keep the conversation light if you can, but don't avoid talking about the details of the event if the person brings them up and needs to talk. Save the deep listening for later, when the person's immediate physical and emotional survival needs have been met and they are able to talk calmly about the situation.

Post trauma
PTSD, or Post Traumatic Stress Disorder, is a condition in which the nervous system and brain get hijacked by an old memory and the emotions associated with it. The symptoms may include a number of rather distressing emotions and behaviours that can trouble the client significantly and that feel out of the client's control to change.

A bit of supportive listening never hurts, but it takes the advanced skills and knowledge of a therapist trained in treating trauma to resolve PTSD, using specialized brain-based techniques that are outside the scope of the non-professional helper.

Suicide

Most people who feel desperate enough to want to die first try to talk with someone about the misery they feel. Most often that person is a friend or a relative rather than a doctor or a therapist.

Empathy is the best tool for a helper to use in these early conversations. If the person opens up to you, offer to take them to a doctor or a therapist with more training to respond to suicidal thoughts. If the person has attempted suicide and lived, they will need some careful counselling by a professional. Supportive listening has a role to play in the short term, but it's best to refer the suicidal person to a professional.

Beware of suicide attempts in progress. It can be very dangerous to get in the way of a person who is trying hard to die. Even so called "empty threats" of suicide can be risky for a helper. I once was asked to talk a drugged-up dude with a knife off a bridge in the middle of the night. It was the scariest thing I ever did as a helper, and I would not do it again.

Even if you think the person does not really mean it, if there is a weapon involved or if the person is clearly highly agitated, call the police and keep your distance. Listening skills are useless in this kind of situation anyway. Your support might be helpful a few days later when the drugs have worn off and the person is interested in talking. Check out the section on suicide in Chapter 6 for more tips for responding in a helpful way to suicidal thoughts.

In some places, the police are trying a new approach. If the circumstances do not involve a weapon and no crime has been committed, they may call in a mental health team or may even leave the scene if a suicidal person seems agitated by an armed police presence.[13]

Charging in with an armed uniformed presence may trigger the distressed person into taking suicidal action, or may prompt the person to turn their weapon on the police. This approach aims to reduce harm to both the suicidal person and the police.

If you are asked to be part of such a response, think twice. What you can accomplish as a helper is limited and the risks can be high. Consider leaving a mental health response to professional helpers.

Depression

It's not always easy to see depression. Think of Robin Williams. He made millions of people laugh and presented himself as a happy, funny guy, when inside he was struggling painfully. Depression does not always lead to suicidal thoughts, but it is a risk that must be taken seriously. The role of the helper in responding to depression is to give the client an opportunity to talk when he is ready to and to refer him to a doctor or a professional therapist for treatment.

Spousal assault

Intimate partner violence is painful for a helper to witness, especially if the victim returns to

---

[13] washingtonpost.com/national-security/2022/09/23/calls-when-person-is-suicidal-some-police-try-new-approach/

her abuser. We feel helpless, and frightened for her. This type of violent relationship is complex, and exceptionally hard to influence from the outside.

About all that a helper can do is be available to talk when the victim is ready. Pushing your own ideas about what she should do is pretty much guaranteed to make her flee from your help and go back to her abuser. The best resource for a woman stuck in an abusive relationship is to try to connect her with a woman's support service that specializes in intimate partner violence, or with a feminist therapist.

Organic mental health issues
Mental health issues such as bi-polar disorder, phobias, psychosis, dissociative identity disorder (formerly known as multiple personality disorder), schizophrenia and obsessive-compulsive disorder (OCD) are most definitely territory for professional helpers. Refer the client to a doctor, who will in turn refer the client on either to a psychiatrist for diagnosis and medication, or to a mental health specialist for consultation to manage this type of disorder.

If the client already has a diagnosis of one of the organic mental illnesses, the only role for a helper is to be a considerate friend. Even compassionate listening has limits in its helpfulness, because a client with one of these disorders is often not in touch with reality.

Substance abuse
If you've been through an addiction yourself and managed to beat it, then you might have some useful advice for a person who is still struggling. Alcoholics Anonymous (AA) is an excellent resource for a problem drinker and Narcotics Anonymous (NA) for a drug user. Alanon and Alateen are supportive for family members of a drinker.

If you have not ever been through addiction and recovery, then trying to advise a client on an addiction is not very useful and may be harmful. The best resources are AA and its associated groups, addictions counsellors, and treatment programs.

Sexual assault
There are few traumatic experiences more damaging than sexual assault. The informal helper has a role to play, especially soon after the assault, when the victim may need non-judgmental, practical help with getting to a hospital, enduring a rape kit investigation, meeting with police, or going to court. Treatment of the psychological issues that so often develop following sexual assault is a job for a professional therapist.

Violence
Immediate, in-your-face violence is territory for the local police, who are trained and equipped to deal with people who are losing it. Listening will be mostly useless and unwanted during an episode of violence. The client may violently reject support you offer at that time. They are unable to think rationally when in the throes of violence. Stay the heck away until all has calmed down and the person is capable of calm, rational thought. Then offer your support.

While the violence is going on, the only role for a helper is to try to keep others safe. For example, if a man is beating up his partner, perhaps calling the police, then getting the kids out of the house to safety will be the most useful things to do.

Where can I refer my client for more help?

You as a helper need to be familiar with all of the referral possibilities in your region. On the next page are some examples of services you may find available to back you up:

• Professional therapists • Lawyers, legal aid service • Legal information service • Police • Victim support services • Crisis intervention phone line or drop in centre • Shelter for women • Homeless shelter • Soup kitchen, food bank • Mediation service • Women's counselling or information centre • Addictions counselling • Rehab counselling • Sexual assault crisis centre	• Spousal assault support program • Housing assistance programs • Mental health information centre • Walk-in medical clinic • Parenting supports • Social services agencies • Child protection service • Welfare support service • Used clothing store • Used toy and clothing exchange • Job bank • Career counselling service • Suicide prevention service • Drug users' safe injection facility • Parole, probation counselling • Military families supports

There may be others in your region. Research each possibility, if you are not already familiar with what they offer. Here are some questions to ask:

- What services do you offer?
- Who can access your services? Who cannot access your services?
- How can a client access your services? Do they need to be referred by a doctor or someone else? Do they need to bring ID or other documentation?
- Is there a cost to the client for your services? How much? If yes, what payment options are possible?
- What is your philosophy? Is this a values–based or faith-based service? Does a client need to agree with your philosophy in order to receive your services?
- How long can you provide services to a client? Is there a time limit? If that limit is reached, what happens next?
- What would cause you to deny service to a client?
- What are the education and background of the people working at your service?
- Are you able and willing to work in partnership with me / my organization to mutually

support clients?
- To whom are you accountable? To whom do you report? How?
- How do you maintain confidentiality?

Rapid self care

There is a lot written on the subject of general self care, so I will not duplicate that information here. Try to keep yourself as healthy as possible, physically and emotionally, so you will be in the best position to give whatever is needed to help others effectively.

Sometimes an intervention can be very stressful. You may find it tough to stay focused on the client and their emotions if your own are blazing. Sometimes you may find that you must quickly finish up with one crisis situation then move rapidly to another, with not much time to decompress in between. Police officers, physicians and nurses will be familiar with this challenge.

Here are a few techniques that will quickly help you to centre and calm your feelings (the pros call it "Self Regulation"). There is more on Self Regulation in Chapter 5. First, breathe. Imagine that you are breathing right down to your toes, and keep your breaths slow and deep. Try to make your exhale longer than your inhale.

Start with this rhythm:

- In for a count of 2, hold for 2, out for a count of 4.
- When your breathing has relaxed a bit, expand to 3, 3 and 6. Then 4, 4 and 8.

Next, drop your jaw. Relax your jaw and mouth. Relax the whole bottom part of your face, and relax the roof your mouth. Relax your shoulders—imagine your shoulders are melting towards the ground. And unclench your belly if it is tight. If any strong emotions are stuck in your body, tap your knees in an alternating pattern (left, right, left, right) while you focus your attention on the physical sensations in your body.

Try not to think, avoid visualizing whatever you have just seen, don't try to understand it or make sense of it. Don't try to minimize or change the physical sensations. Just notice where in your body you feel the physical sensations, and pay attention to them as you tap and breathe. Imagine you are sending loving awareness to your physical sensations. Keep this up for two or three minutes, or until your emotions dissipate.

Still some emotions lingering? If so, try this technique, known as "The Eye Roll":

- Keep your head more or less stable. Focus your eyes on the floor.
- Now slowly raise your eyes until you are looking up at the ceiling.

It's remarkable how such a simple action can have very peaceful and satisfying results! These actions all activate your parasympathetic nervous system, the "calm down" system. (More about this in Chapter 5.)

Key take-away points

- Plain, ordinary empathy and compassion are essential tools for the helper.
- Being authentic is important, but not always easy, and there are limits. Authenticity for a helper is honesty, with discretion.
- It's not about you or what you may value. If you find yourself pushing, back off.
- The client is (usually) in control of the agenda, and that's okay.
- Don't blab! Don't blab to the client or about the client.
- Accept that sometimes there is very little we actually can do to be helpful, and adjust your Teflon cape.
- The client is their own best resource, and helping the client problem-solve is usually the most productive approach.
- Call in the big guns when you know you are out of your depth.
- Know the resources in your region you can refer a client to when more help is needed.
- You can quickly centre yourself with a few simple techniques.

Activities to consolidate your learning

- Do whatever it takes to get past your own issues, whatever they may be, before diving into a helping role. Maybe consider a few visits to a therapist to work out any kinks that might get in the way of being compassionate and empathetic for your clients. Even if you think you are healthy emotionally, it can't hurt to test your confidence in yourself first.
- Learn and practice self regulation techniques. (More about these later.)
- Research legislation and regulations about privacy, confidentiality and sharing of information that apply where you live, to make sure that your organization's policies and procedures reflect those requirements.
- Talk with other staff and volunteers in your organization, as well as with other pros and experienced helpers, about the limitations they have encountered when it comes to helping others. This may help you to prepare for the helplessness that may accompany "failure" when you experience it.

For more information, check out the resources here:

    seawinds-education.mykajabi.com/o-pt-in-to-resources-for-the-non-therapist

4: What on earth should I say?

This chapter presents the key skills that will make you as helpful as a pro. Every therapist uses these skills many times every day. Fortunately, they are not tough to learn, so you can, too!

The main purpose of these skills is to help clients better understand themselves and their situations, and develop their own solutions for their issues. They also:

- Help the client be more precise about what she wants to get across.
- Help you, the helper, make sure you understand properly what your client is trying to say.
- Keep the conversation flowing when it might otherwise get bogged down if the client is confused or having a hard time expressing what is important.
- Help the client explore current issues, explore the past and its contributions to the present, and make plans for future change.

Key Skill 1: Listen actively

We all know how to listen. We do it all the time, right? Yes, but in a helping exchange, we need to listen more carefully, more skilfully and with **intention**.

Listening with intention means listening for specific types of information, for specific purposes. For example, are you listening to get important information quickly? Does the client's safety depend on you learning where she is, or what her symptoms may be? Are you listening to understand your client's dilemmas or conflicts? Are you listening for cues that your clients may be thinking about suicide?

Each of these would be best served with different techniques to elicit information from the client.

It could be a real problem if we miss something critical. That means we need to use some special skills that we would not necessarily use in an ordinary conversation with a buddy.

Listening is the most important thing a helper does. Listening underpins all else we do. Conveying to the client what we have heard when we listen is the heart of this key skill.

Why is just listening so important? Every human has an innate desire to be seen and heard. So many people trudge through their lives feeling invisible, unimportant, unworthy of notice; or perhaps even avoiding notice, especially if they have a history of people hurting them. When we reveal our inner dark corners and know we have been heard and seen, we feel connected to our listener. We feel supported and cared for, which provides hope that our lives can improve.

As you and your client progress through a helping encounter, and the client feels heard and seen, her trust in you increases. With trust, the client is usually able to open up even more, to explore the roots of the problem issue, and to face the tough stuff.

How do we listen actively? We pay attention. Remember the discussion about how to achieve authenticity in Chapter 3? We need first to clear out all of our own issues, thoughts and feelings so they don't get in the way. We need to turn off our own inner dialogue in order to focus on the client's words and body language. If you find yourself thinking more about what you will say or do next, rather than about what the client says, you may miss something important.

Next, we need to let the client know that we have heard not only the words but also the thoughts and feelings that are partly hidden. Ideas that are hinted at, or parcelled out in small bits, or ideas that seem conspicuously absent are often the key ideas that need to see the light of day.

The next step is to let your client know that you have heard her accurately. We do that by "active listening", using paraphrasing and reflecting back what the client has said and the feelings expressed. This way we are actively engaged in the dialogue.

Active listening is the process of giving back to the speaker what you see and hear to help the speaker better express himself and to clarify that you have correctly interpreted what the speaker wanted to say.

Guidelines for Active Listening

- Give your complete attention. Show respect, acceptance, empathy.
- To build trust, let the other person set the pace. Don't push faster or further than the person wants to go.
- Be patient. Allow plenty of time and do not interrupt.
- Don't be afraid to simply hold silence.
- Do not argue or criticize, as it is likely to cause the other person to clam up or become angry. Even if you "win", you lose.
- Don't feel you have to "solve the problem". The best solutions usually come from the person with the problem. Focus instead on acknowledging what you have seen and heard.
- Listen to what the other person is saying and how they are saying it.
- Watch for non-verbal cues to the person's feelings. Use your eyes as well as your ears for listening.
- Do not avoid the "tough stuff".
- Be aware of both the facts and the feelings in what your client is saying.
- Reply using your own words to describe what you have heard.
- Be honest. Let the other person know if you don't understand something they say to you.
- Keep focused on listening. The best way to do this is to stop talking yourself!

In active listening, the listener is as involved in the conversation as the speaker. Active listening becomes "empathic listening" when the listener is able to show understanding of the speaker's feelings.

There are several overall skills and attitudes that are an important part of active listening.

Show respect

It is important to show that you respect your client, even if you disagree with her. This is especially important when the topic is controversial, when you have strong opinions about the topic, or when your client is angry or upset.

- Respect your client's opinion, even if you disagree with it. Hear it out, point out its strengths. The other person has a right to their beliefs. If you are in a helping role, put your own values and opinions on hold, because they should not intrude on the helping process. What are important are your client's opinions and values, not yours, and how they affect their current thinking and feelings.
- Respect your client's feelings, even if you would not feel the same way in a similar situation. Do not make her feel small or inadequate for feeling the way she does.
- Respect your client's suggestions, think about them and point out their strengths, even if you are not in complete agreement with them. If you have doubts or you disagree, or you think they may create further problems for your client, say so gently but assertively, and do not criticize her position. She would not have come to you for help if she were 100% comfortable in her current situation in life, so she is probably feeling vulnerable. She is probably going to accept support rather than challenge more readily, especially in the early stages of a helping interview.
- Give body language signs of respect by being warm and interested in what your client says. Do not appear withdrawn, cold, uninterested, or preoccupied with your own thoughts and feelings. Do not use your body to say, "I don't like what you just said," when your words are supportive.
- Beware of enthusiastically talking so much that you jump in to speak while the client is still talking. You may think you know what is coming next and try to complete the client's sentence for them. While you may think this is a great way to show that you are in sync with the client, the client may feel stepped on, insulted or disrespected that you do not care enough about what they are saying to actually listen.

Show acceptance and empathy

One of the most important skills in helping others is developing sensitivity to the feelings, or emotions of the client. Most people feel better understood and more comfortable when the listener conveys a concern for us and sensitivity to how we are feeling. It is true whether we are feeling good or badly. Having someone take notice of our feelings helps us feel accepted and understood. Knowing the other person cares about the outcome of the exchange satisfies a basic human need. Often helpers find that simply ensuring that their client feels seen and heard can go a long way toward building trust, so that the client leaves you feeling better than when

Kate Tompkins

they arrived.

Be clear as to what your own feelings are about the conversation and separate them from your thoughts and opinions. Be careful not to allow your emotional reactions to be created by warped thinking, or allow your feelings to shape your helping words. Concentrate on what your client is saying rather than what is going on in your own head and gut.

"Showing empathy" means being able to get right under your client's skin and see the world from his point of view, then letting him know that you have seen and understood.

> When meeting with a stroke survivor, be aware they may have speech difficulties, either understanding what you are saying or expressing what they want to say. Just reassure them that you are there for them and encourage them to take the time they need.
>
> Remind them that they have something important to say and that you want to hear what that is. If possible, check with family members or caregivers to see what, if any, hints they may have to facilitate conversation.

- Try to imagine what your client is feeling, even if the situation is unfamiliar to you.
- Be willing to listen to and witness any emotion your client is feeling and needs to express. Just be there, and be open to it, even if it feels a bit scary to witness.
- Do not avoid talking about feelings that are intense or frightening to you if the client wants to talk about and show them. Even feelings that might make you feel uncomfortable, such as angry or hurt feelings, should be acknowledged. This will help you to discover what is on your client's mind and respond appropriately to his needs. If you need to, protect yourself by pulling on your "Teflon cape".
- Encourage your client to talk about anything which is on his mind. Don't shy away from thoughts of suicide or self-harm. Being able to express these thoughts, knowing their helper will treat them seriously and respectfully, can help someone in distress a great deal.
- Treat everything your client says seriously. The way you react when someone opens up to you can affect your client's day, month, even her whole life in ways you might not begin to anticipate.
- Use the skills of paraphrasing and reflecting feelings, which are covered a bit later in this chapter, to show that you have heard and understood the thoughts and feelings expressed.

Use voice and body language to show you are paying attention
The pros call these "attending skills". Attending means showing a person "I am with you", "I hear you", "I am paying attention to you." It involves using posture and voice to good effect.

- Face your client so that you can look easily at her face. Do not turn any part of your body away from your client. Turning your back on someone while they are speaking is a sign to some people that you are rejecting their ideas, or rejecting them as a person.

- Try shifting yourself and your chair to the right a bit so that your left eye and your client's left eye are aligned. This conveys a feeling of convergence: right brain to right brain[14]. In other words, your calming brain is in sync with your client's upset brain. This is a trick trauma therapists use to soothe and calm your client's brain with your own brain's self regulation. (See Chapter 5 for more on self regulation.)
- Use an open posture. Avoid crossing your arms and legs. Crossed arms or legs can be interpreted as meaning "I am not listening" or "I disagree with what you are saying" or even "I don't like you." But at the same time, ensure that you arrange yourself in a way that does not telegraph any possible sexual energy. For example, be wary of displaying plunging necklines or tight pants, simpering postures, spread legs, or crotch-obvious presentations.
- Lean towards the other person at times when it is appropriate, especially with the upper body. But keep it real and natural, a response to what you are hearing. Anything less than authentic will stick out like a sore thumb and destroy trust immediately.
- Keep appropriate eye contact with your client. Be sensitive to the amount of direct eye contact the other person is comfortable with. In some cultures, some people interpret direct eye contact as aggressive, while others are quite comfortable with lots of direct eye contact. Watch for the ways the client uses her eyes, such as looking down or away while you or she is talking. This does not necessarily mean she is failing to pay attention or does not agree with you (though it might mean just that). It may mean she is listening intently, looking away to better focus or to respect you. In such a case, adjust your own level of direct eye contact by looking away for some of the time while you are speaking and observe how your client responds. Go with whatever seems to make your client feel most comfortable.
- Use a pleasant, non-threatening, interested tone of voice, neither too loud nor too soft for the nature of the conversation or your location. If your voice is dull, flat, bored, quivering, or hesitating, or if you laugh at inappropriate times, it can be distracting, and can convey judgments or feelings you do not wish to convey. With practice, this will become

> Its about being willing to give up your time and be there for that person. There is nothing more disheartening when you are in crisis and you need something than having your helper check their watch and say 'I'm here to help you. I've got 10 minutes, what is it?' Shop stewards need to know 'what is the policy?', and 'what is the human condition?' Can we do something to help this person to feel validated. When it affects you, it's important.
>
> Let's figure out how to fix your environment. Everyone has the right to a safe healthy workplace, let's see how we can get that back for you.
> - Reyhan Sarikaya, Chair Health & Safety, Public Service Alliance of Canada, Northern Region

---

14 The right brain does most of our emotional stuff. The left eye is connected to the right brain, and the right eye to the left, more rational and logical, side of the brain.

- natural.
- Relax! Concentrate on your client instead of on yourself, then attending postures and voice will come naturally.

Do not avoid feelings

The facts and details of a situation may be very important in helping, and some of the time will be the main focus in the conversation. But even more important are the feelings which your client has about the situation. Acknowledging those feelings is a critical helping skill.

The ability to correctly interpret your client's emotions can mark the difference between a useful helping interview and one that misses the mark. We detail the "how to" of this skill in the next section.

Key Skill 2: The body cannot lie

Have you ever noticed that your client's words and her body language do not seem to match? The words may say, "I'm fine," but the body may be saying, "Help!"

The pros call it "incongruence." When you spot incongruence, you have a golden opportunity to learn more about your client's deepest emotions and about the conflicts she may be having between her thoughts and what her body feels.

Human beings are very complex creatures. Whenever we consciously experience any emotion—joy, sadness, fear, anger—we are usually aware first of some unexplainable physical sensation.

All emotion has a physical basis that the entire body experiences. Our brains release chemical substances, called hormones, which cause specific physical reactions in the body: a quickening of the pulse, sweaty palms, paleness of the skin as blood rushes away to the body's core, a tense knot in the belly, clenched fists. Then we use our brains to try to assess what those sensations mean. We learn to label these reactions as emotions.

There are three types of body language cues to be aware of, involuntary cues, conscious cues and vocal cues.

Involuntary cues

Involuntary cues, such as sweaty palms and pale skin, are physical reactions that just happen—we have no real control over them. They are in fact produced in an automatic way by the sympathetic nervous system.

When our brains detect something we should be afraid of, another part of the brain directs the body to release adrenaline. Adrenalin in turn tells the breathing to increase and the heart rate to speed up. We are preparing for a "flight, fight, freeze or appease" reaction. We inherited this physical reaction from our evolutionary ancestors and share it with all members of the animal kingdom.

Involuntary cues such as shallow rapid breathing and perspiration and flushing or paling of the skin are the same for all people, no matter where or how they were raised. An African hunter will feel the same rush of fear when faced with an angry lion as will a Cree hunter cornered by an angry grizzly bear.

It is a person's thoughts that determine how they interpret their own body's responses to the "emotion" hormones. Pleasurable excitement and fear look exactly the same, and feel pretty much the same in the body. How a person interprets their situation creates what they think they are "feeling."

For example, a person steps on stage to deliver a presentation or sing a song, and sees a big audience, all looking at her. Her palms may become sweaty, her breath may come faster, she may feel her heart beating strongly in her chest. What is she feeling? To know that, ask, "What are you thinking?"

> What to do? Ask! Try this: "I notice that your face is flushed and your hands are tight. What is going through your mind right now?"

If she thinks it is fun to be on stage, that the audience will applaud no matter what she does and will think she's great, she may be thinking, "Wow this is fun! I love it up here!" She is probably experiencing her body's physical reactions as thrilling excitement to be doing what she loves so much.

However, if she thinks she will make a fool of herself, she really does not know her lines, she expects to be nervous, or she has decided the audience will make fun of her, then she thinks something like, "Why am I up here? I can't do this." And thus, she feels scared.

It is the mind which makes sense out of the body's visceral responses. This is why it is often difficult to correctly interpret a person's emotions simply from casual observation.

Voluntary cues
The second type of body language cues are voluntary reactions. These are habits we learn, such as hand gestures and tone of voice.

From the time we are born, we learn voluntary cues from our families, friends, neighbours and the media. How we learn to show our feelings can be different for one group of people than for another. These cultural differences can cause quite a bit of confusion.

For example, in northern Canada, many older Inuit have learned from their earliest days that looking away from someone else's eyes shows respect for that person. Many Inuit raised in the traditional ways see direct eye contact as being rude, an invasion of the other person's privacy.

Imagine yourself living for ten months of the year in a tiny snow igloo, more or less on top of half a dozen other people, jointly making it through stormy weather, freezing temperatures, starvation, love making and all the daily moments of life with people close enough to be touching most of the time. It is not difficult to imagine how looking away from someone who is experiencing a strong feeling can allow that person at least a bit of privacy. That communication pattern is changing, but the tradition is still evident, especially in elders.

Most people raised in southern Canada, however, tend to have a different view of eye contact. Looking someone straight in the eye and holding that contact is thought to be a sign of self confidence, and trust in and respect for the other person. A person who looks away may be labelled as being dishonest, or lacking in self confidence.

Imagine a police officer, raised in, say, Toronto, with the best of intentions to serve and protect, who is posted in a small Arctic town and meets Inuit elders for the first time. With his direct eye contact and firm handshake, he thinks he is being appropriate and friendly.

But the elder when she gets home complains to her family about yet another aggressive white cop who should have stayed in the south.

Appropriate use of space also has a cultural basis. North Americans are used to more space around their bodies than are those of Asian heritage. A North American visiting China may feel that their personal space bubble is being invaded in a hostile way when others seem to crowd "too close".

Hand gestures are specific to local regions and to language groups. For example, what does a hand flipped under the chin mean to you? Nothing much? If your family is Italian, that gesture might have a very specific meaning that does not translate in a way you might expect.

The careful observer can pick up emotional cues from a surprising variety of sources, some of them very subtle. Our faces have an incredible range of motion. Signs like smiles, eye contact, eye movement and tension lines are fairly obvious; but there are infinite, subtle, tiny movements of the facial muscles, known as "micro expressions", that we pick up without ever being aware of it.

> Inuit traditionally used another signal that visiting southerners have found confusing: raising the eyebrows can mean "I agree" or "I like this" or "Yes." Wrinkling the nose can mean "I don't like this", "I disagree", or "no".
>
> I was rather confused when I first asked a question of a student and received a wrinkled nose as a reply. Being a fairly naïve transplanted southerner at the time, I totally misunderstood and took the person to task for not answering me.
>
> Needless to say, I lost some respect that day.

Our bodies are also very expressive. The way we sit or stand, the gestures of our hands, the amount of space we place between ourselves and the next person, shrugs of the shoulder—again, these are only the most obvious of a myriad of subtle cues our bodies give out. And we tend to attach meaning to them all, based on our own habitual communication styles.

The task of the observant communicator is to learn to watch for the body's signs and signals, to identify even the subtle messages, and to distinguish the emotions behind those cues. This requires practice. It also requires thought: what is the real meaning of what we observe in other people's body language cues? Do they mean the same thing to me as they mean to the other person?

Remember that many emotions look alike, and it is important not to jump to conclusions about how the other person is feeling. And since many people will not tell you directly what their feelings are, or cannot find a word to name their emotions, it is often necessary to identify the 'feeling note' in the other person's voice. You can do this by asking yourself:

- How would I feel if I were in the same situation? How would most people feel?
- What has my client said about how she feels?
- What feelings show themselves in my client's body language and voice?
- How do I usually feel when I speak in that tone of voice? How do most people feel when they speak in that tone of voice?

- What does that gesture or communication style mean to the other person? What does it mean to me? Am I correctly interpreting the other person's meaning?

Another issue is that many people cannot name their emotions; they only know they feel bad. You can help such a client by naming the body language cues you have noticed, and offering a menu of possible emotional choices. For example:

"I see that your hands are tight, and your jaw is clenched. Do you feel angry right now?"

You can start with the four major emotional states: "mad", "sad", "glad" and "afraid". Most people can tune into those possibilities. Then you can further refine the choice. For example, if a client is "mad", is it because of frustration? Or fear that they don't know how to express? Or pain they are afraid to express? (Anger is so much easier and feels so much more powerful than fear or pain. Much anger is actually some other emotion that has not been expressed openly.)

Vocal cues

There are many types of vocal cues to pay attention to. The tone of voice can either match the words chosen, or not. When there is a conflict between the voice tone or the body language and the words used, it can help to gently point this out to the speaker. You could say something like, "I hear you say that you are feeling all right, but I notice that your hand is clenched and your foot is tapping. Could it be that we have missed something important to you? Is there more you would like to tell me?"

Pointing out discrepancies between words and body language cues can help to identify circumstances in which your client is trying to hide his or her true thoughts or feelings, especially if he is embarrassed, or afraid what he says will not be treated with respect. However, it must be done gently and tactfully, and with obvious care for the client's welfare, if it is your intention to maintain openness and clear communication. A challenge of this sort which is thrown out aggressively can stop open discussion in its tracks.

The qualities of a person's voice have an important role to play in expressing emotions, including the following:

- Loudness or softness
- Spacing of words
- Speed of speech
- Choice of words to emphasize
- Cadence (lilt)
- Pauses
- Sighs
- Silence
- Crying, laughing, shouting

Be careful not to jump to conclusions if you are listening to someone whose first language is not the same as your own, even if you are both speaking in the same language for this conversation. There are many vocal patterns that are peculiar to specific languages that do not have the same meaning in other languages.

We tend to make judgments about what we hear, if it does not match the vocal patterns we are used to hearing. We are usually not aware that we are making these judgments because the sound of our own language is so basic to who we are. It is very easy to make mistakes in identifying another person's feelings if we are not aware of some of these patterns.

It is important to 'check out' a person's feelings using more than just voice tone as a guide, especially if the speaker's first language is not your own. Look for signs of emotion in the body language and face movement of the speaker to confirm or correct assumptions drawn from voice tone.

Spoken English in North America has a sparkling array of dialects, based on geography and culture. These dialects show themselves largely in non-verbal information such as those traits above. For example:

- Long silences are uncomfortable to some people, who may want to jump in and say something to "fill in the gap" which is uncomfortable to his ear. However, to some others, silences mean the speaker is thinking, and are not uncomfortable. You can often offer help and comfort to a friend in need by sitting in silent companionship. A laid-back speaker may interpret the more animated speaker's haste to fill in a silence as being aggressive, even if it was not intended that way.
- In most dialects of English, the voice goes up at the end of a sentence to indicate a question. You know the difference between "It's cold outside." and "It's cold outside?" by the lilt in the voice. It is easy for an English speaker to unconsciously assume that any sentence ending with an upward lilt in the voice is a question, or perhaps shows uncertainty or confusion on the part of the speaker. However many languages contain much more lilt than English does and the listener would be making a mistake to assume that a speaker of such a language is not speaking with confidence if the tone doesn't sound 'right' to the English speaker's ear.
- English speakers tend to leave longer pauses between sentences than do speakers of say, French or Spanish, and shorter pauses than, say, Japanese speakers. When the speakers of two different first languages get together in a conversation, the result is often misjudgment of the others' feelings. Pauses that sound "too long" can be interpreted to mean 'that person is slow, or doesn't know what to say, or is unhappy, or a bit stupid'. Pauses that sound 'too short' can be interpreted to mean 'that person is hostile and aggressive, or selfish or arrogant'.

Keep in mind that the speech patterns of a person's first language carry over to other languages they speak. The lilt of an Irish-born Gaelic speaker will be heard when that speaker converses in English. The brief pauses between sentences sometimes heard in French are the norm when a Francophone is having a conversation in English. English speakers who learn another language will carry their familiar speech patterns into the way they speak their adopted language.

Notice the conversations following. What thoughts and emotions do you anticipate each individual will experience? Human nature being what it is, what judgments do you think each is making about the other on the basis of their interpretations?

Two speakers of a language with short pauses between speakers

Two speakers of a language with long pauses between speakers

Speakers of two different languages with different pauses between speakers

The trick is to become aware of your own speech patterns and watch how others are interpreting them. Notice other people's speech patterns and identify how you are interpreting them. Don't assume that what seems comfortable and familiar to your own ear is "right" or universal.

When a listener can correctly identify the feelings of the other person in a conversation, rather than making assumptions which may be false, it is possible to begin to understand their point of view.

Key Skill 3: Ask helpful questions

In English, we use questions more often than any other communication tool for gaining information. It is easier for most people to ask a direct question than to use any other technique to find out what we want to know. However, questions are also the most often misused tool in our collection of communication skills.

There are several problems with asking questions:

- Questions tend to make the client feel defensive. Asking a question gives the impression that you have a reason for asking and that you have a use for the answer. This may suggest that you wish to be more powerful than the speaker and somehow control what he or she does.
- Questions used to fill a silence, or because the helper is nervous and doesn't know what to say or do next, take away from the client the opportunity to think and to say what they want to say. Direct questions take control away from the client in favour of the helper.
- Questions are sometimes asked because the helper is curious. Again, the suggestion may be that the listener has the right to probe into the private thoughts of the speaker, which may be a misuse of control.
- Asking a lot of questions may suggest that the helper can solve the problem, if he has enough information. This takes away from the client the opportunity to solve their own problems, to take the credit for what works, and to learn from what doesn't work.
- Asking questions, especially "Why?", can give the message that you disapprove or are displeased with what the client has said or done.

In spite of these potential issues, most of us in North America ask a lot of questions, so let's look at how to do so in a helpful way.

What makes a question helpful?
There are basically two types of questions: **open-ended questions** and **closed questions**.

Open-ended questions basically require a long answer, inviting the speaker to say as much or as little as they wish. It is like opening a door wide and saying to the speaker, "You may do as you wish." Open-ended questions usually evoke more response from the other person, because they feel like they have control.

Closed questions can usually be answered with a simple yes or no, maybe, or I don't know. They invite the client to talk about only what the helper wants to hear. It is like opening a door a crack and saying to the speaker, "You may do only what I want you to do." Closed questions are often the most effective way to gather specific information, facts and details. However, at the same time, they are also the most effective way to cut off communication. For example, if I ask you a closed question, here is what is likely to happen:

Helper:
Does this child custody plan work for you?

Client:
Yeah, it's okay.

The client is not really given much of an invitation to tell the helper very much. To find out more, I will probably have to ask another question.

However, if I ask an open-ended question, I will probably have better results:

Helper:
How would this child custody plan work for you?

Client:
Well, it's not too bad. I like the weekend access. But I'm worried about the handovers at school. My child's father cannot be counted on to stick to a schedule. My lawyer is quite anxious to get this finalized, but I'm not sure it's the right choice."

> **Effective questions**
>
> Use open-ended questions frequently to build trust, to draw out the client's true thoughts and feelings, and to explore deeply.
>
> Use closed questions sparingly, to gather factual information and to limit the conversation.

Now we have some more detailed information to work with.

Open-ended questions tend to be more effective in most helping circumstances because they give responsibility to the client to decide just what and how much to say. The client is likely to give you more information simply because he thinks it is his choice to do so. Closed questions place control in the hands of the questioner to shape the conversation and generally narrow the focus and minimize expression of opinions and emotion.

When do I use closed questions?

- When you want to narrow the focus of the conversation.
- When you want to reduce the expression of opinion and emotion.
- When you need to gather specific information quickly, for example in an emergency.

When do I use open-ended questions?

- When you want to explore a situation and find out as much as you can.
- When you want to build trust and rapport.
- When you don't know where the client might want to take the conversation.

Kate Tompkins

Here are some examples of open-ended and closed questions. When would the open-ended question be the best choice? When would the closed question be the best choice?

Open-ended questions	**Closed questions**
How do you feel about what happened last night?	Are you still angry today?
How is the new equipment working out?	Is the new equipment easy to use?
How are you and the Board getting along these days?	Are you and the Board still fighting?
How will this computer work out for you?	Is this a good computer?
How do you feel about the new policy?	Is the new policy too restrictive?
What do you need from this discussion?	Will you accept my terms?
How do you plan to respond to this proposal?	Will you hire me?
How are you?	Are you happy?
How does the news sit with you?	Are you mad?

Here are some examples of ways to begin an open-ended question:

- How do you feel about...?
- What do you think about...?
- What is the best way to do this?
- What is likely to happen if you do that?
- What would you like to do?
- How can I help?
- Where do we go from here?
- What would you like to see happen?
- If you could have anything you want, what would it be?
- What is the most important part of this for you?
- What would you like for me to do?
- What are your plans?
- What would you add?
- Is there anything else you want to say?
- What else did we talk about?
- How was your week?
- What brings you to me today?
- I'm curious about...
- Tell me more.

Pseudo questions
The simple question can actually be a real problem-maker for both people in a conversation. In fact, many so-called 'questions' are not really requests for information at all. They are, in fact, a passive-aggressive attack. They may be a way for the questioner to offer an opinion without coming right out and saying what is on his mind. In order to avoid having his idea tossed out,

he will phrase it as a question in hopes of forcing the other person to agree with him.

These 'pseudo questions' are actually a way for the questioner to try to gain some advantage over the other person. Consider these examples:

Pseudo question	Implied meaning
Don't you think that this class is boring?	I think this class is boring. You should think that way too.
Isn't it true that you missed a lot of work last month?	Gotcha! You missed a lot of work. You'd better agree with me.
No one would steal without a good reason, would they?	You might steal stuff. You'd better have a good reason.
You don't really want to leave your job now, do you?	I don't want you to leave your job, and I want to convince you of that too. You would be making a wrong decision if you chose to leave your job now. I know better than you.
Wouldn't you rather hold the conference in Antigonish?	I want to hold the conference in Antigonish, and you should want that, too.
If you were in charge of the meeting, wouldn't you handle it differently?	You'd better handle it my way.
How about asking me first before you offer the job to someone else?	You were wrong to offer the job to someone else, but I don't want to say so openly.
When are you going to fix that window?	Fix the window. You should have done it already.
Weren't you the one who wanted it this way?	This is how I am doing it. You should want it this way.

In each of these examples, the questioner is trying to gain control. He is trying to suggest the 'correct' answer, to punish the other person, to force him into some action, to 'set her up for the kill', to trap him, to provoke a fight, or to force her approval of something the questioner wants to do.

Questions of this type do not improve communication. Rather than opening the door for further discussion, they tend to do a very good job of cutting off any open or honest conversation. This can be a huge mistake in a helping situation.

What if the client has not yet revealed that she feels suicidal, but the thoughts are there under the surface, and she is desperately seeking the right opening to tell you? Closing off communication could result in disaster.

Kate Tompkins

Double questions
Now test yourself: why are these questions less than totally helpful?

- "Do you want to go to the store or do you want to stay home?"
- "How do you feel, or how would you like to feel, and what are you going to do about it?"
- "Are you upset about this, or....?"
- "What does your partner want to do, and what would be the result if she did?"

Which of these possible responses is correct?

- Which question is the client supposed to answer? It's confusing for the client.
- Double questions imply that the client may not know the answer or is not smart enough to come up with their own answer.
- Some people might assume the second possibility is the one you want to steer the client towards, even if she feels more comfortable with the first option.
- The client may think the questioner is in a hurry and is trying to push the client towards an outcome that will sew things up quickly in the way the questioner wants.
- If the client's first language is something other than English, the client is likely to be quite confused about what the interviewer is trying to say.

These are of course all correct! It makes me grind my teeth when I hear radio interviewers accosting a guest with confusing double questions.

To avoid double questions, relax, slow down, ask a simple open-ended question, then quietly listen for the response. If you don't see what you need to know in the client's body language or voice, you can always ask a new follow-up open-ended question.

Culture and questions
There is another problem with asking questions: the way we gain information about another person tends to be tied to our upbringing. While many people in Canada usually accept a direct question as commonplace, others find questions, especially closed questions, to be an extremely rude invasion of privacy.

People have a right to guard private thoughts and feelings as their own, and to accept probing from another person only when they choose. Certainly, direct closed questions would be very inappropriate for someone who felt that way.

The person seeking information must respect the other person's privacy and invite him or her to talk through other techniques, such as paraphrasing or possibly an open-ended question. Careful observation of body messages will often tell the curious person all he needs to know.

Questions do, of course, have their place. It is the responsibility of the helper to choose the most appropriate communication tools for any given situation. If a question is in order, phrase it so as to improve communication rather than to harm it.

The Miracle Question
Pros often use the miracle question to encourage a client to think about what could be, and to take steps towards creating the desired situation. Here is an example of a miracle question used when working with a couple:

Helper:
What if, overnight while you were sleeping, a miracle happened? You wake up, and your relationship is suddenly a 10 out of 10. It's fantastic. What would that look like? What would it feel like? What would you be doing? What would you say? What would your partner say and do? Close your eyes and see a clear picture of what your life would be like if that miracle happened. What do you see?

Client 1:
I see us walking together in the garden. My partner looks at me with affection in her eyes. We hold hands and do stuff together. She tells me what is in her mind and we have a calm, quiet conversation that ends in a kiss. I give her a massage; I know she likes that.

Client 2:
I see us doing the dishes together. He helps with the vacuuming, without my even needing to ask. I feel warm and affectionate to him. He goes grocery shopping without bugging me to make a shopping list. Then he brings me home flowers and we sink into the couch and watch TV together while we hold hands. I make him his favourite chocolate cake, just 'cause.

Helper:
That sounds like a really nice picture. Now let's try an experiment. Each of you pick a day sometime this week, but don't tell your partner which day you choose. From the moment you wake up to the moment you fall asleep, for just that one day, behave as if the miracle has already happened. Everything is great. Do and say everything as if your relationship is wonderful, a 10 out of 10, in spite of whatever your partner might do or say. You act exactly as you would if such a miracle actually did happen. Then just observe. Notice any changes you can see in the way your relationship is for that day. What do you do differently? What does your partner do differently? How do things change because you acted differently? How do you feel during that day? Then next week, you can reveal which day you chose and share what you learned from the experiment.

The Miracle Question helps clients to see that life can improve, and that there is a role they can play to make it so. They can see the impact of their choices on others, and experience how it feels to create a different dynamic in their relationship. They also can see more clearly what their own thoughts, triggers and emotions are, and see if any misperceptions have been in control, getting in the way of marital bliss.

Here is an example of using the Miracle Question with a child:

Helper:
Let's play a game. See this magic wand? If you wave your magic wand, you can make wonderful stuff happen. Now what if when you go to sleep tonight, you wave your magic wand, and when you wake up in the morning, you have no anxiety. Poof! It's all gone. Like magic, a miracle happened over night and it's gone. Now close your eyes and imagine what that would feel like. What would you notice in your body? What would you do differently if you had no anxiety? What would you say to your friends?

Scaling questions

Another very useful tool is the scaling question. This tool asks a client to rate on a scale of 0 -10, or 0 – 100, what level an emotion might be at this particular moment, or how much the client actually believes some thought. Scaling questions imply that an emotional sensation can change over time, and that the client may be able to do something to manage that emotion. It might also imply that a thought, for example a negative impression of oneself, might also be changeable.

Here is an example of using a scaling question to look at change and progress:

Helper:
If 0 is "none at all", and 10 is "completely overwhelming", how strong is this feeling right now?

Client:
I'd say a 6.

Helper:
A 6? That is progress! Yesterday you said your anger was at an 8. What made the difference for you?

Client:
I realized that I was thinking about it wrong.

Here is an example of scaling questions used to help shift a client's negative thinking pattern:

Helper:
You tell me that you think you are a bad person. What number between 0 and 100% would you give that thought? How much do you actually believe it right now?

Client:
I guess 80%?

Helper:
Okay. Now let's flip that thought, how would you word the exact opposite thought?

Client:
I know I am a thoughtful person. People say I am.

Helper:
Okay, great. What evidence do you have that this is true?

(Have the client share evidence of being a good person).

Helper:
Now give this thought a number between 0 and 100%.

Client:
50%.

Helper:
Okay, great. So that adds up to more than 100%. Now how is it possible that you can believe both thoughts at the same time?

A discussion follows about how what we focus on becomes our reality, how our thoughts about ourselves often become warped, how we often ignore evidence against our negative thought, and that, in some corner of our minds, we know the negative thought is false. So let's choose to focus on the positive thought instead.

See Chapter 5 for a tool that can be used to help the client understand this concept.

Questions to fill silence
Have you ever made this common mistake: Have you ever blurted out some question, whether appropriate or not, to fill a silence?

Some people are really uncomfortable with silence and will yak about anything in order to escape that uncomfortable feeling. However sitting quietly with a client in distress can be very calming, a very valuable support. The client probably feels comforted by your steady presence and may be too tired, or too hurt, or in too much pain, or too much shock to be able to talk. Why on earth would you make a client in distress have to listen to your babble?

The client may think he is not supposed to talk about whatever is on his mind if the helper is babbling. The helper trying to fill silence is liable to

> When sitting with a client who is not talking, it can be helpful to visualize that you are holding the time and space you are sharing as your client processes their thoughts and feelings. You can visualize a white light surrounding both of you and supporting the client as they process and you hold the silence for you both. While sitting in silence you can also try matching your breath to that of the client. Breathe in when they do, out with them. This can also create an unspoken bond that facilitates the client-helper relationship.
> - Christina Baxter, Chaplain

miss some important piece of information or to make incorrect assumptions. Don't be afraid to simply sit in companionable silence with your client. Use your attending skills to let your client know you are there and paying attention, and let your client take the lead with the conversation, unless the situation demands that you take charge for the sake of safety or to guide a client who cannot manage on their own for the moment.

Be the quiet anchor for your client. This is a type of support that may best be given by informal helpers, since the pros often just don't have time to sit with a client.

Being silent but making it clear that you are still there, still listening whenever the client is ready to speak, is a great way to elicit more information. Letting silence sit gently during a helping conversation can be quite revealing.

Sometimes the client needs time to organize their thoughts, and will reveal what you need to hear in their own time. The client may feel driven by the silence to dig deep and reveal the most crucial information to fill the gap, which may give the helper important clues that might not have come out otherwise.

Silence also avoids judgment or anything else that the client might find off-putting. If you have the sense that your client is not yet revealing something important, you can use silence to ferret out what the client cannot yet say.

Silence can save a life!

Guidelines for asking useful questions

- Do I really need to ask a question right now? Can I use some other communication tool instead?
- By asking a question, am I trying give a message that is better not given?
- What other alternatives can I use?
- Would a closed or an open-ended question help the conversation more right now?

Key Skill 4: Be a mirror for your client

Paraphrasing facts and details, and reflection of feelings

Paraphrasing is a way to let the speaker know that you heard and understood. It also helps you to be certain that you understand correctly what the speaker said. Paraphrasing concentrates on the facts and details of a speaker's message.

> On YouTube, find the video "It's not about the nail"

As helpers, our task goes further than simply being a listening post for the client to sort out their issues. We need to zero in on the personal, emotional and cognitive issues that are important to our clients' health, safety, happiness, and sanity. While paraphrasing begins that process, we need to go a step further to be truly effective. We need to respond to the feelings that a client shows us.

Reflecting emotions is very similar to paraphrasing, except the focus is not on facts and details, it is on feelings and perceptions. It is like holding up a mirror so that the speaker can see herself more clearly.

Let's take a look at how paraphrasing and reflection of feelings can shape a conversation.

Example 1

Client:
My damn roof leaks! It drips on the bed and my wife had to replace the pillows. We can't afford that, and was she ever pissed! She bitches that the linoleum needs replacing in the kitchen, the family needs another bedroom, and the sink is cracked. How am I supposed to deal with all that with a bad back? And the damn bank has threatened to take back the house!

Paraphrase:
You do have a lot of things to think about right now. The problem with the bank seems to be the most immediate problem.

> **Effective paraphrasing and reflection of feelings**
>
> 1. Acknowledge the most important part of the message.
>
> 2. Keep the focus on the speaker, not on someone else.
>
> 3. Probe for deeper meanings.
>
> 4. Listen for what is not said.
>
> 5. Combine interest in both facts and details, and on emotions and personal impacts for a well-rounded response.
>
> 6. Focus mostly on the emotions in a therapeutic conversation.

This response helps to focus the speaker on the issues that are of most immediate importance, which can be quite helpful if the speaker is rambling or confused or feeling overwhelmed.

Where will the conversation go from here? Probably to a discussion about how to deal with the banking issue. The listener can re-direct the flow of conversation toward household maintenance issues later, if that seems important, but deals with the most immediate issue first.

Let's try a reflection of feelings instead:

Client:
My damn roof leaks! It drips on the bed and my wife had to replace the pillows. We can't afford that, and was she ever pissed! She bitches that the linoleum needs replacing in the kitchen, the family needs another bedroom, and the sink is cracked. How am I supposed to deal with all that with a bad back? And the damn bank has threatened to take back the house!

Reflection:
I would be frustrated, too, having to deal with all that. And worried as well.

Where will the conversation go from here? Probably to the client's feelings about the situation. This may lead to the most critical issue for the client—that he feels helpless to change the situation, and that a resulting feeling of inadequacy due his back issues may be affecting his marriage. He has already hinted at that.

His anger may really be a way to say that he is scared. Do not focus on his anger, which may amplify the client's feelings and distract him from the real issues. If you feel uncomfortable with his anger, take a deep breath and redirect the client to his underlying feelings instead.

Example 2

Client:
My wife's drinking is badly affecting the entire family. She has lost her job, money is tight, we might lose our house. I have tried negotiating with the bank, but they don't really listen, I am sure I got nowhere. I cannot pay the mortgage this month unless I let the power bill go for another month. And of top of that, I was called into my boss's office yesterday. I slipped up on a project I am working on. I just can't concentrate on what I'm doing. I'm always worrying about money and trying to figure out what to do. So now I have been warned, so I might lose my job too. This is a disaster! I don't know where to start. What should I do?

Paraphrase:
You have some serious issues to deal with right now. Which of your money problems are you most concerned about?

Client:
Well, the bank. I guess I can hold onto my job for now, I can worry about that later. Do you know a good mortgage broker?

Where will the conversation go from here? Probably to plans to get his family's finances in order, which will help the client stay focused and not panic, running about in several unproductive directions at once.

Let's try a reflection of the speaker's feelings:

Client:
My wife's drinking is badly affecting the entire family. She has lost her job, money is tight, we might lose our house. I have tried negotiating with the bank, but they don't really listen, I am sure I got nowhere. I cannot pay the mortgage this month unless I let the power bill go for another month. And of top of that, I was called into my boss's office yesterday. I slipped up on a project I am working on. I just can't concentrate on what I'm

doing. I'm always worrying about money and trying to figure out what to do. So now I have been warned, so I might lose my job too. This is a disaster! I don't know where to start. What should I do?

Reflection:
I can hear your worry in your voice. It must be a really scary position to be in.

Client:
It is. I'm worried sick. And not just about the finances. I am also worried about my wife, and what to do to help her. And how can I protect the kids?

Where will the conversation go from here? Probably not to financial planning, which can wait, but to his emotional state of mind. Is he okay? Is his health okay? Is he making good choices to manage his stress? Does he feel any helplessness or desperation that might lead to even darker places? Does he need any assistance for his kids or his wife?

Example 3

Client:
My partner is a real piece of work. He is very controlling, he won't let me spend time with my friends. He gives me an allowance to spend on the house. But God help me if I can't pay all the bills on the little he gives me. Things get much worse on the weekend, when he is drinking...and the amount of money that he spends in the bar on Saturday nights! I could do the grocery shopping with that bar bill! I budget very closely, but I usually don't have enough to look after myself after the family's needs are taken care of.

Paraphrase:
You do have some legitimate concerns about this problem. Clearly you have thought about the money issues in a lot of detail.

Client:
Yeah, fat lot of good it does me though.

> When a client mentions what they are feeling, it is temping to respond "I know just how you feel." Do your best not to respond in this way because it can feel to your client that his experience is being minimized or trivialized. It may also feel like the conversation has now become about you and not about the client. Yes, we all know what it is like to feel grief, anger, and loneliness. But what we don't know is how it makes our client feel.
>
> Use your recollections of similar feelings to create empathy. Then using active listening techniques, reflect back to your client what you have heard and what you have seen in facial expression and body language. This will give your client an opportunity to correct any misunderstandings and will let them know you are a caring participant in the conversation.
>
> - Christina Baxter, Chaplain

Where will the conversation go from here? Likely to concerns about money management. And how she might manage in this tight situation.

Let's try a reflection of the feelings she hinted at:

> Client:
> My partner is a real piece of work. He is very controlling; he won't let me spend time with my friends. He gives me an allowance to spend on the house. But God help me if I can't pay all the bills on the little he gives me. Things get much worse on the weekend, when he is drinking… and the amount of money that he spends in the bar on Saturday nights! I could do the grocery shopping with that bar bill!
>
> Reflection:
> You mentioned that he is controlling, and that things are worse on Saturday nights. And you seem to be talking fairly calmly about your money issues, but I hear some distress in your voice. I have a feeling there is more you want to tell me.
>
> Client (beginning to cry):
> He hits me. Sometimes he bruises my eyes and last month he broke my arm. Every damn Saturday night! I'm so afraid of him! I can't go on like this.

By the client acknowledging the feelings she hinted at, the conversation has gone someplace very different, and she has been able to reveal the real trouble she needs help with. The money issues can wait until she is safe.

Acknowledge the most important part of the message
Sometimes it is tough to choose which of the speaker's words to focus on. It might seem easiest to focus on the most obvious things the speaker is saying, but this may not be the most effective response.

Example 4

> Client:
> I'm very depressed. Since I lost my house and my son in that fire, I feel lost. Like there is no reason to get up in the morning anymore. I just want to die.
>
> Poor Response:
> You seem to be less than your usually happy self today.

What is the likely response to this comment? The speaker may be hurt or angry that his words have been taken so lightly. You may be the first person he has opened up to. In any case, this is probably the end of the conversation, for any trust the client may have had in the listener is likely to have evaporated.

Let's try again:

> Client:
> I'm very depressed. Since I lost my house and my son in that fire, I feel lost. Like there is no reason to get up in the morning anymore. I just want to die.
>
> Better Response:
> It's important to you to feel that you have security and a home and family. I know someone who can help.

Where will the conversation go from here? Probably to a discussion of a community resource that might be able to offer some assistance. Helpful, because it addresses the client's needs immediately.

But there is a more important issue: the speaker is suicidal. So it is best to zoom right in on that strong emotion.

> Client:
> I'm very depressed. Since I lost my house and my son in that fire, I feel lost. Like there is no reason to get up in the morning anymore. I just want to die.
>
> Even Better Response:
> I know it must be terrible to feel suicidal. I can imagine how lost you must feel.
>
> Client:
> I'm in a deep hole. I don't know how to get out.
>
> Even Better Response:
> I want you to know that you are not alone. Things must seem pretty hopeless to you right now, but I know someone who can help. And you and I can keep talking now for as long as you like.

By acknowledging how the speaker feels inside, the listener gives the speaker hope and a sense that the situation might in fact have a solution.

When people hint at suicidal feelings, it is important to address them head on. Do not try to put them aside. If you are not sure what to do from there, refer the speaker to someone who does, but do not ignore the comments or allow them to be swept under the carpet.

Keep the focus on the speaker, not on someone else.

Kate Tompkins

Example 5

> Client:
> Why do you think my boss does that?
>
> Poor Response:
> Perhaps he didn't get along too well with his mother.

You have just taken the conversation away from the speaker to talk about her boss instead. This will likely stop the speaker from saying much more that is important.
  Let's try again:

> Client:
> Why do you think my boss does that?
>
> Better Response:
> I'm not sure. But I can see that it is important to you to understand why your boss acts the way he does. How does his behaviour affect you?

So now where will the conversation go? Probably to a discussion of how the speaker feels about the situation at work.

Adjust your Teflon Cape
Being a mirror for your client helps him to see himself more clearly, which can lead to seeing his own strengths and coming up with his own solutions. This is absolutely the time to ensure that your Teflon Cape is securely in place. The focus **must** stay on the client's experiences, thoughts and feelings, and not on your own.

Probe for deeper meanings
When you are learning to paraphrase and reflect, you will likely begin by repeating the speaker's words in your own voice. Doing so can be useful, because it at least lets the speaker know you were listening. However, it is not as helpful as trying to get at the deeper meaning of what the speaker has said. It's like telling a friend that "I really have a craving for a piece of chocolate cake" and having your friend respond with "Well, you really have a craving for chocolate cake." You know your friend heard you, but that's about all you know. And your friend will likely be annoyed enough to end the conversation.

> Client:
> I don't think I should have ever gone to college.
>
> Weak Response:
> College isn't the right thing to do.

Client:
Yeah, I guess so.

Most likely, that will be the end of the discussion. Let's try again:

Client:
I don't think I should have ever gone to college.
Better Response:
It sounds like you think you made a mistake.

Client:
That's it exactly. I have never admitted that to anyone. I don't know what to do. I have to stay in this job for a few years until I pay off my debt to the government, and I don't like the job. In fact, I have been having trouble sleeping lately, just worrying about being stuck here. What is going to happen to me and my family?

Choosing to aim directly at the deeper meaning in the speaker's words usually leads to a more in-depth discussion of the issue.

*Listen for what is **not** said*
Try to "read between the lines". In other words, listen for what is not said, or what is hinted at but not said directly. Often when a person begins to say something and then changes his mind, he is hinting at what is really important to him.

Client:
Things have been bad for a long time. My mom and I have been fighting each other all winter. My step-dad and I don't get along at all and I am afraid they are going to kick me out. He is a bit of a jerk, and I really miss how things used to be, before he came along. And now...well...now I don't know what I'm going to do.

Good Response:
Things have been piling up on you.

Client:
Yeah. It's kind of hard right now. I don't know if I will be able to stay at home much longer.

This response is not bad, because it lets the speaker know you have heard her concerns, at least superficially. But what about that last bit? There seems to be another problem hinted at which the client has not talked about yet. Notice how much further the conversation goes when you acknowledge that hint.

Client:
Things have been bad for a long time. My mom and I have been fighting each other all winter. My step dad and I don't get along at all and I am afraid they are going to kick me out. He is a bit of a jerk, and I really miss how things used to be, before he came along. And now...well...now I don't know what I'm going to do.

Better Response:
You were going to say something more.

Speaker:
Yeah. I had not planned to tell you this, but you seem to be a good person and I trust you. I was going to say that I'm pregnant! Mom will go berserk and my stepdad will kick me out for sure. And what about school? Oh God, what am I gonna do?

Now that you know what is really going on with this client, you are in a position to respond in a way that will be appropriate and useful.

When do I choose to paraphrase facts and details?
Focus in on the facts and details in these circumstances:

- When you need to gather details quickly, as in an emergency.
- When the circumstances do not really support the client opening up and being vulnerable, such as in a public place.
- When you need to control the conversation, such as managing a troublesome client whose interest is not really obtaining help.

When do I choose to reflect feelings?
Focus in on the feelings in these circumstances:

- When the interview is a helping encounter. Feelings are the bread and butter of a therapeutic conversation.
- Whenever the client expresses, displays or hints at any emotion.
- Whenever the topic is one of personal importance to the client.
- Whenever you can imagine yourself feeling something significant in a similar situation.

Can I combine a paraphrase and a reflection of feeling?
Yes. In fact most responses in a helping conversation will be some combination of a focus on facts and on feelings. If there is a choice, choose to focus on the feelings first, then move on to deal with the practicalities of the situation later.

On the next page are some ways to begin a paraphrase or a reflection of feeling:

- If I understand you correctly, you are saying...
- So you are saying....Is that right?
- It sounds like...
- From your point of view...
- It seems to you...
- In your experience...
- From where you stand,...
- As you see it...
- You think...
- What I hear you saying is...
- Let's sort this out. The most important thing is...
- You have talked about...
- You were going to say something more...
- You seem to have left something out that is important to you.
- Could it be...?
- Here are the choices we have talked about....Did that include everything we have talked about?
- I can hear...in your voice.
- I can see... in your face.
- I notice that your hands are...
- You must feel...
- You mentioned...
- I would feel...too.
- I can imagine...
- Things must seem...
- You mean...

Key Skill 5: Avoid giving advice

Giving advice can be a very dangerous communication tool. Here's why:

- When you give someone advice, the client is likely to become dependent on you. The client may think she needs you to make decisions for her.
- When you give advice, you are assuming that you know what is best for the client. A parent or elder may have more experience than a child and can offer some assistance in handling difficult situations. However, most adults prefer to discover what is best for themselves. Most of us do not know better than others what is best for them. Encouraging the client to come up with his own solutions is a foundation pillar in therapeutic listening.
- The client may interpret your giving advice as indicating a lack of respect. It is like saying, "You are unable to explore the options and to make your own choices."
- Giving advice creates a "no-win" situation. If the advice works, the client cannot take any credit for solving the problem. If the advice doesn't work, the client may blame the helper, instead of taking responsibility for their actions themselves. This takes away the opportunity for the person with the problem to learn from their own mistakes.
- Giving advice usually does not help the person with the problem understand their situation more clearly. They may leave the conversation just as confused and upset as when

> People know best what is best for them. We are just here to let them discover it for themselves.
>
> - Patricia Couchoir,
> Transitional Housing Manager

they came in, maybe more so.
- How people receive advice depends on both cultural norms and individual personality. For example, people who grew up with aboriginal elders may be perfectly comfortable with receiving advice, accepting it as being the usual way that knowledge and information is passed from one generation to the next, especially if it comes from someone older than themselves. People who grew up independently may resist being told what to do, since they think they can manage their affairs perfectly well on their own. Many people may tend to resist advice, since, in Canada, the most widespread cultural traditions do not celebrate advice as a standard way of learning.

The main risk with giving advice is that the person with the problem is not part of the problem-solving process. Helping is something that is done to them. After receiving advice, a person with a problem may, for a short time, seem relieved and may feel that the pressure has been eased or removed from them. This will not last, because the person has not taken an active part in the solution, and thus has not dealt with whatever caused the problem originally.

Key Skill 6: Avoid self-disclosure

It can be very tempting to tell your client all about your own story, about how you solved a similar issue, implying that the client should do the same thing. I'll bet you can guess by now why this is a sand trap. Did I hear you say, "Because it takes focus away from the client and how he sees his issues"? You are correct! Did you also say, "It robs the client of the satisfaction of learning from his own mistakes"? Right again! And maybe also, "What's right for me may not be what is right for my client"? So true! Oh and one more thought: "It is not up to me to lay my burdens onto my client". Yup, 'nuff said. (Remember "authenticity with discretion and boundaries"?)

I can also hear you wondering if you should say something like this: "Yes but...I can maybe show you a new perspective that might be useful for you." Well yes, that might be true, if it is done well. For example, speakers at AA meetings publicly share very personal, intimate details of their struggles and achievements, which can model possible happy futures for others in the meeting who are beginning their journey of sobriety. In this case, listening to others' self dis-

> If you try to tell people what the answer is you are going to get yourself into a whole lot of trouble. I always said just slow down, take some deep breaths, relax, and I think you will come up with your own answers. I never gave a solution to anybody. I am not God, I don't have the answer or the solution. I'll guide you down that path and you tell me the answer. When you start giving people answers that's when you get yourself into trouble, and them. That's the best counselling you can give anyone. After they come to an answer, then the professional help can be given to them. Finding that reason why they need help, then getting them the help is easier. They have to realize what got them there.
>
> - Mary Desmond, Corrections Nurse and Community Activist.

closure is part of what people come for.

You could reduce the possible risks of self disclosure by asking the client if he is interested in hearing about your story, keeping your comments very brief, and quickly returning the focus back to the speaker. Try something like this:

> Well, yes, I did deal with something like that once, and I learned a lot from the experience. I can tell you about it if you need to hear it. But what would you like to do?

The best way to use your own experience therapeutically is to quietly model the type of life skills that would set an example for others.

Key Skill 7: Probe, summarize, reframe and confront helpfully

(and with humour!)

Probing
Probing is a combination of paraphrasing and asking questions. Probes are designed to obtain information from another person. Asking the right questions can result in clear answers.

Be careful using probes, as they may be interpreted as controlling. Ask yourself first, "What is my intent in using a probe?" If it is to correctly understand or to discover information you need to know in order to help your client or to keep your client safe, a probe is warranted. Otherwise, it may be wiser to take some different direction with your client to maintain their trust.

Since probing can backfire, use it sparingly, gently, and respectfully. Try infusing humour into your probe. Humour can go a long way toward disarming hesitation or resistance and encouraging a client to open up more.

Probes have many uses. For example:

- To encourage a client who has been vague to say more.
- To help the client get back on track if she strays from your questions, or her response has nothing to do with your question.
- To encourage the client to say more when her response has been too general or you are not clear on how she feels or thinks.
- To ferret out the truth when you suspect the other person is not being completely honest or is covering up important feelings or information.
- To encourage your client to talk when he does not respond at all.
- To clarify a response that is unclear or doesn't make sense.

On the next page are helpful probing openers:

- Could it be that...?
- I wonder if...
- Would you buy this idea:...?
- What I guess I'm hearing is...
- Correct me if I'm wrong, but...
- Is it possible that...?
- Could this be what's going on, you...?
- This is what I think I hear you saying...
- You appear to be feeling...
- It appears you...
- Perhaps you are thinking...
- I sense that you may feel...
- Is there any chance that you...?
- Maybe you feel...
- Is it conceivable that...?
- Maybe I'm out to lunch, but...
- I'm not certain I understand. You're feeling...
- It seems that you...
- As I hear it, you...
- ...is that the way it is?
- ...is that what you mean?
- ...is that the way you feel?
- Let me see if I understand. You...
- Let me see if I'm with you. You...
- I get the impression that...
- I guess that you're...
- If I understand you correctly, you are saying that...
- Can you expand on that a bit more?
- Can you give me an example?
- How strongly do you feel about...?

Summarizing

During long conversations, it may help to stop and summarize what has gone on so far. This is especially helpful if the conversation has been tense, a lot of information has been covered or the client is upset or confused. It makes sure that nothing important is forgotten or left out, and helps the client focus on what is most important, instead of getting lost in unimportant details.

Summarizing also allows the speaker to correct any misunderstandings the listener may have about what has been said.

Follow these steps to summarize:

1. Make an opening statement, then describe what you think has been said and how the client has felt about it:
    - "Let's go over what we have talked about so far. You mentioned..."
    - "Here are the choices we have thought of so far..."
    - "Let's review this."
2. Ask the client to either agree or disagree with your summary:
    - "Is that right?"
    - "Has that got it all?"
    - "Did that include everything we've thought of?"
    - "Did I forget anything?"
3. Ask the client to correct any part that was not right:
    - "What did I leave out?"
    - "What else did we talk about?"
    - "What would you add?"
    - "Is there anything else you want to say?"

Reframing

Reframing is the skill of helping the client see and think differently about their situation. It's all about planting the seeds of possibility.

Our brains are designed to seek out problems, to see the negative first. Pros call this a "negativity bias". That was a useful survival skill when we were living in the midst of carnivorous predators and countless dangers to our survival, but in today's modern world, that skill can actually make our lives hell.

If we let our brains have free rein in a relatively safe situation, we risk becoming anxious due to constantly worrying about what might happen that could harm us. We start seeing the worst in every situation and cannot enjoy the good and the beauty surrounding us. We miss out on happy relationships and make it impossible for joy to exist. We also tend to skew the truth when we allow a negativity bias to be in control, because we close our minds to the possibility of some other explanation, some other way to see the world, some other way to solve a tough problem.

> Being able to see a situation from a different point of view can help you feel better and uncover new ways to manage a problem or situation. Simply put, sometimes we can't see the forest for the trees. And often, seeing that broader picture can help us tremendously. This is what reframing is. Reframing, in the therapeutic sense, is about looking at a situation, thought, or feeling from another angle.
>
> - Jor-El Caraballo, Talkspace.com

Whew! Sounds exhausting, doesn't it? Doing all that makes it tough for happiness to bubble up inside. A negativity bias with free rein destroys relationships, creates depression and anxiety, and generally makes life miserable.

It's also important to note that our emotions are created directly by our thoughts. If I wake up in the morning and think, "I wonder what crap I'll have to deal with today," what do you suppose my day will be like? I am likely to feel down, discouraged, negative, even angry for the rest of the day. But if I wake up in the morning and think, "What a beautiful sunrise!" then I have a better chance of seeing my day and all the people in it in a positive way.

How do we helpfully challenge a client's negativity bias? By reframing. That means flipping a thought around to see it another way. For example:

> Client:
> My kids are out of control since my wife and I split. They are deliberately trying to defy me. I cannot get them to be kind to each other or their mother. I am a failure as a father.
>
> Helper:
> Are your kids trying to give you a message? It sounds like they are confused and scared. What do they need from you right now?

This parent now is looking at his children's needs rather than focusing on their bad behaviour.
Here is another example:

Client:
Since my accident, I have been quite emotional. My emotions are off the wall, in fact. I'm broken. You can't ever heal me. I'll never be the same again.

Helper;
You are worried about your future. That's understandable, but let's look at your progress so far. You have managed to reduce your stress level, you are back to work and getting through your day. That is good progress! How did you make that happen?

Now the client will be focusing on the strengths she already has in her personal tool box, and what else she might do with those strengths, rather than being overwhelmed by all of the negative thoughts her brain is all too eager to supply her with.

Here is another example:

Client:
I am such a failure. I slipped again! Here I thought I was OK finally but I ended up in the bar with my buddies after bowling on Tuesday. I might as well give up.

Helper:
You tell me that you slipped this week, but you did a great job of staying sober last month. What worked for you then? How can you bring those great strategies into your life again today?

Yet another example:

Client:
I am frustrated. I am slipping with my diet plan. It seems like I can never manage to go any further, so I am sabotaging myself.

Helper:
I want to let you know that you are doing great! You can go further, because you have come this far. Take a look at this chart for yourself:

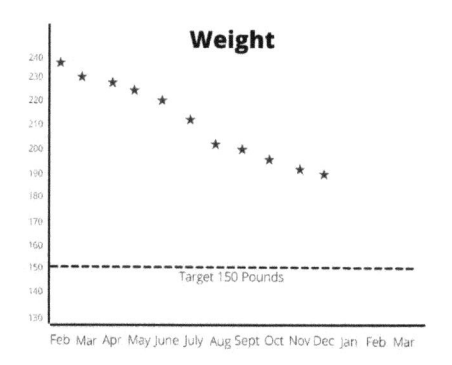

Now the client can see that in fact her progress has been steady and is still heading in the right direction, even if she feels frustrated at this moment. That will give her hope and confidence to keep on going with her plan.

And one more:

> Client:
> I am so depressed. I can't even get out of bed in the morning.
>
> Helper:
> So you have been depressed.

Notice how the helper restated the client's words into the past tense? It opens up the possibility that the client can feel something different tomorrow. Now the client will be thinking about what he needs to do to make that vision happen.

Remember the actress with stage fright? You can help her to think differently about her emotions. Instead of focusing on her fears, you could help her reframe her thoughts by thinking that the sensations she feels are the body's way to say, "I want to do a good job," rather than fear of failure.

Supportive confrontation
Supportive confrontation is the art of challenging the client while still ensuring your support. One of the simplest ways to confront helpfully is to point out inconsistencies and discrepancies. Our old friend humour can help with that task.

If the details of a story are told one way today and another way tomorrow, there is an inconsistency. If the body language says one thing and the words say another, there is an incongruity. These are often gold mines of important information to be tapped.

Inconsistencies and incongruities are signs that the client is not completely aware of what she is saying and that there is something important underneath her words. That may be due to a number of reasons. Perhaps she is confused. Perhaps her memory of the incident is incomplete, which sometimes happens after a traumatic event. Perhaps the event happened decades ago and her mind has actually altered parts of the memory to be comfortable for her to recall. Perhaps she is attempting to deny or avoid a painful memory. Perhaps she thinks she cannot face the truth, or she fears that perhaps her listener does not want to hear the gory details and may abandon her. Perhaps she fears that bringing to light some nasty details will make her so emotional that she will be unable to cope.

> "Framing the conversation from our own experience is helpful, as is the use of "joining" language to establish common ground. We honor the goodness in the other while describing the gap between our expectations, assumptions, and/or commitments."
> - Flip Brown
> businesscultureconsultants.com

Whatever the reason, inconsistencies and incongruities should be acknowledged to see where they take the conversation. For example:

- I see that your foot is tapping and your hands are moving a lot, although you tell me that you feel relaxed. Is there something on your mind that needs to get talked about?
- I'm confused. Last time we spoke, you mentioned that your husband never hurt you, but today you tell me that he tossed you against a wall. Can you clarify that for me? What really happened?
- You say that your family is your first priority, but you also tell me that you chose to do 5 hours of house cleaning on the weekend when they wanted you to go hiking with them. I am confused. What can you do to give your family the priority you want to give them?

It is important that you can point out inconsistencies and incongruities in a way that does not make the client feel judged, challenged or belittled. If your approach implies that you think the client lied to you, you will break the client's trust and you will likely miss the opportunity to bring to light an important issue. The client needs to feel that you are on her side, even when you are gently challenging her.

Supportive confrontation is a skill that must be used carefully. If you use it too early, before the client has learned to trust you and you two have built a supportive alliance, it may backfire. The client may evaporate, feeling attacked and betrayed. Relationship building is an important first step before attempting confrontation.

The purpose of supportive confrontation is to help the client understand how his choices are affecting him and how his warped thoughts are keeping him stuck. If your agenda is something else, don't do it!

To confront supportively, follow these steps:

- Identify and describe the core inconsistency, incongruity, ambivalence or mixed messages you have noticed.
- Assure the client of your caring and support using your attending and respecting skills.
- Identify and acknowledge the inconsistent feelings that likely accompany the inconsistent thoughts, using open-ended questions and reflections of feelings.
- Try using humour to defuse any resistance the client may have to looking at his choices.
- Help the client analyze their own inconsistencies and incongruities. Try being curious about how the client would explain these inconsistencies, rather than judgmental about seeing something different than you expect from your client. Both your own perspective and the way the client sees the situation may change dramatically with this simple step.
- Try being "unattached to the outcome", as eastern philosophy thinkers would say. In other words, remember that the client needs to come up with their own solutions, not ours.
- Present the situation as a challenge rather than as a problem, or a partial success and progress rather than a failure to complete important tasks, or perhaps as a hidden strength forgotten or not yet recognized.

Rapid creation of trust, connection and cooperation

If you need to build a sense of connection and trust quickly, the two most effective skills are to reflect obvious emotion (describe the body language you see and what you suspect that might mean emotionally to the client) then follow up with an open-ended question (to learn what is foremost on the client's mind). This two-step rapid-connecting technique works well in all types of circumstances, including emergencies.

For example:

- I see that you are in pain. How can I help?
- You look like you are trying to choose which way to go. What is your main concern?
- I can see indecision written all over you. What can I do to help you decide?

Key take-away points

- Listen with intention. Listening actively is the number 1 key skill.
- Show respect for your client's opinions, feelings, suggestions.
- Use attending skills to show acceptance, empathy and attention. Take what your client says seriously. It might matter a great deal more to your client than you realize.
- Do not avoid feelings or the "tough stuff."
- Learn what your client's involuntary and voluntary body language cues and vocal patterns communicate and note ways in which they may differ from your own familiar patterns.
- If you must ask a question, use closed questions to gather essential information quickly and to limit conversation; use open-ended questions to build rapport and trust, to learn what is on your client's mind and to help her to explore deeper.
- Use specialized questions such as the miracle question and scaling questions to help your client explore further what could be in their lives.
- Don't be afraid of silence.
- Use paraphrasing content to gather and highlight facts, and reflection of feelings to explore emotional reactions. Focus mainly on emotions in a helping conversation.
- Listen for what is not said as a clue to essential concerns.
- Avoid giving advice and talking about yourself.
- Probe, summarize, reframe and confront supportively, after a therapeutic relationship has been developed.
- To build trust and connection quickly, use a 2-step approach: a reflection of feeling followed by an open-ended question.

Activities to consolidate your learning

1. Give this client a useful paraphrase or reflection of feelings:

   Client:
   I have a terrible problem with money. My boss has covered for me once, but I am afraid he won't do that again. I borrowed some cash from my employer's business account without him knowing and now I can't pay it back.

   You:

2. Write a useful paraphrase or reflection of feelings for this client:

   Client:
   There are so many different choices I could make. I just don't know which to choose. I could go back to school and get my grade 12. I could move in with my parents and help out at home with the younger kids. I could move to Halifax and try to find a job. I could just sit here and get stoned. Quite a life, eh?

   You:

3. Find a partner you like and trust for a role-playing exercise. The conversation should be: "How money and I get along". Take turns, and make it real. When you are the speaker, talk about you and your money. When you are the listener, use paraphrases and reflections of feeling to respond to your partner. Try to "read between the lines" and get to the deeper meaning of what your partner is saying.
   After a few minutes, switch around. If you were the listener the first time, now you be the speaker. If you were the speaker the first time, now you listen.

4. Replace these closed questions with open questions:

   Closed:
   Do you still want to work here?

   Open:

   Closed:
   Are you going to sue the Council now?

   Open:

   Closed:
   I know it's been difficult for you and the work team, but you don't really want to fire him for his drinking, do you?

   Open:

Kate Tompkins

    Closed: Do you want to conclude this negotiation now?

    Open:

5. Find a partner you like and trust for a role-play exercise. The topic of the conversation should be: "How I feel about my body."
    When you are the listener, make sure everything you say is a piece of advice to the speaker.

- What happens to the conversation?
- When you are the speaker, how does it feel to be given advice?
- When you are the advice giver, how does it feel to give advice?

6. Respond to the following speech using paraphrases, reflections of feelings, questions, probes, reframes or supportive confrontation.

Client:
Well, this sure is a big mess. Look at those kids out there, looking sneaky. I'll bet they're off to sniff glue or something. My wife spent $1200 last weekend—on what? Nothing much that I could see. How am I supposed to—oh, never mind. It doesn't matter all that much anyway, I guess. Now how about them Blue Jay's? Reminds me, there's a game on this weekend. TV got broke yesterday though. It kinda—slipped (har har), slipped off its table, you know what I mean? Bitch. She'll get what's comin'. Better to watch a game on TV, though, than to put up with those idiots I work, er, used to work with. Damn bunch of 'em are idiots. The meeting on Wednesday was quite the humdinger, I can tell you. Lots of fur flying! That new grader operator is a dolt. Drove right over the edge of the cemetery last week! I'll bet he rolled over a few of the old folks, if you know what I mean. Bought your lottery ticket for this week's draw yet? It's a bigg'un!

Your summary:

If you want feedback on your activities, try sharing with a partner or a pro therapist. If you want more practice with these skills, try enrolling in an on-line course, such as the ones listed in Chapter 8.

For more information, check out the resources here:

    seawinds-education.mykajabi.com/o-pt-in-to-resources-for-the-non-therapist

5: Freebies to swipe

This chapter offers simple tools you may swipe to use with your clients. All are either non-proprietary and in common use, or are products of my own experience. All can be used, with some thought and preparation, by non-therapists.

All of the documents I have created are copyrighted, so, while you are welcome to use them yourself, I ask that you respect my professional experience, my need to earn a living (I have a mortgage to pay, too!) and copyright law by doing the following:

- Do not use my materials for any financial gain. Do not sell them to clients, and do not incorporate them into your own or your agency's resources to line your pockets or your agency's bank account.
- Do not distribute any of my resources to anyone outside of your own immediate organization. By all means show them to your co-workers if they would be of use for helping clients. But please do not send them out to any other office, organization, board or agency, to the media, or to the public. If there is something you really like and want to make wider use of, please ask me for the rights to do so.
- Do not use my resources for training your staff. If you need staff training, I can provide a custom training program just for your organization, or encourage them to register for my next course offering. For information about courses, please consult Chapter 8.

These activities should work well with clients who are relatively sane, calm and capable of thought and self analysis. I would NOT recommend using these tools under these circumstances:

- Your client has a diagnosis of, or is suspected of having, one of the organic disorders, such as dementia, bi-polar disorder, psychosis or schizophrenia. (Leave working with this client to a pro therapist, psychiatrist or a doctor.)
- Your client has lot of trauma in their background which has not been resolved through therapy. (Working with PTSD is a job for a pro therapist.)
- Your client is experiencing high emotions, is very upset or confused. (Wait until your client is in a calmer frame of mind.)
- Your client exhibits tendencies towards violence or mental or emotional instability. (Leave working with this client to a pro therapist.)
- Your client's basic survival needs have not been met. (Help them find safety, shelter, food, water, medical attention, sleep or whatever other help is needed. Leave using

these tools until some other time when your client's life is more stable.)
- Your client has some agenda other than exploring his life. (Meet the immediate needs; forget your own agenda.)
- You do not have a private, quiet, comfortable place to meet.

I recommend trying out the tools with friends or co-workers to become comfortable with them. It also helps to see how different people might react to a tool. Some might help to strengthen relationships and co-operative thinking on your team if your group tries them together.

There are five types of tools in this chapter:

- Tools for exploring the past
- Tools for exploring relationships
- Tools for creating a better future
- Tools for improving mental health and awareness
- Self-regulation tools
- Triage and response tools

Tools for exploring the past

Timeline
This very simple tool can help a client explore his past and its contributions to his present, and identify trends, patterns, and gaps. It's also great for developing rapport with your client if you work on-line together.

How to use it
Start by having the client assemble a piece of shelf paper about two feet long, or several sheets of printer paper taped together, and pens or markers in different colours. Next, have your client draw a horizontal line across the centre of the page.

Under the line, the client can print years or ages. Then, under that, the client writes in important events, places he lived, or people who had a significant impact on his life. Above the line, he can write in emotions he recalls being significant at the time. He can use the coloured pens to highlight details, date ranges or repeated emotional responses. You can work on the timeline together or, if he needs time to think about it, he can complete the timeline at home for you two to look at another time.

A completed timeline might look and work like this:

Timeline

Age	Event	Feelings
0		Can't remember
3		
5	father leaves the home	Angry, sad, confused
8	mother remarries	
10		
12	raped by stepfather	Angry, sad, betrayed
15	abortion	Lost, scared
18	University	
22	Married John	Can't remember
25	husband has affair	Angry, sad, betrayed
30	Started new business	
32		Excited, hopeful

Ask the client to lead you on a guided tour of his timeline, pointing out the key items. You can encourage him to analyze the picture he has created with questions and reflections such as these:

- "I see that your dad left when you were five years old. That must have been a confusing time for you."
- "You mentioned that you felt angry after your dad left. And I see that you have felt that way a few times since. How much of that anger still exists for you?"
- "How did your husband's affair impact you?"
- "You have not said anything about your university years. How were they for you?"
- "In what ways do you think your early years affect you today?"

Cautions

Be careful not to put words in your client's mouth. You may be able to see clearly some patterns or points of significance, but it is the client who needs to discover them.

Don't offer any solutions. Completing this timeline can be a starting point for a client, and can bring important reflections or "ah-ha!" moments. But if there are some lingering post-trauma symptoms or significant emotional impacts that are causing problems for the client today, then resolving them is territory for a pro therapist. The helper's job is just to begin the process, to awaken awareness.

Time travel journalling

This is an exercise in journalling. It can help to keep track of one's life, thoughts, emotions, and dreams.

How to use it
Assist the client to gather a notebook to write in, pens, etc.

To log current events, encourage her to make a journal entry every day. In her entry, she can make note not only of significant events of the day, but also persistent thoughts, emotions, and observations about her day. She can then review her journal regularly to note her progress.

You can use this journalling tool to explore the past as well. Have your client begin to write about past events as if they were current. Encourage her to imagine she is writing just after the past event. She can imagine the thoughts she recalls having at the time, and the emotions that she felt, to create a faithful record of the past event. She can then look back to review the past events and also look at her present to see what echoes there may be now in her current thoughts and emotional habits.

Time travel journaling can also help paint the picture of a sparkling new life a client wants to create. "If you can imagine it, you can likely create it," is an old saw, but it's true. Have the client write as if the new life were already a reality, have her describe what steps she took to create that new life—and voila! She has a blueprint for change that she already believes will work.

These questions might help her to analyze her journal writing:

- "What trends do you notice? Are there any familiar patterns, thoughts, or feelings that repeat over time?"
- "Do you see any significant changes in your moods over time?"
- "In your past events, how did you feel? How did you get past those feelings at the time?"
- "Do you recognize those old familiar feelings in your present? What triggers them?"
- "Do you see any patterns re triggers, people, places, objects or events that typically precede a familiar mood?"
- "What does this tell you?"
- "What would you like to do about it?"
- "How can I help?"

Cautions
Reliving past events can bring up some strong emotions. This is an exercise in developing awareness that you should introduce when the client is fairly calm and stable. I would caution against using it when the client is in the throes of strong emotions or events that will require a lot of her emotion and attention.

A client who is known or suspected to have a lot of trauma in their background, or to have PTSD, should probably not do this exercise without the support of a pro therapist to do trauma treatment. But clients who are more or less OK can have fun with this activity and can learn some interesting bits of information.

If you glean important information from this exercise, your client may need to talk more about her patterns. Just listen and help her draw conclusions. If it seems that she is distressed or needs to explore some difficult memories, then it is time to call in a pro therapist.

Kate Tompkins

Free-flowing art
This is a fun way to help your client simply express himself freely, without words. Sometimes, trying to find words to talk about what is on our minds is tough, especially when emotions are running high or after a trauma. No artistic skills are required: even someone who "cannot draw a straight line" can happily do this exercise.

How to use it
Gather together paper and paints. Finger paint or watercolour paint in jars or tubes work well. Long sheets of white shelf paper or brown wrapping paper work well, but you can tape together ordinary printer paper to make a larger canvas. The paper should be big enough that the client can swing his arms over a wide sweep and lean into the task.

Gather music and any technology available to play it out loud or into headphones. The type of music does not matter a lot; whatever the client wants is fine. Something instrumental and sweeping works well for many people.

Spread the paper and paints out on a large table and have your client don old clothes that don't mind getting dirty, or a huge apron. Spread newspapers or some other form of protective covering on the floor. The client can choose favourite colours to work with, and squeeze or dab some onto the side of the paper.

Have your client start by closing his eyes and, using his fingers, sweep over the paper in big, broad motions, in time to the music, without any intent to draw or create anything in particular, simply responding to the music. The movement should be a total body exercise. Encourage your client to lean right into the task and let their entire body swing to the music while keeping their fingers on the paper and in the paints.

This step helps the client to relax into the activity and suspend self judgment. Sometimes doing only this step is all the client needs to open up and allow their emotions to flow. You might move directly from this activity into a conversation about what is happening in your client's life and how he feels.

When the client fills up the paper in front of him, or feels ready to move on, you can slide the paper down to expose a fresh, clean "canvas".

The client can venture into using motion and also colour to express specific thoughts and feelings. If the spirit moves him, your client can also begin to paint specific scenarios or people from his past that impact him today.

Sometimes it feels safer to paint a picture than to use words to describe the same scene. For example, a child may think that he is not supposed to accuse a family member of abuse using his words, but feels safer to depict the event or his feelings about it in art.

Regardless of what the client chooses to paint, follow up with a conversation about what the client was thinking and feeling as he painted.

Cautions
This activity can open doors the client may not yet be ready to walk through. Its main value is to encourage the client to express thoughts, emotions and memories that do not come out easily in speech. Keep things light and fun.

If the painting is very dark or frightening, or if it depicts some form of trauma or the feelings expressed are intense, it is time to call in a pro therapist to help the client process the memories and feelings.

Tools for exploring relationships

Sociograms

A sociogram is a drawing depicting a client's relationships with family, friends, and community. The client can add lines of communication and association, and indicate the strength and quality of specific relationships, patterns of interaction and other types of information. To see different examples, search online for "sociogram" and you will find many.

Sociograms help to develop rapport and to begin exploring where the client sits with the others in his life. Drawing a sociogram can reveal hidden thoughts about relationships and hopes about future liaisons. Social isolation becomes obvious, and so do conflicting demands based on relationships.

The client can also portray qualities such as strengths shared among family members.

How to use it
Assemble paper and markers or pens in several colours.

Have the client start by drawing a star at the centre of the page with his name beside it. Then he places symbols to represent his family members in a circle around the star: a box for male, a circle for female. In the next layer out, he places symbols for friends, coworkers, and other contacts. He can add another layer for community contacts.

Then the client adds lines to represent the nature of their relationship with each person in his sociogram. The client can get creative here. For example:

- Larger squares and circles for people of significance in the client's life; smaller symbols for others.
- A strong full line for a close relationship; A weak line for a weak connection.
- A two-way arrow to indicate mutual attraction, or a one-ended arrow to show unreturned attraction.
- Different colours to show the nature of the relationship. Perhaps red to show a relationship of conflict, blue to show a comfortable relationship.
- The client, especially a child, might want to add in stickers, photos or graphics (like a happy face) to illustrate an important person or relationship.

A completed sociogram might look like the example on the next page:

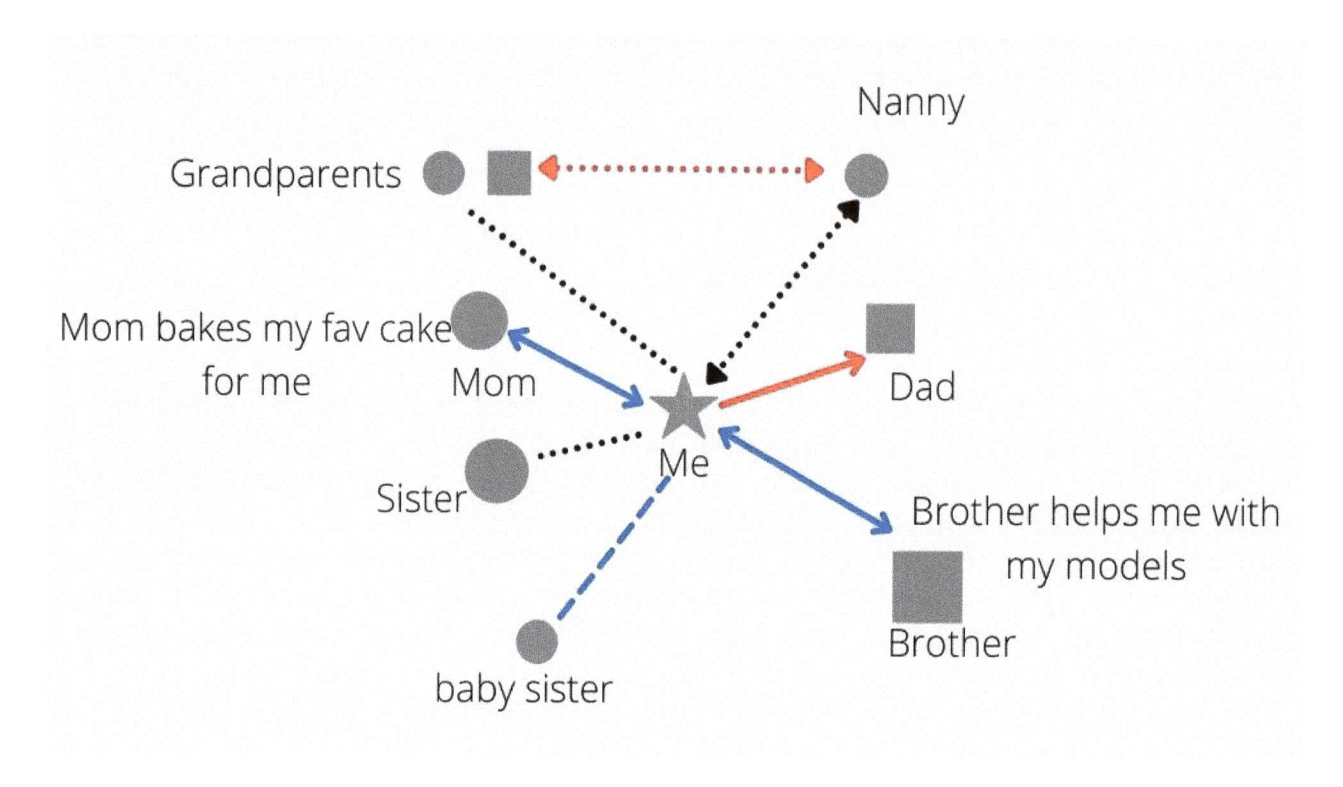

To help the client think about his sociogram, try asking questions such as these:

- "Who can you count on, no matter what?"
- "Who is in charge in your family?"
- "Who would you tell a secret to?"
- "Who would you prefer to stay away from?"
- "Who do you feel close to? Who do you feel distant from?"

Cautions
Simpler and cleaner is better. Too much information can cloud what is important. It's better to make multiple sociograms to explore different relationships than to try to cram it all into one messy, unreadable diagram.

Sociograms might seem complicated, but relationships tend to be complicated. They also change over time. If I lose someone from my circle, the entire landscape of my world changes.

Stick to just relationships, or add in strengths, such as "We can talk to each other" or "We help each other". If you have your client add in information such as mental health issues or alcohol use or violence, you run the risk of further developing that pathology rather than strengths. Leave that type of analysis to the pros.

Assertiveness, passiveness or aggressiveness

The assertiveness continuum is a way for a client to see graphically what his relationship choices have been, and how they effect him. This is another tool to awaken awareness to the need for change.

How to use it

Describe the different points on the continuum. Assertiveness is not always an easy concept to understand, especially for those raised by aggressive or passive parents. Many people have difficulty separating the points. Some people seem to leap back and forth between passiveness and aggression, unwilling to seem weak, and going overboard on the dominance and control behaviours to make up for it. Finding that balance, opting for being transparent and honest, regardless of other people's reaction, is not always easy. The best any of us can do is try to find that assertive balance point as often as possible, so we can feel proud and easy about our choices.

One of the ways to help the client see the impact of his choices is to examine how other people react to him.

- "What happens when you choose to be passive. How do you feel? How do others act around you?"
- "What happens when you choose to be aggressive? What do others do in response?"
- "When you choose to be assertive, what results do you see?"

The Assertiveness Continuum

Emotions I feel

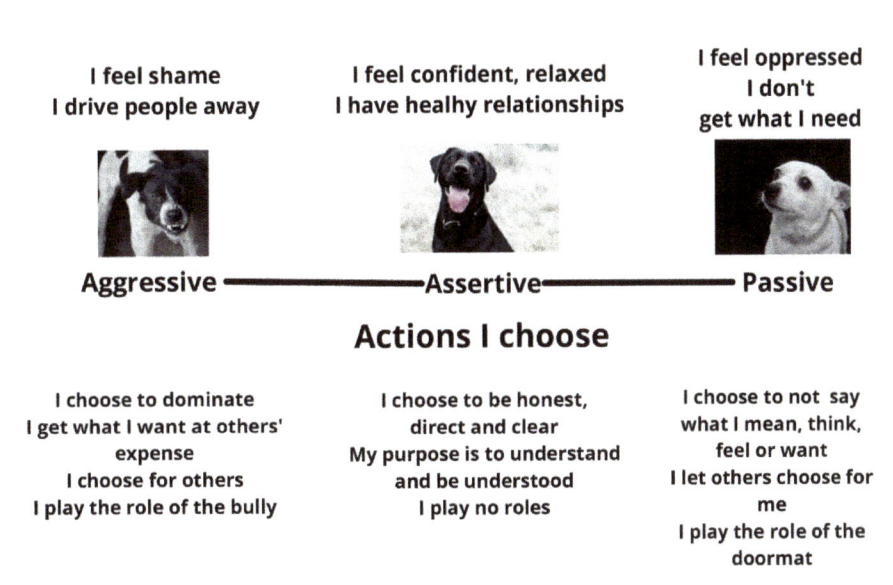

I feel shame I drive people away	I feel confident, relaxed I have healhy relationships	I feel oppressed I don't get what I need

Aggressive ——————— Assertive ——————— Passive

Actions I choose

I choose to dominate I get what I want at others' expense I choose for others I play the role of the bully	I choose to be honest, direct and clear My purpose is to understand and be understood I play no roles	I choose to not say what I mean, think, feel or want I let others choose for me I play the role of the doormat

Cautions
Make sure you can model what assertiveness can look like, before trying to have this discussion with your client. Actions speak louder than words!

Ensure that your client is the one to draw conclusions from this diagram. If you point out to the client all of his passive or aggressive behaviour choices, it could damage his self esteem, his trust in you, and his willingness to look at himself any further.

A simple tool for communicating the tough stuff assertively

When you are helping a client develop her assertive skills, this tool can't be beat. This is a simple, five-step formula for assertive communication, especially for talking about the tough stuff. I have used this tool effectively in the bedroom and in the board room. It was inspired by a tool for connecting taught by PD Seminars at Havens on Gabriola Island, British Columbia.

These are the five steps:

1. "I notice" — Talk about what you have observed, using your five senses. Include enough detail so that the other person knows what you are talking about, but not enough to overwhelm. No emotion or judgment at this point, just observation.
2. "I think" — This step comes from your head. Ask for information or provide it; offer your opinion; talk about whether you agree or disagree, like or dislike, approve or do not approve.
3. "I feel" — This step comes from your gut. Talk about how the situation impacts you emotionally. Use emotion laden words. (For example, I feel proud, loving, scared, angry, frustrated, uneasy, hopeful.)
4. "I want" — Try to establish a contract. Talk about what you are willing to do or not willing to do, what you want more of, what you want less of. Perhaps you might ask for what you want and offer something in return.
5. "I intend" — This step details what you intend to do in response to the other person's choices. It is about consequences, either positive or negative.

For more detail on this tool, check out the resources link at the end of the chapter. Go to the section on resources for Chapter 5 and look for *The 5 Easy Steps For Talking About The Tough Stuff.*

How to use it
Anyone can use it, including children, with a little practice. You can deliver the steps in any order, but for learning how to use it, I recommend following this order:

1. (After demonstrating the formula) "Did you notice how often I used the word 'I' and how infrequently I used the word 'you?'" Saying "I am upset" is a totally different message than, "You stupid jerk, look what you did". Using lots of "I" statements means "I am taking responsibility for my own needs, I am not dumping them on you". Using a lot of

"you" statements will produce hostility from the other person. Using "I" statements defuses conflict. If I am talking about what I see, what I think, what I feel, it is difficult to argue with that.

2. The step where we talk about our feelings is crucial, if your purpose is to deepen and strengthen a relationship. When we share the deepest, darkest, cobwebbiest corners our heart, mind and soul, we become vulnerable to the other person. It is that vulnerability which creates true intimacy. We would leave out that feeling step if someone is in our face abusing us, or in some workplace situations where the expression of feelings is not valued. In the case of abuse, we use just step 1 ("This is what I see") and step 4 ("Do it again and I will charge you with assault".) In a workplace that does not value open emotional communication, we would use steps 1, 2, 4 and perhaps 5 but not talk about feelings.
3. The third thing that makes this formula so powerful is the last step, where we talk about what we intend to do in response to the other person's choices, since most people do not include this thought in ordinary conversation. Some people think of it as "natural consequences". For example: "If you touch that hot stove, naturally, you will get burned."

Consequences can be the promise of a reward or the threat of a punishment, or both, although rewards work better in most circumstances. To be effective, consequences need to be:

- *Reasonable and feasible*—ones that you can actually carry out. There is no value in threatening a consequence that you don't follow through on when needed. If you say, "Hit me again and I will call the police and charge you," and your partner hits you to see what you will do and you do not charge him, what have you taught him? You have taught him that there are no consequences. "Go ahead and do what you want; I will not stop you," is the unspoken message.
- *A match for the severity of the offense*. If the problem is that he hits you, and you cower and declare that if he hits you again you won't like it (imagine me saying that in a mousy voice and passive body language) then your consequence will have no weight, and he will laugh at you. If the offense is that you don't like the fact that he chews gum and you announce that if he chews gum again, you will call the police and charge him, that is just as ludicrous. Be prepared to be laughed at again.
- *Seen by the other person as actually being a significant consequence*. If I want my child to clean up his room, and offer an extra 30 minutes of TV when the child hates TV and prefers to play with his Xbox, then my intended reward will have no interest to the child. If I promise to take away his Xbox if he does not clean up his room, that might have more impact on him since it matters to him.

After you explain the five steps, demonstrate how they can be used. Here is a script you can use or adapt. Let's say that I am dating a guy. I'll call him Bill. We went to a party last night and he got very drunk, which I did not like, so I sit down with him the next day and say this:

1. Bill, I noticed last night that you drank eight beers and three shooters, and I think I also saw a glass of wine.
2. I am curious to know, is that how you typically drink, or was that an unusual night for you?
3. Last night I was embarrassed to be seen with you, and today I feel uneasy, because I don't know where we are going with this relationship.
4. I am not interested in getting involved with a heavy drinker.
5. If you want to continue to drink like you did last night, I will not pursue a relationship with you, because I don't want to be around that. But if you want to stop drinking, I will back you 100%, I will go to AA with you, whatever you want. But you need to make a choice.

That was an example of a shaping message. Here is an example of a "feel good" message, using the same five steps:

1. I noticed you at the party last night. You have such a radiant smile, it lights up your whole face.
2. Are you single?
3. I am quite attracted to you.
4. So if you are single, I would like to get to know you better.
5. I promise to try to keep that smile on your face!

After you demonstrate the assertive communication formula, have the client role play.

- First, the client should choose a relationship that is comfortable and devise a message of thanks or appreciation, using the five steps, and pretend to deliver the message to an empty chair where the person receiving the message supposedly sits. This one is easy and will give your client confidence to tackle more challenging messages. Ask the client how it feels to deliver that message.
- Next, have your client imagine a relationship where there is some minor issue that might be changed, nothing with too much emotional content, and again role play delivering the message.
- Next, the client should tackle some more crunchy situation with a lot of emotion attached to it, and role play delivering that message. By now, it should become easier and more comfortable to use these five steps to get the message across.

As with any new tool, we need to practice for it to become easy to use. Encourage the client to find excuses to use the communication formula at least three times during the week, to cement it in his brain.

If couples are learning this assertive communication tool together, they might tape the list to the fridge and pull it out any time they have a disagreement, and take note of how it changes their usual communication patterns.

Cautions

This tool is very powerful. Using it effectively enhances communication so much that it has a tendency to change relationships, and not always in the way you might intend.

When I began using it, I noticed that I was no longer interested in people who were not prepared to be just as direct with me, and they were no longer interested in me, for being so direct. I began to attract people who were more honest and transparent than anyone I had ever spent time with before, and I was attracted to them. So my circle of friends changed, and I dumped an important personal relationship that was not what I wanted.

Introduced into a shaky relationship, the communication formula can either make or break the relationship. If both parties are willing to use it effectively, their relationship can go from 0–100% in moments. However, if only one party is interested in being this honest and the other refuses, then it will very quickly become evident that the relationship does not have the healthy foundation it needs to be able to survive. It's quite informative, either way.

Make sure you can model assertive communication well yourself before trying to teach the use of this tool.

If you don't like my scripts, invent your own. Just make sure they actually follow these five steps faithfully.

Setting boundaries

This is an extension of the assertive communication formula. Setting boundaries is a way of teaching others we are involved with about how we want to be treated.

Setting boundaries happens in all relationships, although we do not always recognize that we are doing so. Often, we have assumptions about how our partners should behave, and expect that our partners should have the same assumption of good behaviour—that is a boundary, whether it is expressed openly or not.

When the relationship involves abuse of any kind, setting boundaries can either change the relationship profoundly for the better or break it, just as with using the assertive communication formula. Don't think of setting boundaries as being a nasty threat. Think of it as saying out loud what you already assume, so that there will be no misunderstandings. Think of it also as an opportunity to strengthen your relationship while discussing what you both need from each other.

We set boundaries about lots of issues, such as how money is handled, how children should be raised, monogamy and fidelity, abuse.

On the next page is the basic template for a boundary statement:

	Action	Consequences
HOT BUTTON		
This is always unacceptable		
This makes me very uncomfortable		
This makes me uncomfortable		
This is quite irritating or annoying		
This I can tolerate		
This I like and would like more of		
COOL BUTTON		

How to use it

Start by having the client choose one issue that is of importance in their relationship. If there is more than one issue to set boundaries about, then each issue should be on a separate boundaries sheet. Keep it simple, and deal with the easy issues first to gain confidence, then move on to the tough stuff. If there are a number of issues to set boundaries about, advise your client not to attempt to dump them all on the other person at once; rather, deal with them one at a time.

Note that the template looks a bit like a thermometer, with "Hot" at the top and "Cool" at the bottom. The behaviours the client writes into the left column and the consequences in the right column will escalate from the bottom towards the top.

Begin at the "cool" end. Have the client imagine what she is comfortable with, and would maybe like more of. If the issue is abuse, then perhaps "He gives me a back rub" could be the entry in the left column in the bottom box.

Now go to the top, the "hot button" end, and imagine the very worst that might ever possibly happen, even if it has not ever happened before. If abuse is the topic, then perhaps "He beats me" would be at the top of the left column.

Next, fill in escalating behaviours in the intervening boxes in the left column.

Now it's time to think of consequences to match the behaviours. These need to escalate just as the behaviours did, and have the same qualities as did the consequences in step five of the assertive communication formula: reasonable, feasible, doable, matching the offence in severity, seen as being consequential to the other person.

On the next page is a sample boundary statement regarding abuse in a relationship:

Issue: Safety, Abuse

	Action	Consequence
HOT BUTTON		
This is always unacceptable	You hit me or push me. You sexually assault me.	I call the RCMP and charge you with assault. I will end the relationship.
This makes me very uncomfortable	You shout at me.	I will end the relationship.
This makes me uncomfortable	You insult me or purposely embarrass me in public.	I will leave you temporarily until I feel safe again.
This is quite irritating or annoying	You criticize me.	I will distance myself emotionally from you until I feel safe again.
This I can tolerate	You disagree with me.	I may disagree with you and make my own choices.
This I like and I would like more of	You ask for my opinion and respect my ideas.	I will engage with you in respectful conversation.
COOL COMFORT		

Kate Tompkins

Here is a sample boundary statement for financial management in a relationship:

Issue: Money

	Action	**Consequence**
HOT BUTTON		
This is always unacceptable	You steal money from my account	I call the RCMP and charge you with theft. I end the relationship.
This makes me very uncomfortable	You cannot explain where our money went. Or You hide expenses and withdrawals from me.	I will hire an accountant to learn about our or your financial affairs. If this happens more than once, I will end the relationship.
This makes me uncomfortable	You give away money or buy things for others that was meant to pay our bills.	I will arrange our account so that you cannot access it without my permission.
This is quite irritating or annoying	You spend more of our money than we agreed on, or you spend it in a way we did not agree on, or you make important purchases without consulting me.	I will keep my own money separate from yours.
This I can tolerate	You overspend from your own personal account.	I will ignore what you do with your own account as long as it does not affect my money or my security.
This I like and I would like more of	We develop a budget together and talk about it regularly. Or we review statements and expenses together and negotiate needed changes.	We will both feel comfortable about money.
COOL COMFORT		

After drafting up a boundary statement with your help, the client will want to look at it again in a few days to be sure she still likes it. She might want to tweak some of the boxes at a later meeting.

Once she is happy with it, she can practice delivering it to her partner, using the 5 steps of the assertive communication formula. Coach her to speak confidently and clearly, to hold her head up high and her back straight. Suggest that she write out what she intends to say to her partner, so it will come more easily when she delivers her message. Then she might imagine what he will say in response, and plan out what she will say next, for 2 or 3 rounds of conversation. If she has a bit of a script ready, she will feel more confident and deliver her statement more comfortably.

It does not matter whether or not her partner likes her boundary statement or whether or not he agrees with it. It is fair game to ask for clarification if he does not understand some point, but whether he actually likes it is irrelevant. This is how she wants to be treated and he has the choice whether to respect her boundaries or not. If he chooses to honour her boundaries, then everyone gets to live happily after. If he chooses to cross one of her boundaries (some partners will do so, just to see what happens, wondering if she really means it) then her job is to follow through on the promised consequence, immediately. That is the only way he will learn to respect her boundaries.

Cautions

As with using the assertive communication formula, setting boundaries will provide a great deal of information to a client. If she is unsure whether or not to stay in a relationship, especially an abusive relationship, this exercise can be worth gold. If there is basic respect and love present, but he just does not know how to behave well, or he is dealing with issues of his own and is not really aware of how his actions effect her, then possibly her partner will listen to her, decide to honour her boundaries, and change his behaviour choices. An abusive relationship can be turned around quickly by setting boundaries.

However, if his motivations have more to do with power and control, aggressive domination, or narcissistic manipulation, he is more likely to toss her boundaries aside and do what he likes, regardless of what she wants or needs to be safe. She will know now that attempting to turn the relationship around to be safe and respectful is not going to work.

Now comes the interesting part. People who come to that realization sometimes have the strength and confidence to turn around and walk out the door. However, many people, especially women, who have been stuck in an abusive relationship for some time, will find it very challenging or maybe even impossible to leave an abuser. This is a complex issue, which I address in more detail in Chapter 6.

Be aware that, for a helper, it can be very painful to watch an abused woman return to her abuser. Pull out that Teflon cape! Just be there for her the next time and the next time and the next time that she tries to leave, knowing that she has your support no matter what her choices. Maybe the next time will be the charm and she will succeed in leaving him to create a wonderful safe new life.

How to assess relationships

If your client has been in an unhealthy relationship for a while, she may begin to forget what a healthy relationship looks like. That is especially true if her family did not offer a great role model for her when she was growing up.

There are lots of resources online, just search for "healthy relationships" and many sites will pop up. I put together this inventory from my experience meeting couples and learning what worked for them.

How to use it

Keep in mind what a healthy relationship looks like so you can compare that image to what your client describes. When there is a trusting relationship between you and your client, you may be able to gently point out differences between what the woman has described and what you know to be healthy.

Have your client check off all the characteristics in the inventory that she sees in her own relationship. If there are lots of positive traits she can check off, that is a sign that her relationship is thankfully solid. Traits she was not able to check off are directions for possible growth for the couple.

If she finds that she cannot check very many boxes, or if the inventory sheds light on some glaringly obvious issue, that is information she can use to consider making changes in her life, such as setting boundaries or deciding whether or not the relationship is worth keeping.

Then have her complete the "What Do I Want My Life to Look Like?" exercise and create her action plan. "If you can dream it, you can create it."

Cautions

Approach this exercise gently, as a light, fun exercise that can provide some useful information. It can be stressful, even traumatic, for some to contemplate a relationship they are invested in and realize that it may not be what they fantasized it to be.

Again, allow your client to decide what, if anything, to do about her new understanding.

The Non-Therapist

A healthy relationship

Check the ones you see in your relationship	✓
Your partner values what you have to say. Your partner asks your opinion, and listens when you tell him your opinion. Your partner thinks you are a good person, and tells you so, often. Your partner values your skills, both at home and at work, and thanks you for your contributions to the home and family life. Your partner is polite to your friends, even if he does not like them. Your partner speaks to you with no hostility in voice or body language. Your partner does things to protect you, care for you, make your life better. You know for sure you will be welcomed warmly when you come home. Your partner asks you what you want and need and then does what he can to do those things for you. Your partner is kind to you. Your partner likes you and your values about how to treat people. Your partner follows through on promises to you. Your partner wants for you to be happy. You both enjoy having sex, and have sex regularly at times that work for both of you. Most of the time, you have lots of positive feelings for your partner. Usually, you both look for solutions to issues rather than blaming or finding fault. You and your partner both look for opportunities to be affectionate. As parents, you are both lovers and partners. You can communicate honestly. No lying, deception, secrets, frequent arguments. You can both let go of the past and focus on the present. You like looking after each other's needs. You are in the relationship because you want to be, not for obligation. You like living together. Your visions for the future are similar. Your values about how other people should be treated are similar. You have a workable arrangement for handling money, which both of you honour. You are not afraid of your partner. Ever. When you and your partner have disagreements, you can talk about them kindly. When you have strong disagreements, you both fight fairly. *More —>*	

Kate Tompkins

	✓
Check the ones you see in your relationship	
You have similar ideas about how to raise children and can talk about how to do so without stress or disrespect.	
You and your partner are able to create mutually-agreeable plans for your future.	
Your partner respects your boundaries.	
When you and your partner have disagreements, you can talk about them kindly. When you have strong disagreements, you both fight fairly.	
You have similar ideas about how to raise children and can talk about how to do so without stress or disrespect.	
You and your partner are able to create mutually-agreeable plans for your future.	
Your partner respects your boundaries.	
You and your partner appreciate each other's sense of humour.	
You and your partner are able to share your deepest emotions.	
You and your partner both trust the other to a significant degree.	
You enjoy each other's companionship, and enjoy doing at least some things together, while respecting each other's needs for privacy.	
You are able to create a balance between togetherness and individuality that works for both of you.	
You and your partner are able to be honest with each other and trust each other to be truthful.	
You are both able to compromise on occasion without giving up your most important needs.	
You each have your own identity, which does not depend on your partner's.	
You and your partner both support the other to pursue new hobbies and make new friends.	
Neither of you is dependent on the other to the point where you cannot function without the other.	
You each make the other feel loved, wanted, and appreciated.	
You feel valued, accepted. You feel a deep emotional connection.	
You are able to spend quality time together regularly.	
You have fun together.	
You have relationship rules, or boundaries, which you both understand and commit to.	

Am I in an abusive relationship?
Admitting to anyone that a relationship is abusive is not easy. The imagined stigma of being in such a relationship is especially challenging for professionals, whose public image relies on seeming to be well put together.

This brief survey may help someone, man or woman, stuck in an abusive relationship, to realize what is happening. This is another tool for enhancing awareness of the need for change.

How to use it
The survey is fairly straightforward. All that is required is to check off some boxes.

Encourage your client to look over the survey once she has completed it. There is no specific score or threshold that screams out "abusive relationship!" However, if they checked even one box, that is a sign that the relationship needs first aid.

This survey applies equally to men and to women, regardless of whether it is a same-sex relationship or a hetero relationship.

If your client has checked off more than one box, the help of someone who specializes in supporting victims of domestic abuse is called for. Help her look for a shelter, or a support program, or an agency in your region, and an experienced therapist.

Cautions
Remember that your support is not conditional on what choices she makes. Supporting her will go much further than attempting to convince her (or him) that visiting an agency for information and support would be a good idea because it is your idea of what should happen.

Kate Tompkins

Am I in an abusive relationship?
Not sure? (Or maybe you just don't feel good about admitting it?) Well – lets find out!

Check off any of the following that you experience in your relationship.	✓
My partner has threatened me, my children, or some other family member, or my pets with violence.	
My partner has pushed, shoved or tripped me purposely.	
My partner has hit, bit, kicked, or punched me.	
My partner has cut, burned, or used a weapon against me.	
My partner has tortured or mutilated me.	
My partner has yelled at me.	
My partner has called me names, insulted me, mocked me, humiliated me, or used abusive language against me, in public or in private.	
My partner has prevented me from seeing my friends and family.	
My partner has treated me with contempt or emotional coldness, or my partner has isolated me from meaningful contact.	
My partner has raped me or threatened to rape me.	
My partner has touched me sexually without my consent, forced me to engage in sexual activity against my will or forced me to have sex without contraception.	
My partner has deliberately given me a sexual illness or infection.	
My partner has controlled my finances or my income, taken my money without my permission.	
My partner has controlled access to my financial information or records.	
My partner has prevented me from getting a job that would bring in my own money.	
My partner has forced me out of my house, or forced me to give away control of my house.	
My partner has not given me medical help when I needed it.	
My partner has not provided me with food or basic necessities of life when I needed them.	
My partner has done other things that were meant to control, belittle, hurt or deprive me.	

Are my children being treated abusively?

For some parents, realizing that their partner is abusing their children is the wake-up call they need to take a serious look at their relationship. A mom who is suffering abuse may be more likely to take action on her kids' behalf than for herself.

This brief survey will help a parent look at how their partner's behaviour is effecting children in the home.

> Thank you to the Centre for Research & Education on Violence against Women & Children at Western University for inspiration.

How to use it/cautions

The notes in previous exercise about unconditional support and seeking the help of a specialized agency or program apply here, too.

Kate Tompkins

Are my children being treated abusively?
Sometimes the abuse is directed at our children as a way to hurt us.

	✓
Check any of these abusive actions that you have witnessed or know about.	
My child has witnessed or heard a parent being abused.	
My partner treats my children as if they were a possession, or as if they exist for his benefit.	
My partner constantly criticizes my children or makes them feel bad about themselves on purpose.	
My partner tells my children they are stupid or worthless or will never amount to anything.	
My partner ignores or neglects my children.	
My partner deliberately withholds food, medical care, or other necessities of life from my children.	
My partner threatens to abandon my children or leave them behind.	
My children have been forced to watch porn or sexual activity, to take off their clothes or watch someone else undress, or have nude photos taken.	
My children have been forced to touch someone's genitals or to allow someone to touch theirs.	
My children have been forced or enticed to have sex with an adult or with another child.	
My children have been kept in the home and not allowed to leave or not allowed to see family or friends.	
My children are constantly watched, monitored, or controlled, including phone and internet activities, beyond the requirements of safety.	
My partner has engaged in any other activity meant to control, belittle or in any way harm my children.	

How to make a safety plan
A plan to stay safe is a top priority for anyone who is in an abusive relationship. To be useful, the plan needs to address what to do in situations when safety is threatened, where to go, and what to take along. The following guide is a way to start making a safety plan.

How to use it
Help your client think through what might happen and what she would need to do to keep herself and her children safe. This is not always as simple as it may sound. There is a draw towards minimizing the danger, because actually admitting it means it becomes real, and she would need (or thinks she *should* need) to do something about it.

Encourage your client to be realistic, to see things as they really are, and to think practically. Recalling her concerns for her children might help her to see the situation as it is.

Cautions
Anyone who needs a safety plan very likely also needs the support of a shelter, program or agency that specializes in helping people respond to abusive relationships. Encourage her to reach out, and take her by the hand to visit those supports if she needs to lean on you.

Making a safety plan
Having a safety plan that works for you is a top priority, regardless of whether you decide to stay in the home or leave. To make your plan, you will need to think through all the actions you need to take to keep yourself and your children safe.

Here are some suggestions for things you might do. Take one action at a time and start with the one that is easiest and safest for you.

- Tell someone you trust about the abuse.
- Think about your partner's past use and level of force. This will help you predict what type of danger you and your children are facing, and when you must leave.
- Tell your children that abuse is never right, even when someone they love is being abusive. Tell them the abuse is not their fault, and it is not your fault. They did not cause it and neither did you. Teach them it is important to stay safe when there is abuse.
- Plan where to go in an emergency. Teach your children how to get help. Tell them not to get between you and your partner if there is violence. Plan a code word to signal your children they should get help or leave.
- Don't run to a place where your children are, as your partner may follow and hurt them as well.
- Create a plan to get out of your house safely and practice it with your children.
- Ask your neighbours, friends and family to call the police if they hear sounds of abuse and to look after your children in an emergency.
- If an argument is developing, move to a space where you can get outside easily. Don't go to a room where there is potential access to weapons (such as the kitchen, workshop, bathroom).

- If you are being hurt, protect your face with your arms around each side of your head, with your fingers locked together behind your head. Don't wear scarves or long dangling jewellery.
- Park your car by backing it into the driveway so you can leave more quickly if you need to, and keep it fuelled.
- Hide your keys, cell phone and some money near your escape route. Pack a bag with basic essentials for yourself and your children and hide it someplace safe where you can easily grab it.
- Have a list of phone numbers to call for help. You can keep a rolled-up piece of paper with emergency contact numbers in a small tube such as an old lipstick or lip balm container that looks like nothing special in your purse.
- Call the police if it is an emergency. Your local shelter or police may be able to equip you with a panic button/cell phone.
- Make sure all weapons and ammunition are hidden or removed from your home.

Emergency grab bag packing list

- Important papers, such as the following. You can store copies on a thumb drive, or in a safety deposit box that your abuser does not know about.
  - Birth certificates, Social Insurance cards, and passports or immigration papers for you and your children.
  - Health insurance cards for you and your children.
  - Financial records, including recent bank statements and stocks or mutual fund records.
  - Housing documents, such as rental agreements, mortgage statements, or the title or deed.
  - Your most recent credit report.
  - The title or lease paperwork for your car.
  - Statements for any retirement plans.
  - The past two years' tax returns.
- Medications and toiletries for you and your kids and any pets you will take with you.
- Two or three changes of clothes.
- Small toys, books, amusements for your kids.
- A "clean" cell phone that your abuser does not know about.
- Lists of phone numbers for emergency help, close supportive friends, taxis.
- Spare sets of car and office keys.
- Bank cards, and some cash, including coins for parking meters and vending machines at hospitals or shelters.
- Small family heirlooms.
- Photos of anything in the house that is worth significant money, or large family heirlooms too big to take in a bag.
- Evidence of abuse, such as photos of bruises and wounds or damaged property; threat-

ening notes; copies of police and medical reports.

Understanding the cycle of violence

Understanding how violence cycles in an abusive relationship can help to predict what is likely to occur.

How to use it
If your client is resistant to the idea that her (or his) relationship may be abusive, have her look at "The Cycle of Violence" graphic. It seems to be easier for a woman to look at the cycle diagram and compare it to her own changing relationship first before tackling the more challenging "Am I In An Abusive Relationship?" and "Are My Children Being Abused?"

Once she has accepted that her relationship may be abusive, help her to accept the larger picture by putting abuse into a broader societal context.

Many of the horrific mass shooting incidents that have plagued society recently have begun as domestic violence. The man assaults his partner, then goes on to attack others in order to further satisfy the need he thinks he has for what he might call 'revenge' or 'justice'.

Abuse by a man towards a woman, or towards a male partner, exists in our society because society allows it to exist. Not because victims are stupid, weak, timid, or don't stand up for themselves. A man chooses to be abusive because our male-dominated society allows it and, some might say, encourages it.

It does not have to be that way. We can stop the abuse.

Cautions
It is important that your client does not start to blame herself once she realizes she is in an abusive relationship. Even if, for the sake of survival, she may have instigated some of the abuse which occurred in her relationship, she still is NOT RESPONSIBLE. Even if she has returned to an abuser, possibly several times, she is still NOT RESPONSIBLE for the abuse. She needs to receive that message loud and clear. **Violence is the choice of the violent person**. She does whatever she needs to do in order to manage it, to try to keep it to a minimum, and to survive.

There is a role for her to play to escape the abuse, but she must not be blamed if she has not yet taken those steps. It takes time. There are many reasons why a woman does not leave an abusive relationship or returns after she has escaped, which we will look at more closely in Chapter 6.

After awareness has been awakened, the next step is to take action to change the pattern, although it might take several turns around the cycle before that can happen.

What is the cycle of violence?

The cycle of violence theory looks at the repetitive nature of a perpetrator's actions that hinder a victim's ability to leave an abusive relationship. The theory provides an insight into this by illustrating how the behaviour of a perpetrator can change very dramatically, making it difficult for the woman to leave. Women who have experienced violence may recognize this cycle.

Dr Lenore Walker developed the cycle of violence theory in 1979. It describes the phases an abusive relationship moves through in the lead-up to a violent event, and its follow-up.

There is no specific time period for moving through the three phases of the cycle of violence. The couple may move quickly from explosion to explosion, or it may be years between events. In some relationships, the cycle starts off slowly: the first violent event may be a few years into the relationship, and it may be another few years before the second event occurs.

But then the cycle starts to speed up, with shorter and shorter times spent in the honeymoon and build up stages, and with violent events occurring frequently.

There are three phases in of the cycle of violence:

1: Tension-building

Tension between the people in the relationship starts to increase and verbal, emotional or financial abuse occurs.

This phase can be very frightening for people experiencing abuse. They feel as though the situation will explode if they do anything wrong. The behaviour of the abuser intensifies and reaches a point where a release of tension is inevitable.

2: Acute explosion

The peak of the violence is reached in this phase. The perpetrator experiences a release of tension and this behaviour may become habitual. Some partners may actually provoke a violent episode at a time and place where she thinks she can control the level of violence rather than wait for her partner to explode more dangerously.

3: Honeymoon phase

- Remorse: At this point, the perpetrator may start to feel ashamed. He may become withdrawn and try to justify his actions to himself and others. For example, he may say, "You know it makes me angry when you say that."
- Pursuit: The perpetrator may promise to never be violent again. They may try to explain the violence by blaming other factors such as alcohol or stress at work. The perpetrator may be very attentive to the target of the violence, including buying gifts and helping around the house. It could seem as though the perpetrator has changed. At this point, the target of the violence can feel confused and hurt but also relieved that the violence is over.
- Denial: Both people in the relationship may be in denial about the severity of the abuse and violence. Intimacy can increase. Both people may feel happy and want the relationship to continue, so they may not acknowledge the possibility that the violence could happen again.

Over time, this phase passes and the cycle begins again.

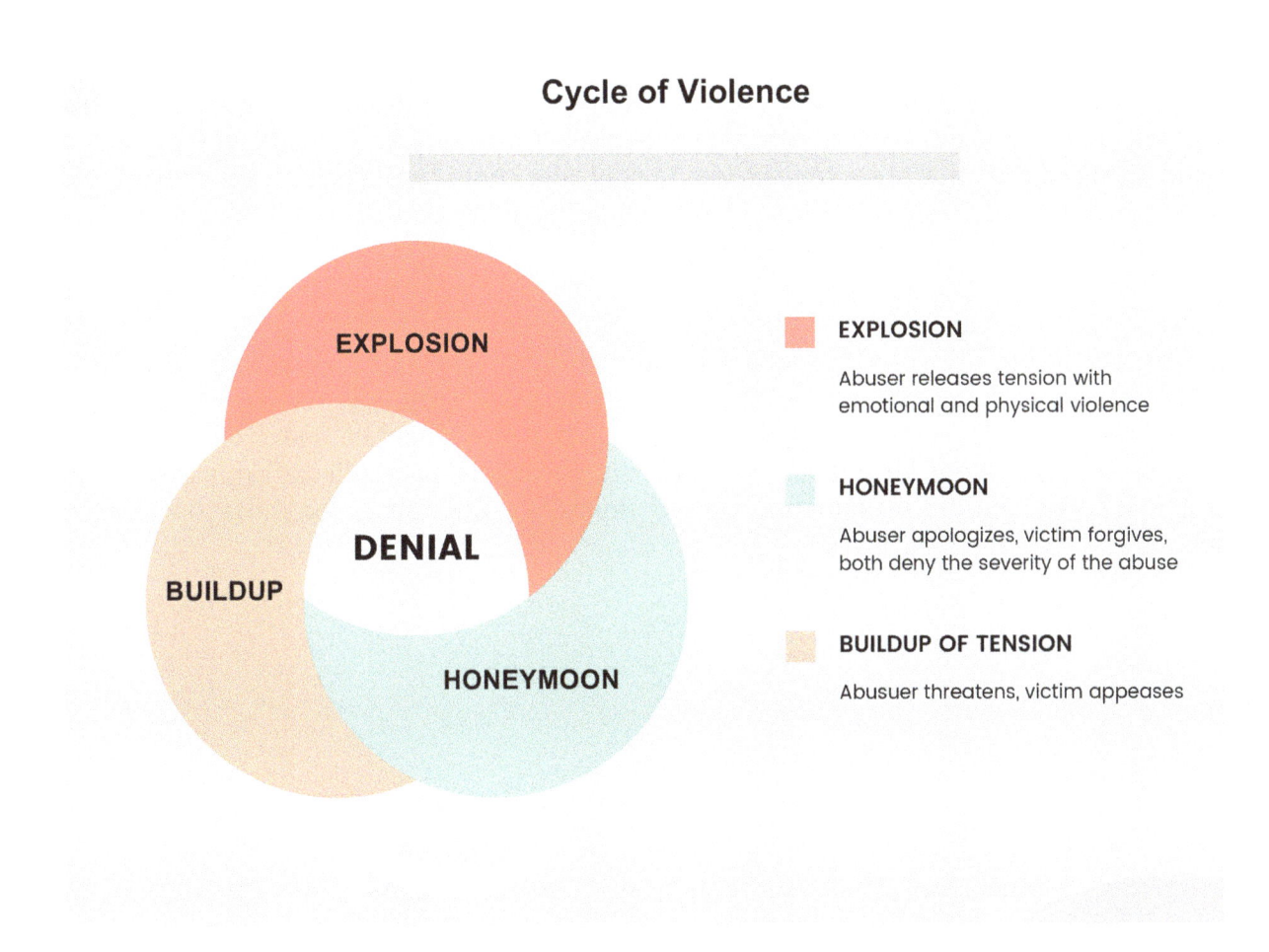

Cycle of Violence

EXPLOSION
Abuser releases tension with emotional and physical violence

HONEYMOON
Abuser apologizes, victim forgives, both deny the severity of the abuse

BUILDUP OF TENSION
Abusuer threatens, victim appeases

Should I stay or should I leave?

After awareness has been awakened, a victim of intimate partner violence needs to make a decision that is exceptionally tough to make: "Should I stay or should I go?"

This brief survey will help her think through the decision. If she can find at least one good reason to leave, it might save her life.

How to use it

Present this survey as a tool to assist in her decision-making. It might be helpful to encourage her to look critically at her reasons for staying in the relationship and decide which really are true and so significant that they compel her to stay. She could rank each of her reasons from most compelling to least significant and try to come up with plans to neutralize some of the reasons to stay.

Cautions

Again, resist the temptation to try to steer her towards the outcome you see as being best for her. (Are you seeing a pattern in this bit of advice?) It is amazing how resistant some people can be to the idea that their relationship is dangerous and they might be better off out of it.

There are many reasons for not leaving an abusive relationship which can appear to be both valid and insurmountable to someone lost in them. See Chapter 6 for more on this phenomenon.

Should I stay or should I leave?

There are many reasons why you might choose to stay in your abusive relationship. Do any of these apply to you?

Possible reasons to stay	✓
I don't have transportation of my own to leave when I need to. There is no shelter for abused women in my area. I am afraid that staff in a shelter won't understand me or my culture. I am afraid that staff in a shelter may judge me harshly for not leaving sooner. I am afraid of what family and friends might think if they know what has been going on. I am afraid that neighbours, family and friends may judge me harshly if I leave my relationship. I am afraid my abuser will hurt me or kill me if I try to leave. I don't trust police, courts, the justice system or the law. I fear I would not be treated well. I live in a small town or a rural area. I am afraid of everyone knowing about my situation. I have lost my self confidence, or I have been beaten down so much I don't think I have the energy to make a big change in my life. I don't have family or friends whom I can count on to support me if I decide to leave. I have a physical or mental health issue that would get in my way. It would be hard for me to carry through with a big change. I fear that my colleagues will lose respect for me if they know what my life has been like. I would feel like a failure, or that I have not tried hard enough. I would feel like a failure because I am a professional. I should have been able to solve this situation. There is something wrong with me. I don't deserve to be happy. I should be punished for something I did. I don't have any money to support myself and my kids if I leave. I still love my partner in spite of the abuse, and he loves me. I want my kids to be in their own home with both parents. I don't want my kids to grow up without their father. I just don't believe it is possible to live a life without abuse. I don't know how to leave. I don't know where to start. Some other reason?	

Possible reasons to leave	✓
I am sick and tired of being hurt, afraid and demoralized.	
I am afraid he will kill me. I want to live.	
I am afraid he will hurt my kids or damage them emotionally.	
I don't want my kids learning that abuse is normal and should be tolerated or excused. I want my kids to grow up in a healthy home.	
I want my self-confidence, self-esteem and pride back.	
I want to be the person my colleagues think I am.	
I want the respect of my friends, family, and community for standing up for what is right.	
I trust that I can find appropriate supports for me who understand me.	
I am ready. I have done all I could to try to make my relationship work. It is time to go.	
I deserve to be happy and safe.	
I trust myself to figure out whatever I need to do to leave safely.	
I know I can find, save or earn enough money to survive on my own.	
I have, or can get, professional counselling to help me work out any personal issues that might get in my way.	
I have survived abuse for a while now. It has made me stronger. I know I can be okay on my own.	
My faith or my spiritual beliefs will sustain me through a big change.	
I want to be a role model to my kids, and to my community. That means I need to be healthy and happy and demonstrate what good choices are.	
I tried to set boundaries, but he did not honour them. I cannot trust him to do so, even if he says he will.	
My kids are starting to act abusively. I want them out of this environment.	
I see other couples who have a good relationship. I want a healthy relationship, too.	
I have a friend who is supporting me to leave. Now is a good time.	
I want to like myself again.	
Some other reason?	

The escape plan worksheet
The escape plan worksheet is a way to encourage a victim who is planning to leave an abusive relationship to think about how to do it safely.

How to use it
Help her to think through her situation logically and courageously.

Help her come up with alternatives. For example, you could help her to research a shelter close by and the local police to learn what assistance they can provide. If she does the research herself, she is more likely to actually make use of the resources available to her.

Cautions
In order for it to actually work for her, her plan needs to be *her* plan: ideas that she initiates and can see herself following through on. Making the plan herself will help her to develop strength and conviction. A plan that is "done to her" may not ever see the light of day.

Kate Tompkins

Escape Plan Worksheet

Plan, plan, and plan again. Your success in leaving depends to a large degree on how well you are able to plan ahead of time. This chart may help you keep track of what you need to think about before making your move. Check off the steps you have completed

Task	Notes	✓
Save, borrow, or find enough cash to pay for: • A couple of hotel nights, food, gas • Extra clothes if needed • Rent down payment • Utilities down payment		
Review your safety plan and make any changes needed. Plan the details: Where will you go? When? How?		
Pack a grab bag and hide it someplace your abuser won't find it—at work, at a neighbour's or friend's place. See "Make a Safety Plan" for a list of what to pack.		
Assess your current safety. For example, are weapons removed from the house? Are keys to weapons storage cases hidden? What is your abuser's current state of mind? The safest time to leave is when your abuser is away from home.		
Arrange for help. If the police are responding to your emergency call, leave with them and go directly to a shelter or another safe place your abuser does not know about. If you are able to plan a more orderly exit, the local police may be willing to go with you to stand guard while you gather up your stuff to leave. Ask a women's shelter for help. Ask a male friend to go with you, or maybe a large group of supportive women friends.		
Stick to your plan. Remind yourself about why you need to leave: you deserve a safe happy life, and believe that you can create one for yourself and your kids. Enlist the help of friends, therapists, women's advocates to lend you their support. Don't be too hard on yourself if things don't go exactly according to your plan. Carry on with your escape as best you can and be open to new ideas about how to create a new safe life.		

Understanding consent
Although "no" and "yes" may seem self-explanatory, apparently to some people they are not. Understanding what consent looks like and what it does not look like could be important game changers for your client.

How to use it
The videos listed here may or may not still be accessible when you search for them. The internet being what it is, if you cannot open these, try searching online for "consent"; that is how I found these.

These brief clips are funny and engaging, so your client can more easily absorb the information without feeling pressured or blamed.

Preset viewing these clips as a fun exercise that might provide some useful information.

- youtube.com/watch?v=TBFCeGDVAdQ
- youtube.com/watch?v=laMtr-rUEmY

If the issue of consent is key to the person you are helping, perhaps you'd like to search for others you like.

Tools for creating a better future

What do I want my life to look like?
This is a fantasy exercise to help a client imagine what their life could be like and plan feasible steps towards that goal. It is general enough to be useful in a variety of circumstances.

How to use it
The directions are included in the exercise.

Cautions
Ask yourself these questions:

- Would this exercise be suitable for the person I want to help? Why or why not?
- Do I need to tweak it in any way to make it more suitable for the person I want to help?
- What benefits might come to my client if I introduce this tool?
- What is my client's emotional state right now? Are there any risks to their continuing well being?
- What do I need to do to make this a productive, helpful exercise for my client?
- What materials do I need to gather? What space can I use that will be quiet, private, and conducive to this type of thinking?

- What is my own emotional state today? Am I calm, relaxed, able to focus on my client? Is there anything I need to do to prepare myself emotionally for this meeting?
- Is there anything else I need to think about?

What do I want my life to look like?

You know the old adage—if you can imagine it, you can create it, you can make it happen. If you can't imagine it, how can you ever take steps to create the life you want?

You can start off with thinking about what you don't want. But the magic happens when you think positively. Try to phrase your ideas as "can do", desirable goals. Imagine the ideal you'd like to reach, even if it seems unattainable right this minute.

Many people speak of feeling overwhelmed and hopeless until they find the right supportive help and come to see a way out of whatever their mental prison might be. Then all their dreams can come true. They are able to do whatever it takes to create a safe, happy, and satisfying life.

I encourage you to be fearless, and to be brutally honest with yourself.

Sit down with a supportive friend, helper, counsellor or advocate to do this exercise. You might want to have a big piece of paper handy, maybe a large pad of flip chart paper, and some pens or markers, to keep your great ideas from floating away.

Ask yourself: What is my reality today? What is actually happening in my life?
- What parts of it are great?
- What parts of it are good or at least tolerable?
- What parts of it are difficult?
- What parts of it are unacceptable?

Now try relaxing as deeply as you can manage. Close your eyes and allow your mind to wander a bit. Then imagine yourself one year from today, living your ideal life. Imagine lots of details.
- Imagine where you are. Imagine sights—buildings, trees, meadows. Notice shapes and textures, shadow and light, movement and stillness, straight lines and curves, colours and textures.
- Imagine smells—pine sap and damp earth? The sea? Your perfume? Flowers in your garden? Something cooking?
- Imagine sounds—traffic, laughter, wind, waves, voices, birds, music?
- Reach out in your mind and touch something, like a wall or a tree trunk. What is the texture, what is the temperature?
- Imagine what you might be wearing, what your face looks like, what your body language says.
- Imagine who is with you and what you are doing.
- Imagine how you feel emotionally.
- What does this great new life look and feel like?

Now brainstorm a list of your strengths with your support person. What do you have going for

you now?
- How are your health and physical strength?
- What personality traits will help you create the new life you want?
- What skills do you have? They might be skills from work or from your volunteer activities or your social life.
- What are your financial assets?
- What property do you control and can access?
- What people resources can you access for help? Support people and organizations? Friends? Family?
- What other useful strengths do you have?

Now brainstorm a list of the challenges you face.
- Do you have health issues you need to address before you can make any major changes?
- Do you have mental health issues that might get in the way?
- Do your finances need topping up or straightening out?
- Is there information you need? Skills you need to develop?
- Are you isolated from friends and other supports?
- How are your relationships?
- Are there any other challenges you need to address?

Now it's time for a plan. With the help of your support person, list the most important things you need to do to prepare yourself. If you are not too overwhelmed, list any additional tasks to do that you can think of. List whom you will approach for help, what resources you will need.

Making a worksheet like this might help you develop your action plan:

My Action Plan for Change

Issue or Challenge I Face	Resources and Help I Will Access; Actions I Will Take	Results I hope to see

On the next page is an example of a filled-in worksheet:

Issue or Challenge I Face	Resources and Help I Will Access; Actions I Will Take	Results I hope to see
I feel sick from stress.	See my doctor about my stress and my stomach issues	My stomach will settle down.
I am probably depressed.	Research local therapists. Book an appointment with one.	I will feel hopeful and more energetic than I do now.
I am overdrawn at the bank. I need to pay off some bills.	See a financial advisor. Maybe see a bankruptcy trustee for advice.	I will have some accessible cash in my bank account. I will have control over my own money.

Create a future history

This is a variation of the time travel journaling exercise, aimed at developing a picture of a possible future that your client could create. It can help your client to see that hope does exist for her, that change is indeed possible, that a better future is within her grasp, and she can create it. Not only does this activity help her to lift herself out of despair and hopelessness, it provides a plan of action and the energy to get started on the new plan.

How to use it

Have the client imagine what she would like her future to look like, using the previous exercise (or any other similar fantasy exercise you may already have in your tool box).

The next step is for her to create a picture of what she wants her life to be like in one year's time. Depending on the interests and skills of your client this could be in almost any format. For example:

- Artwork, depicting her living her good life, complete with details about the other people she will have in her life and her surroundings.
- A journal entry dated 12 months from today, talking about her life over the year. Include details about how she got to be where she imagines she will be in a year. If she is facing challenges that may not be resolved in 12 months' time but might be in two years, then the entry can be dated two years from now.
- Her obituary, as she would like it to read. What would the reader of her future obit learn about her life, her accomplishments, her attachments, her dreams and her plans?
- A short story about how she turned her life around and created a beautiful, juicy life.
- A stand-up comedy routine in which she pokes fun at herself, her life, her trials and tribulations, and what she has accomplished over her lifetime.

- A song about her wonderful new life.
- A dramatic scene which she role plays, showing her as the heroine who beats all the odds and comes out the other end happy and content.

Cautions
If she is depressed, it might be easy for her slip into negative thinking. Creating a pessimistic picture of her possible future is exactly what we do NOT want to happen. This exercise should be done when she is relatively stable, and feeling more or less hopeful. You may need to remind her to think positively and hopefully and to be future oriented. If she slips into pessimistic thinking, help her to reframe her thoughts and start again.

Three mirrors
This is a fantasy exercise that allows a client to create a clear picture in their minds of what their future could be.

How to use it
Explain that this exercise will help your client to imagine the future she wants to create.

Start by helping your client to relax, as deeply as possible. Any relaxation exercise will do. You are welcome to use a relaxation recording listed on our website:

seawinds-education.mykajabi.com

When your client is well relaxed, then play this recording:

dropbox.com/scl/fi/5h6rfo7nse9ovnq5cldnu/Three-Mirrors-Exercise.mp3?rlkey=miqqyjxgk92r8b5exq9htw7p8&st=y3wdr0yj&dl=0

After she has completed the second recording, help her to assess what she created by asking questions such as these:

- "What did you see in the past mirror? How old were you? What did you learn about your past self from this mirror?"
- "What did you see in the present-day mirror? What did you learn about your current self from this mirror?"
- "What did you see in the future mirror? Where were you? Who was with you? What were you doing in your beautiful future? How did you feel?"
- "What pieces do you need to put in place in order to actually create the beautiful future you imagined?"
- "Where would you like to start with that process of creation?"

Cautions
With a focus on creating a beautiful future, there are not too many risks with this exercise. If she becomes pessimistic about her ability to actually create the future she has imagined, help her reframe her thoughts to be more optimistic and to allow for infinite possibility.

Tools for improving mental health and awareness

A simple CBT exercise to rewrite mental scripts
Cognitive behavioural therapy (CBT) is the gold standard treatment for mild to moderate depression, anxiety and many other issues. CBT is one of the most extensively-researched techniques in psychotherapy. We **know** that it works. The basic premise is that our thoughts create our emotions, and that we can turn around many unwanted emotional states by learning to think differently about life.

This simple tool is a great place to start, prompting the client to think critically about their own thoughts.

How to use it
Ask the client to draw a vertical line down the centre of a piece of paper. At the top of each column, he writes "I Am". Encourage the client to write in the left-hand column a few words to describe a significant thought he has about himself. We are shooting here for the good, the bad and the ugly, no holds barred.

It works best if the client does this step fairy quickly, not taking time to assess each statement: just pump out the thoughts. Half a dozen thoughts are adequate to begin.

Next, choose one to work on. The chosen thought should be one that causes a problem for the client, probably a negative thought, not necessarily rational.

Ask the client to give the thought a percentage between 0 – 100% that describes how much he actually believes that thought.

Then ask the client to flip that thought, and to come up with a new thought that is more or less the opposite of the negative thought, and write that new thought in the right-hand column opposite its evil twin on the left.

Ask the client to make note of evidence from his life that would prove that positive thought true, and write that under the positive thought. Now ask the client to give the positive thought a percentage between 0 – 100% that shows how much he actually believes this statement.

On the next page is what the completed worksheet might look like:

I Am	**I Am**
Smart	
Too fat	
Unkind, selfish 60%	I am thoughtful, 85%.
I over think things	
I get too emotional	*Evidence:*
Never going to be happy	
No one will ever want to marry me	- *I always remember family birthdays and anniversaries*
Professional	
Musical	- *I notice how others feel and ask how they are doing*
Overly dramatic	
	- *I give what I can to charity*
	- *I make sure my elderly neighbours have help when they need it*

The next step is to have the client look carefully at their observations. Almost always, the numbers for the two thoughts will add up to more than 100%. Then you can encourage the client to analyze his observations with questions and reflections such as these:

- "These two thoughts are pretty much opposites. How is it possible to believe them both at the same time? How is it possible that you can believe 60% that you are selfish and unkind, yet at the same time, you believe 85% that you are kind and thoughtful? That adds up to more than 100%. Why do you think that the numbers add up to more than 100%?"
- Some parts of our minds know that there is a different perspective to look at, which is why your client can also believe the positive thought at times. It is common to believe both the positive and the negative thought, to differing degrees at different times.
- You could point out that what we focus on becomes our reality and that often our thoughts about ourselves become warped. When we get used to that warped thought, we often ignore evidence that our supposedly "true" negative thought may be untrue.
- "When are you most likely to believe the thought in the left column? When are you most likely to believe the thought in the right column? Why do you think that is?"
- "You have gathered some evidence that the thought on the right is true, so why would

you give the thought on the left any airtime?"
- "Which thought do you think is the truth? If both thoughts have some truth, what do you think would happen if you were to choose to focus on the thought on the right?"
- "I notice that you have gathered some evidence that this new thought is true. How does it feel to look at the evidence and think that new thought?"

You can follow up on this reflection by pointing out that our thoughts create our emotional feelings. If your client tells you that he felt down, discouraged, and overwhelmed when he thought the negative thought but feels more happy, hopeful and buoyant when he thinks the positive thought, then you could ask him to reflect on what that might say about his habitual feelings of discouragement. What has he been focusing on, and how might he feel differently if he were to choose to focus on the flipped thought instead?

What conclusions can he make from this exercise? What can he choose to do differently?

By this point the client may realize that he has choice, and that if he chooses to focus on the thought on the left, he will feel bad. But if he chooses to focus on the thought on the right, he will feel much better. The extension of that understanding is that our thoughts create our own emotional reality. That may be a leap for some, but it is a profound understanding that can be life-changing.

This process can then be repeated to examine and flip more of the thoughts on the left side.

Supply the client with several 3"X5" file cards, pieces of paper or cardboard, and a magic marker. Have the client write the positive thought in bold marker pen on several of the cards.

He then posts the cards wherever he can see them frequently in passing, such as on the fridge, or the bathroom mirror, or above his bed. Every time he passes one of the cards, he reads the positive statement out loud at least three times.

The number three seems to have some archetypal significance, which it is said, is why the number three appears so often in art, literature, myths and stories (the three little pigs; three wishes; body, mind and spirit; Father, Son and Holy Ghost; "third time is the charm"; the three primary colours (red, yellow, blue) are needed to mix most other colours; and many more references from many different cultures.) Symbols representing the number three are found throughout history and from different cultures all over the world.

Reading words on a card then saying them out loud requires using more than one of our senses—sight and hearing. Modern brain researchers might say that using more than one sense simultaneously opens up more new neural pathways, thus enhancing the possibility of new behaviour patterns too. Educators know the value of presenting new information using more than one sense to encourage improved recall of the learned material.

It takes about three weeks of fairly continuous repetition for a new, positive thought to become well-established. After a few weeks your client will probably notice a shift towards a more positive outlook and emotional state.

Cautions
Be careful to focus mostly on the positive aspects of what the client brings to this exercise, while avoiding giving too much attention to the habitual negative thoughts. You don't want to

further ingrain those warped thoughts in someone's head. Do acknowledge them, but then immediately direct the client to flip their thought and make that new thought the chief focus for the exercise.

It is often challenging for a person to do that. We can become so focused on whatever thought we have developed, true or not, that our emotions may be running high and it is difficult to leave that thought behind and see any other possibility. Negative thoughts and the emotions they create may have become the only valid possibilities in a client's mind, so that challenging them can seem wrong. He may even resist the new thought.

You may need to assist the client to formulate the words for a valid counter-thought, and to come up with evidence of the new thought. "Remember when you_____? That says to me that you are kind."

It is often quite a stretch for the client to accept that the new thought might actually have some validity and to then believe it and act on it. The client may need reminding to go with that new positive thought.

Any client who has a great deal of difficulty accepting a new positive thought may need to see a therapist to dig deeper into why their negative thoughts seem so much more real.

A mood record to monitor emotional state patterns

The mood record is an important tool in CBT, Cognitive Behavioural Therapy. A person tracks their moods throughout each day over a week or so to see patterns that can provide clues about where our moods come from. The mood record helps the client to recognize the links between their environment, thoughts, and feelings.

How to use it

Search for "mood record" online and you will find several example formats, plus listings of downloadable apps to monitor moods.

Create a simple chart with the hours of the day and a space to write notes every two hours. Record a single word to describe your mood ("excited"; "depressed"; "sad"; "angry"). Note where you were at the time, who you were with, and what was happening.

Have your client track her moods through at least a week, or longer if possible, then look for patterns. For example, if she feels gloomy and depressed every time she walks into her work place, then you can help her explore what it is about the workplace that is causing her to feel badly about being there.

If your client notices that being around a specific person makes her feel happy, then exploring that relationship further might be fruitful.

If they take an antidepressant which seems to wear off by the end of the day, then perhaps a visit to their doctor to reassess her meds might be in order.

If a client records that her moods are dark and suicidal all the time, then getting her to a doctor or to a pro therapist immediately is essential.

Cautions
There is not a great deal of risk using this observation tool. It merely identifies patterns and sheds light on environmental issues that are affecting the client.

A thought record to monitor problem thoughts

Similar to the mood record, the thought record monitors what are called "automatic thoughts", the habitual thought patterns that crowd our heads, and the links between what we think and how we feel.

The idea is that we all have developed thoughts that are not totally rational, and these thought patterns create our habitual emotional states.

How to use it
Present this as a simple but interesting exercise that can have a profound impact on how a person lives their life.

The client first needs to discover what their automatic thoughts are. Remember the discussion in Chapter 3 about the mental thought recordings that become the soundtrack to our lives?

There are many ways to make these discoveries. A client may notice similar patterns and begin to be curious about them. A helper might point out obvious patterns that the client has not noticed. Therapy might root out persistent irrational thoughts. The key here is to understand that most of our habitual thought patterns are there because they once served a purpose. However, carried forward into adult life, those old familiar patterns can be more of a problem than a help.

Most thought patterns come from our childhoods. Automatic thoughts are often irrational because they were acquired when we did not fully understand the context of things that happened or were said to us. To make meaning out of confusing or frightening events, children often weave stories that paint themselves in a bad light, totally unnecessarily. As adults, we understand that our childhood thoughts may not make a lot of sense, but they are recorded on our mental tapes anyway.

When a strong emotion pops up, there is almost always a habitual automatic thought behind the mood. The good news is that the mental tapes with the distressing recordings can be re-recorded. The thought record begins that process.

After the client has kept a thought record for a week or longer, you can assist the client to think about the patterns brought to light.

- "What similarities do you notice in these events? Do you see a pattern in the automatic thoughts?"
- "How often are you aware of those familiar feelings?"
- "What cool thoughts calm down your familiar feelings? Do you notice a pattern?"
- "What do you notice in your life when you can calm down your feelings with a realistic thought? Do your relationships change? Do your choices change? What else changes?"

- "What information do you need to choose realistic thoughts more often?"
- "What changes in your life would you like to make, given this information?"
- "What assistance would you need to do so consistently?"

Following are a template for a simple thought record, and a sample completed record.

You can search online for more thought record templates. The "bible" for CBT tools is *Mind Over Mood: Change How You Feel by Changing the Way You Think*, in which you will find many useful tools. There is a complete listing for this book in Chapter 8.

Date	Situation	Automatic Thoughts	Emotions	What could I tell myself instead?	Rate your mood again
	What was the familiar trigger?	*What exactly were those thoughts? How much do you believe each of them (1-100%)?*	*How bad do you feel (1-100%)?*	*A constructive, realistic, positive thought to change your emotions*	*How do you feel now (1-100%)?*

Date	Situation	Automatic Thoughts	Emotions	What could I tell myself instead?	Rate your mood again
	What was the familiar trigger?	*What exactly were those thoughts? How much do you believe each of them (1-100%)?*	*How bad do you feel (1-100%)?*	*A constructive, realistic, positive thought to change your emotions*	*How do you feel now (1-100%)?*
Nov. 10, 2023	Friend failed to respond as I wanted him to when I felt bad over hurtful comments from another friend. Lack of support from someone I	He is a selfish asshole, he should back me in this issue. 95% I can't really count on anyone. 85% I might as well withdraw from	Angry 90% Hurt 80% Betrayed 95%	He has his own PTSD issues, he cannot handle my emotions right now, he needs to protect himself. In fact my expectations may have been unreal-	Angry 0% Hurt 5% Betrayed 0%

Kate Tompkins

Date	Situation	Automatic Thoughts	Emotions	What could I tell myself instead?	Rate your mood again
	expected it from.	this friendship. 65%		istic.	
Dec 15, 2023	Girlfriend left town to spend Christmas with her sister instead of with me. Lack of support from someone I expected it from.	Alone again. I am always alone, it seems to be my natural condition. 100% I will always be alone. 95% No one really cares about me. 75%	Lonely 85% Sad 90% Resentful 70%	She had no choice, her sister is doing poorly, of course she had to go. It's not about me. I will spend Christmas with another friend, where I will be welcomed. I know she loves me, she shows me in other ways.	Lonely 3% Sad 5% Resentful 0%
January 12, 2024	My dog ran away when I called him. Lack of caring for what I want.	Jerk of a dog! 100% Of course he does not listen to me, no one does. 85%	Annoyed 90% Betrayed 95%	Of course he ran when he had the chance, he needs exercise. It's not about me. He wants to behave, but I need to meet his needs first.	Annoyed 2% Betrayed 0%

As I reflect on what I have recorded, I might make these observations:

- I notice that a go-to thought of mine is to assume that no one cares about me and that I have been betrayed. It would be useful to think about where that thought came from. Was there a time in my earlier years when someone did let me down? Is that reflection

real, or is it an irrational interpretation of something that in fact was different or that had nothing to do with me?
- Following that irrational thought, I notice that my go-to emotions are resentment and anger. However, if I decide that my earlier thought was in fact irrational, look how my emotions calm down and change. I am able then to see things differently, which means I can make different choices.

The process of changing our emotions by changing the way we think is the cornerstone of CBT, Cognitive Behavioural Therapy.

Cautions
This tool cannot be beat for helping people look at themselves and their lives differently. A person who is relatively stable and calm should find it fairly straightforward to use thought records to analyze their thinking, emotional and behaviour patterns to become more aware.

However, a person with significant PTSD may need the help of a pro therapist to clear out irrational thoughts and their feelings using special techniques for post-trauma work.

Self-regulation tools

Self regulation is the process of calming one's self down when our emotions are running higher than we like.

Did you know we have three nervous systems?

The central nervous system is the one we don't need to think about. It runs our brain, heart, digestion and other body functions. The autonomic nervous system is all about our emotions. It has two branches—the sympathetic system and the parasympathetic system.

The sympathetic system is the one activated when we feel love, joy, pleasure, excitement, and also when we feel anxiety, fear, anger, frustration. It gets us out of bed in the morning and drives our activity.

The parasympathetic system is the "calm down" system. It is the one that we engage when we relax.

The two branches of the autonomic system are biphasic and bipolar. In other words, they both can move up and down, and cannot both be activated at the same time. If the parasympathetic nervous system is dominant, then the sympathetic is down. If the sympathetic is up, then the parasympathetic system is down. That's good news, because it means that we can actively do something to calm down when we feel distress.

So here's the thing that matters: It is impossible for a body, in which every single muscle is relaxed to feel distress. It's really pretty simple, not always easy to do in practice; but with practice, it is quite wonderful.

One of the reasons why all of these suggested calm-down exercises works is that they all engage at least one of our five senses—sight, hearing, touch, taste and smell. The five senses are directly connected to the parasympathetic nervous system, the calm down system.

So—you want to relax? Engage your five senses.

These exercises help the parasympathetic system to be dominant, thus squelching the sympathetic system and dampening our emotional feelings.

Which are the most effective? Whichever ones work best for you. You can combine them for even better effect. For example, the jaw drop and the pelvic drop, followed by diaphragmatic breathing, is a popular combination. The peripheral vision and wet noodle is also a popular combination.

Experiment with these. Try out all of them to discover which work the best for you. Then practice them many times a day when you don't really need them to develop muscle memory so it will be easier to use them when you do need them.

Any time you feel a negative thought enter your consciousness, relax. Any time you feel some distress rising, relax. Any time you think about it, relax. Once every few minutes, relax, whether you need to or not.

In a couple of weeks of using these skills often, your body will start to figure out what to do, and it will become easier, faster, and lead to deeper relaxation.

There are other techniques for calming down, but these following are popular and effective.

Cautions

There are no risks with these self-regulation exercises. Anyone can follow them, usually fairly easily.

The Five Senses Inventory, also known as '5, 4, 3'

- Take a mental inventory of five things you can see around you, and list them. ("I see desk, I see lamp, I see carpet…"etc.)
- Take a mental inventory of four things you can feel or touch. ("I feel my shoes, I feel my bum on the chair, I feel my earrings, I can touch my desk…")
- Take a mental inventory of three things you can hear ("I hear a car on the road, I hear my fridge…")

If you need more time, do it all again with five more things you can see, four more things you can feel, three more things you can hear.

The wet noodle

Scan your body. Start at the top of your head and go right down to your toes. Or you can start at your toes and work upwards. Find any muscle that is tight, scrunch it up and hold for ten seconds, then let it go. Try tightening up all your muscles then letting them go to find the feeling of total relaxation.

Find your peripheral vision

- Focus on a spot on the wall straight ahead.
- Keep your focus on that spot, but hold your hands up in front of your face then slowly spread your arms out to the side. Track your hands with your peripheral vision, allowing your field of view to widen and notice what you see in your peripheral vision.

Do this for ten seconds.

Relax your jaw

- Gently allow your jaw to drop towards the floor.
- Drop your tongue. Get it off the roof of your mouth and let it touch your bottom teeth. Relax the entire bottom half of your face and jaw, as if your jaw were melting towards the floor.
- Try to drop the roof of your mouth.
- Hold for ten seconds.

This exercise instantaneously engages the parasympathetic nervous system.

Relax your pelvis

- Sit on your hands, dig around and find two bony points that stick down out of your pelvis into the seat cushion. Put pressure on those two spots for ten seconds, until your body has a felt sense of them.
- Sitting or standing, find the top of the widest part of your pelvic bones in the front on both sides and press on them. Hold that sensation of feeling.
- Draw imaginary lines or pieces of string to connect those four points. The left front hip point to the right front hip point; right front hip to right butt cheek point; right butt cheek point to left butt cheek point; left butt cheek point to left front hip point. That forms a rectangle with one side higher.
- Focus on the edges of the rectangle, the boundaries, and softly expand the rectangle outwards.
- Relax the core muscles in the middle of the square.
- Everything will relax along with them.

This exercise also instantaneously engages the peripheral nervous system.

Deep diaphragmatic breathing

You can teach these breathing skills to your client by demonstrating them yourself. If your client is in the throes of a highly charged emotion, you can simply model the deep breathing yourself and your client will likely follow along. You can remind him to "breathe" if he holds his breath.

- Breathe deeply, as if you were breathing to your toes.
- Slow your breathing down, while continuing to breathe deeply.
- Lengthen the exhale to be about twice as long as the inhale. Try counting:
    - In, 2, 3, 4
    - Hold, 2, 3, 4
    - Out, 2, 3, 4, 5, 6, 7, 8.

    - In, 2, 3, 4
    - Hold 2, 3, 4
    - Out, 2, 3, 4, 5, 6, 7, 8.

- Continue breathing deeply and consciously.
- If you are quite anxious and having trouble breathing smoothly, it might be challenging to breathe this slowly. You could try 1, 1, and 2. When your breath calms down a bit, you could move to 2,2 and 4, then on to 3, 3 and 6, then to 4,4 and 8.
- If you have trouble breathing deeply, try placing one hand over the upper part of your belly and breathing so that you push out against your hand. This helps you feel where your diaphragm is and encourages deep breathing.

Relaxation recording

There are many relaxation recordings and scripts online. Search for "relaxation recording" online and you will come up with literally millions of sites to check out.

You are welcome to make use of this one:

seawinds-education.mykajabi.com/relaxation-recording-10ba0b5c-a5a0-4d80-977f-9cb5135704b3

How to use it
Find a quiet, safe, private place. You might want a blanket to stay comfortable if your body temperature goes down when you relax. Turn off your phone or any other source of possible distraction. Just kick back, with your favourite play back device beside your ear, and enjoy.

Cautions
Be prepared for "couch lock" because you are likely to get deeply relaxed or fall asleep.
Some people find it challenging to relax. Those who are quite physically active, or those with

a high level of energy, or those with ADHD may find it actually stresses them to listen to a recording such as this, because their body is used to nearly constant motion.

If your client is one of those folks who cannot sit still, they may not appreciate this type of relaxation, preferring to move. A walk in the woods can do more for such people than trying to force themselves to lie still long enough to listen to a relaxation tape.

Meditation

Meditation is an ancient practice enjoyed by many people around the world. Meditation has become popular as a way to manage stress, fight chronic illnesses including depression, heart disease, and chronic pain. There are numerous ways to meditate. To see a brief description of several approaches, visit these articles:

- everydayhealth.com/meditation/types/
- nytimes.com/guides/well/how-to-meditate

It's easy to do and promotes calmness, clarity and focus, wellness and happiness. My friend Joanne meditates daily and says she just doesn't feel right if she skips a day's meditation.

How to use it
Try the following approach suggested by my colleague and good buddy, The Rev. Christina Baxter.

> One of the biggest mistakes new meditation practitioners make is to try to mediate for too long a time. Just as you would not begin lifting weights with a 60 pound weight, do not try to begin with a 60 minute sit. Begin with just a few minutes – two or three. Set a timer. As you become comfortable with a few minutes, slowly increase the time as you sit in meditation. A twenty minute session is a good goal.
>
> Before you begin, find a quiet place to practice. If you want to light a candle or burn incense, please do. If you can sit cross legged on the floor, do so, keeping your spine straight. Sitting in a chair is also good – again, keeping the spine straight, with good alignment of your head, feet flat on the floor. I find it helpful to take three deep breaths into my abdomen, letting the breath out slowly. Breathe in through your nose and out through your mouth, with the out breath of equal length to the inbreath.
>
> Then just sit quietly. Some people like to count their breaths to help concentration. Each in and out breath is counted from one to ten then begin again. This is not as easy as it sounds. Quickly you will discover that your "monkey mind" is working overtime, throwing thoughts hither and yon. When you notice these distractions, just take a breath or two and begin counting over again. Also it is tempting to "put hooks" into these random thoughts then build stories to attach to them. Again, when you notice this happening, just let the thoughts go, take a breath or two and begin again.
>
> Do not be discouraged by experiencing intrusive thoughts. It happens to all meditators, no

matter how long they have been meditating. Noticing and dismissing these thoughts, is in fact, part of the practice.

If the thoughts are about something that genuinely needs your attention, just let them go with a promise to yourself that you will attend to it as soon as you are finished meditating. Another thought to dismiss intrusions is to remind yourself that for the time you are meditating, you do not have to think about anything. You can for these few moments enjoy the quiet and solitude. The noises of daily living will still be there when your meditation is over.

When ending your time of meditation, slowly bring your consciousness back to the present. Take another breath or two as you transition back to everyday life. You may even want to make a "Namaskar" (hands held together in front of your heart) as a way to signal that your time of meditation is over and give thanks for the opportunity to practice meditating.

As you practice meditation and appreciate the silence, it will make holding the silence with a client easier. You will have learned to make friends with silence and the peace it can offer.

Cautions

Meditation is easy for some people, but feels challenging and even distressing for people who experience ADHD and those who are nervous or what we used to call "highly strung". They will say they hate having to sit still for so long.

For these people a moving mediation sometimes works better. The practitioner moves his body as if walking, but very very slowly, and focuses on the tiniest movement of each muscle as they move. Practitioners of moving meditations often enjoy moving outside, so they can flood their senses with sights, smells, textures, and sounds to help the walker stay "in their bodies" and "out of their heads."

People who are suffering from post-trauma symptoms may find it too distressing when thoughts and memories of their traumatic experience float to the surface and demand attention. For these people, engaging in a post trauma treatment first helps to clear out those distressing memories and emotions. Meditation then can become welcome, later on.

Therapeutic rocks

You can use these ceremonies with common rocks to help your client let go of behaviours he is ready to leave behind and invite in new healthy behaviours. They can also be used to help transition through different phases of life or to assist with healthy grieving.[15]

How to use them

Here are four ways to use rocks for ceremonial purposes.[16]

---

15 With thanks to ACPE Certified Educator, Gerald L. Jones, MA, BCC
16 Contributed by The Rev. Christina Baxter.

1. Place two clear containers in a selected location. Fill one container with rocks of various sizes and shapes, along with sharpies. Invite people to write names (first names or initials only to protect privacy) or prayers, or other appropriate thoughts on the rocks. Then place the finished rocks in the second container. When the container is full, collect the rocks and place them in a special place in a garden, flower bed, or other location at your premises. We referred to these as "prayer rocks"; however, please feel free to call them by any name that is appropriate for your organization. We also placed a small explanation sign next to the containers explaining the process and inviting people to use the rocks.

> My Chaplain Supervisor, Gerald L. Jones, shared how to use rocks in healing ceremonies. I was a little sceptical at first, but quickly came to realize the powerful healing in these simple ceremonies using rocks.
> We always had a good supply of rocks and sharpies, in addition to a special location on the hospital grounds to place these rocks.
> - The Rev. Christina Baxter

2. After a traumatic episode, invite all those involved to gather in a circle either near the location of the event or, if that is not appropriate, in some other quiet place. Take a rock and invite the participants to each take a turn holding it. They can hold it in silence or they can speak a name, a thought, a prayer, or whatever is helpful for them. When the person is done, pass it to the next person in the circle. Allow each person the time they need (some will linger, some will quickly pass the rock; some will hold it silently, others will say what they are feeling). When the rock has come full circle, wish peace to those who participated as they leave, then place the rock in a special location on the grounds of your building.

3. A two-part ceremony works well for clients who are processing feelings and events. In the first part, provide rocks of various sizes that are preferably flat, and colourful sharpies. Invite your clients to write on the rocks anything that no longer serves them in their journey of growth. Allow them as much time as they need to write on as many rocks as they want. When they are done, place the rocks in a rock garden or, if near water, have them commit them to the water to recycle whatever it is they no longer need in their life. Invite them to acknowledge overnight that they have now created an opening in their life. What is it they want to invite into their life to fill this newly created space? At the next meeting have them again write on rocks what it is they are inviting into their life. Give them as much time as they need. When done, commit the rocks to a garden or water, giving thanks for both the letting go and the welcoming of new ideas, people, goals, etc. into their life.

4. For those who work in hospice/palliative care, when family or loved ones are unable to be with your client at the end of life, place a rock next to the bed of your client. Before placing the rock, hold it and either silently or quietly speak your hopes and wishes for your client as they transition from this life to the next. If an opportunity presents itself, give the rock to the family and explain how it was used at the time of death.

Kate Tompkins

Cautions
The only caution is to avoid giving access to rocks to anyone who has violent tendencies, is actively angry, or for some other reason is likely to use the rocks as a missile or a weapon. Otherwise, everyone responds well to these ceremonies.

Triage and response tools

Triage assessment and response tool for suicidal thinking
On the next page is a summary of suggested actions for a helper to take when encountering a person who is thinking about suicide.

How to use it
Make a copy of this summary and keep it where you can quickly access it when you need it.
　　For more on suicide and how to respond to suicidal thinking, see Chapter 6.

Cautions
The only caution is the need for you, the helper, to stay calm at any stage of suicidal thinking or intent. You need to be a calm anchor for the lost soul in torment.

Does he have occasional thoughts of suicide?

Listen well
Reassure him
Help him discuss underlying issues

Does he have a motivation to die?

Listen well
Help him create a safety plan
Get him to a therapist ASAP
Check on him, watch for changes

Does his manner show depression or decision? Intent to die?

Listen well
Help him create a safety plan
Take him to hospital emergency
Stay with him
Check on him if he is discharged

Has he completed suicide?

Stay calm
Call 911
Secure the scene
Remove and comfort family members, care for kids
Arrange for clean up

Does he have persistent strong thoughts of suicide?

Listen well
Assess motivation, manner, plan and means
Help him enhance protective factors, reduce risk factors
Refer him to a therapist
Check on him, watch for changes

Does he have a viable plan? Does he have the means to carry out the plan?

Listen well
Help him create a safety plan
Help him remove weapons, dangerous medications from the house
Get him to a therapist ASAP
Check on him, watch for changes

Has he attempted suicide?

Stay calm
Call 911
Rescue him, apply first aid
Stay with him if he is discharged
Remove weapons, medications from the house
Comfort family members

Kate Tompkins

Triage assessment and response tool for intimate partner violence
Similar to the triage guide for suicidal thinking, this is a summary of suggested actions for a helper to take when encountering a person who is being abused.

How to use it
Make a copy of the summary on the next page and keep it where you can quickly access it when you need it.

For more on intimate partner violence, see Chapter 6.

Cautions
Every case is different, every person has their own concerns, so remember to listen well and respond to whatever the needs are for today. With abusive relationships, every day is a new opportunity to make a different decision, so go with the flow as much as you can and respond to whatever the client brings to you today.

This guide assumes that the person being abused is a woman, because it is most often women who find themselves in that position. However, the same assessment process and responses apply to men being abused.

The Non-Therapist

Is she safe?

Get her to physical safety
Create emotional safety
Help her create a safety plan
Help her visit local police
Help her cover her tracks online

Is she ready to make big changes?

Help her find therapy for mental health issues
Demonstrate self regulation and stress management techniques
Help her access sufficient cash to make an escape

Does she want to stay in the relationship?

Help her be clear about she wants and does not want
Demonstrate how to create boundaries statements
Teach her to assess the success of her boundaries
Teach her to recognize when it is time to leave the relationship

Is she ready to create a new safe life?

Refer to a therapist to heal from trauma
Help her identify relationship patterns
Teach her to be aware of relationship dynamics and signs of future abuse

Does she have immediate care issues?

Get her to medical care
Help her find emergency housing
Get her what she needs

Does she know where to find help?

Help her obtain legal protection orders
Help her locate agencies, shelters
Help her obtain woman abuse-centered information, counselling
Help her find online supports
Support her to expand her network of supportive women friends

Does she want to leave the relationship?

Encourage her to see a therapist to discuss trauma bonding
Help her to overcome obstacles
Stay patient, offer unconditional support
Help her create a safety plan, and an escape plan
Help her access legal protection orders
Help her enlist help to move out
Help her prepare for court appearances

Kate Tompkins

Triage assessment and response tool for trauma
This tool is a guide for responding to a client in crisis following a traumatic experience.

How to use it
Make a copy of the summary on the next page and keep it where you can quickly access it when you need it.

For more on trauma and post trauma and how to respond to them, see Chapter 6.

Cautions
Again, stay calm. Be that calm anchor when the world has been turned upside down for your client.

Is she safe?

Get her to physical safety

Supply first aid if needed

Create emotional safety

Contact emergency services if needed

Look after immediate personal needs

Calm her down, demo regulation skills

Does she need supportive company?

Accompany her to emergency services

Stay with her or arrange for other company

Avoid trite reassurances

Listen well

Get her moving as much as she is able

Protect her privacy by helping to screen visitors

Does she know where to find help?

Help her locate shelters, agencies

Help her find emergency counselling support

Help her connect with supportive family, friends

Help her connect with financial supports, housing

Is she ready to move on??

Encourage her to resume normal life and social activities, networks and routines

Encourage her to develop new healthy activities and friendships

Support the family to support her

Educate family about trauma responses

Offer help with everyday tasks

Continue to be available

Help her access counselling for PTSD if needed

Key take-away points

- Non-therapists can use these tools to help clients who are relatively stable and sane.
- Try out every tool first to become comfortable with it and be able to predict how clients will respond to it.
- Make sure you can demonstrate or model the skills and ideas yourself first.
- Adapt the tools as needed to be useful for your clients. If you are not sure how, please contact the author for advice.
- Make sure that you are relaxed, calm and focused yourself before using these tools. Make sure your Teflon cape is handy.
- If any issues arise, such as overwhelming emotions, troubling past memories, or anything else that seems unusual or out of place, refer your client to a pro therapist.
- Keep copies of the triage tools where you can easily access them.

Activities to consolidate your learning

1. Gather your friends or co-workers together to practice using the tools. One of you can role play the client, the other the helper. Take note of how the tools worked, how the "client" felt engaging in the activity, the questions that arose, additional materials you need to gather, what your "client" had to say about how their perspective changed as a result of using the tool.
2. Check out some of the additional resources listed for each tool to learn more. Choose at least three tools, research them, practice them, and become proficient enough in their use that you feel confident and comfortable with them. Make these your "go to" tools. Then add three more to your tool box. Then three more.

For more information, check out the resources here:
seawinds-education.mykajabi.com/o-pt-in-to-resources-for-the-non-therapist

6: What should I expect?

This chapter outlines some of the most common issues that a helper is likely to encounter and offers some guidelines for responding effectively.

Suicidal thinking

What you need to know
There may be nothing more frightening to a helper than realizing your friend or client is suicidal. Breathe, drop your jaw, and pull on your Teflon cape.

It is important to remember that when a person is feeling suicidal, he is probably frightened. We are hard-wired to want to live. That is perhaps the primary goal of existence: to continue to exist. So when a person feels desperate enough to say he is thinking of suicide, what he may actually mean is that he cannot carry on with the way he has been living his life, can no longer cope with whatever life has brought to him, and cannot see any other way out of his pain and misery. Yet. Which is **not** the same as "I want to die."

The main jobs for the helper when suicide is in the air are to be a calm anchor, to assess the immediate risk for the client and to help the client access the right kind of help. Our job is to help him feel that he is not alone, that some solutions may be possible, and that hope for the future is possible. But of course, our job is **not** to attempt to force feed those thoughts to our client. It is to create the right conditions and to support him while he comes to those conclusions on his own.

Always take a hint of suicidal thinking seriously, even if you suspect it is not real. If the person truly is thinking about suicide, you may save a life. If the person was being somewhat less than totally serious, and you respond as if they were, the person will probably quickly back down, and may laugh at you, but he still knows that you care about him and would respond quickly if he really did contemplate taking his thoughts further.

So, what if the embarrassed client accuses you of going overboard? You will know you have done the right thing. If you have good reason to ask a person directly about suicide, do so, immediately, directly and without feeling like an idiot.

According to government statistics, every day, on average, at least ten people die by their own hand in Canada. And many more are thinking about it or attempt it. For every suicide, there are at least seven other people profoundly affected by the loss.[17] In small towns, the en-

---
[17] Joseph Sadek, *A Clinician's Guide to Suicide Assessment and Management*, Department of Psychiatry, Dalhousie University, Halifax, Nova Scotia, Canada: Springer Press, date unknown.

tire community is likely to be affected when someone suicides.

According to Statistics Canada, here are the groups most likely to choose suicide:

- Men and boys—three times more often than women and girls
- People serving federal sentences
- People who have lost a family member or close friend to suicide
- People who survived a suicide attempt by a family member or close friend
- Some in First Nations, Metis and Inuit communities, especially youth
- 1/3 of deaths by suicide are among people 45-59 years
- Suicide is the second leading cause of death among youth and young adults (15-34 years)
- Suicide rates are high for seniors, especially those living alone, and especially men

Women have higher rates of self harm, such as cutting or burning themselves. Suicidal thinking and self harm are seen in high rates in 2sLGBTQ people, those who identify as two-spirited, lesbian, gay, bisexual, trans, or queer/questioning youth.

Thoughts of suicide (the pros call those thoughts "Suicidal Ideation", or SI) that just show up from time to time, with the person not going as far as making a plan, are not at all uncommon. If everyone was honest about whether or not the thought of suicide had ever crossed their mind at some point, no doubt a few or several people you know would raise their hands.

In itself, the odd suicidal thought is not a real danger and no panicked response is required. It just means that things in that person's life are not 100 percent wonderful and some positive changes might be enough to send those fleeting thoughts flying out the window. If things change and the person talks openly about suicide or has a plan, then it's time to gear up to help.

How to respond effectively

When your client begins to hint at suicide, you might hear comments such as these, which should raise the red flag in the back of your mind:

- "I'm not sure how long I can go on like this."
- "I'm just so tired of being down."
- "My family would be better off without me."
- "No one would miss me."
- "I won't be around for your birthday next month."

If you hear a comment such as these, ask directly what is going on in your client's head. It is a myth that mentioning suicide will cement the thought and bring it about. That is simply not true.

If a person is feeling bad enough to be seriously considering suicide, then he will welcome your question, as it would give him an opportunity to open up about some very frightening feelings. He will likely be relieved that you have caught on and have opened the door for him to talk.

If he is not feeling suicidal, he will simply say, "No!" and you can both relax. If he hesitates and comes back with something like, "Well, not really, but..." then you have an opening to talk about whatever might be on his mind.

You lose absolutely nothing by asking, and directness not only saves time in what might be a risky situation, it also allows your client to be honest and open up to you. Your client will know that you are aware, you are tuned in to him, and you can handle whatever he might need to say. (Stay calm!)

Try these:

- "Has the thought of suicide ever crossed your mind?"
- "Sometimes when people feel the way you do right now, they start to have thoughts about suicide. Has this ever happened to you?"
- "You mentioned that your family would be better off without you. Does that mean you are thinking of suicide?"

If the answer is yes, follow up with something like these:

- "When was the last time you felt that way?" (If it was years ago with no recent occurrences, then there is likely not a great deal of risk for this client. If it was yesterday, then there is immediate risk and further assessment is needed.)
- "Was it just a fleeting thought, or do you find these thoughts in your head often?" (If it was just fleeting, no big worries, but if the thoughts are persistent, then more assessment is needed.)

Let's take a closer look.

Your client has occasional thoughts of suicide
If, like many others, your client admits that, occasionally, the thought has crossed his mind, but they were only fleeting thoughts that did not fully develop, then the main response is to listen well. If he seems distressed about his suicidal thoughts, assure him that occasional thoughts like this are common and not necessarily a sign that he is actually suicidal.

You might help him explore his thoughts with questions and reflections such as these:

- "What is going on in your life right now?" (Are there issues that are making him vulnerable?)
- "I can see distress on your face. I'd really like to hear what you are thinking right now." (Is the thought of suicide present?)
- "Is there any pattern to when those thoughts come up?" (Are there identifiable triggers that can be addressed?)
- "How do you feel when these thoughts appear?" (What is his emotional state? How worried is he about himself?)

- "What works for you to get past these suicidal thoughts?" (What skills does he have to think things through logically? Does he have close social supports?)
- "I can tell that things have been very challenging for you lately." (Opens the door for the client to reveal his private, frightening thoughts.)
- "It must be difficult to be in your shoes right now". (Acknowledges the challenges and the fact that you care, building rapport and trust so that he can open up to you.)

Your client has strong, persistent thoughts of suicide
If your client admits to having thoughts that are more than fleeting, thoughts that are persistent, frequent or strong, then it is time to refer the person to a pro therapist.

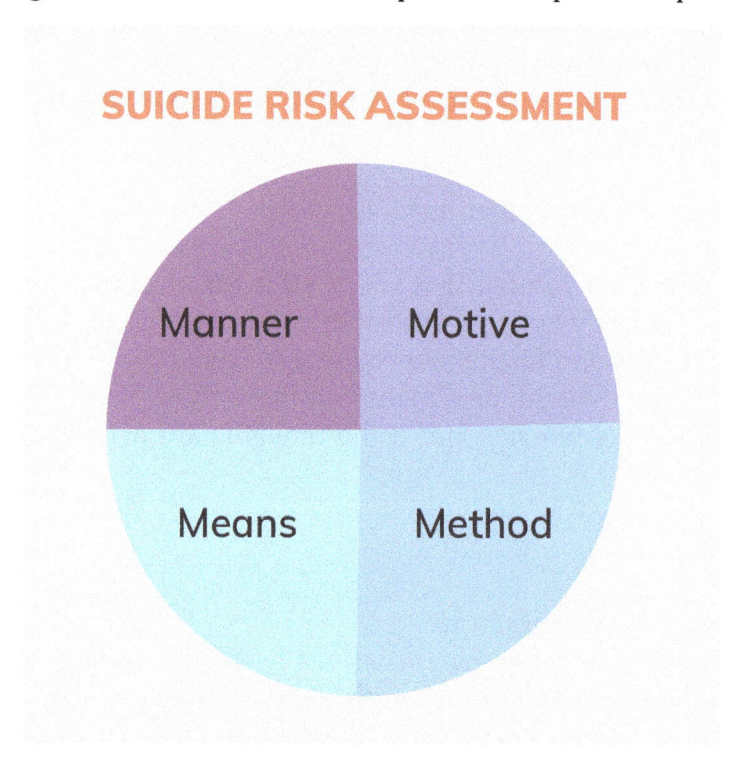

SUICIDE RISK ASSESSMENT

- Manner
- Motive
- Means
- Method

Since it may take a while for the client to be seen by a therapist, and since your client may not actually go to a therapist even when you recommend one, it is also time to get ready to offer more immediate help. To know what to do, it is also time for more assessment. You will need to learn more about these areas of concern: motivation, method, means and manner.

Motivation refers to whatever may be driving his suicidal thoughts, and whether he has the intention to actually kill himself. Many factors can increase a person's motivation to die, and the more that are present, the greater the possible risk. Look for these:

- A previous failed suicide attempt
- A past event that made him vulnerable, such as the death of a parent
- Loss of a family member or close friend to suicide
- Clusters of suicides in his small community
- A recent loss, such as being fired, or his spouse leaving him, or a romantic relationship ending
- A mental health issue, such as depression
- Failure to take medications for mental health concerns as directed
- Recent dramatic change in mood
- Money problems
- Being isolated socially
- Being a man or boy between the ages of 10 and 29
- Being a man over 80
- Being aboriginal
- Previous sexual abuse or other sources of trauma
- Childhood abuse or neglect
- Chronic disability or other impairment
- Frequent moves to new homes
- Lack of access to medical and mental health supports
- Impairment due to alcohol or drugs
- Hopelessness, helplessness
- Being impulsive or aggressive
- Poor judgment or the inability to think rationally
- Legal problems
- Impending incarceration or homelessness
- Serious illness
- Having been bullied
- Easy access to lethal weapons such as guns
- Having written a suicide good-bye note
- Feeling like a burden on family or friends
- Chronic insomnia
- Anything that creates vulnerability for the client
- Having rehearsed a potentially lethal plan and worked out the details
- Refuses, or feels unable, to create or commit to a suicide safety plan
- Inner voices commanding the client to kill himself
- Chronic physical pain or acute severe medical illness

There are factors which help to reduce the risks. These are not necessarily going to prevent your client from doing the deed, but reminding him of them might be what turns him back to deciding to live:

- Having responsibility for others, especially children and pets
- Discovering a reason to keep on with life
- Building new social supports or renewing old ones
- Religion, faith
- Finding a way to reduce stress and enhance ability to cope in a healthy way. Creative pursuits are especially helpful.

Kate Tompkins

These might help to explore motivation:

- "What kind of thoughts have you been having?" (Are they troubling, detailed thoughts starring him as the victim?)
- "When did these thoughts start?" (If they have been going on a long time, that indicates there are motivational risks factors that need to be explored.)
- "How often do these thoughts come up for you?" (If they are frequent and persistent, that is a warning sign.)
- "When they do come up, what do you do?" (Does he choose healthy ways of coping? Does he use alcohol or drugs to temporarily numb the pain? Does he have a support network?)
- "On a scale of 0–10, with 0 being not at all, and 10 being absolutely, how likely are you to try to kill yourself in the next day or so?" (How firm is his intent to die?)

Once you have explored the client's motivation and determined that there is significant risk for your client, you can help to reduce the risks by supporting him to remove or neutralize any risk factors that can be changed and to enhance protective factors he can develop.

Help your client create a safety plan.

- Who will he call if he feels out of control or his suicidal thoughts frighten him? He will need to have the phone number handy.
- Where will he go if he feels in danger from himself?
- What can he do to calm down, think more rationally, take time to unwind?
- What can he do to reduce his own risk factors and enhance his protective factors?

Watch him for changes in mood or an increase in substance use or gathering stuff that could be used for a lethal means of suiciding, such as guns and ammunition, ropes, medications, poisons.

Method refers to any plan the client may be thinking about. The most important assessment is how potentially lethal the plan may be. The most lethal methods are:

- using firearms
- hanging
- slicing blood vessels open along the length of the vein.
- jumping off a bridge
- driving into something solid

These more lethal methods tend to be favoured by men. Less potentially lethal are:

- carbon monoxide poisoning
- poison
- medication or drug overdose
- slicing across the wrist

These methods, favoured by women, are less lethal because they are less certain and slower. (Is the dosage enough? Is the poison toxic enough? Is the substance or medication one that will kill or just make her sick? Is there time to complete the suicide before someone finds her?)

Means refers to whether the client has what he needs to carry out his method.

- If his method is shooting, does he have easy access to guns? Ammunition? (If yes, help him remove them and store them someplace else he cannot easily access.)
- If his method is hanging, does he have rope available? A solid place to anchor the rope? (If yes, help him remove them.)
- If his method is cutting, does he have a sharp knife? (Remove knives from the house.)
- If his method is driving, does he have a vehicle easily available? (Take away his keys until he is in a better frame of mind.)
- If the method is poison or overdose, are the substances available? (Remove them if possible.)
- If the method is carbon monoxide, does he know how to set things up to be lethal?

When exploring method and means, especially if there is strong motivation, this is an occasion when using closed questions can be justified. These might be helpful:

- "When you think about suicide, does it go as far as making a plan as to how you would do it? I'd like to hear about your plan."
- "Have you considered any other plans?" (Not everyone will reveal the most lethal plans right away, knowing you will try to stop them. Be supportive, build that trust and sense of alliance to encourage him to open up.)
- "Have you rehearsed your plan? Thought about all the details?" (Don't help him if not!)
- "Do you have weapons in the house?" (or any other materials he would need for his plan.)

If there is no well-thought-out plan and no easy access to the means, the risk is not as great. In that case, access to therapy to work on the risk factors in his life is appropriate.

If there is no quick and easy access to a therapist, engage whatever supports are available in your community. Even in a smaller isolated community, there is usually someone available to talk to, such as a nurse or doctor, clergy, or social worker.

If there is a well-thought-out lethal plan, the means are easily available, and access to therapy is not handy, you will need to engage others in the community to help you monitor him: call police to do a "wellness check"; take him to the local nursing station or hospital emergency room; take him to a local care agency such as a mental health office.

Be aware that, given the state of mental and even medical health care services currently, it is possible that not much progress will be made; after a brief assessment your client may very well be quickly discharged and become your responsibility again. If that happens, work out your own frustrations privately, pull on your Teflon cape, and continue to just be there for him.

If he has a viable method in mind and the means available to carry out the plan, create or revisit the safety plan.

Manner refers to what you can see of his emotional state, which is a bit more challenging to interpret. Someone who is highly agitated, anxious, or frightened is obviously in distress, and therefore may be likely to act out fantasies and plans for suicide. But that same person is also more likely to seek help before things get out of hand.

What of the quiet person who downplays their distress or hides it? What of the person who seems to be the life of the party, then goes home early when no one notices and blows his head off?

A change in a person's usual manner, or what seems to be an emotional state that is out of sync with the present moment, is a more reliable indicator of risk, especially if he has already revealed the intent to suicide. Watch for changes such as a sudden rise in emotion or, after a lot of emotion, an unexpected calmness. This may indicate that a decision has been made and it will only be a matter of time to gather the required means before he will attempt suicide.

But of course it could also mean that he has taken some healthy action or thought things out and now thinks and feels differently, and that all is well, so don't go off half cocked just because you see a change in someone's manner.

If you are not sure, ask. Assess any risk factors that are present, refer him to a therapist if you still suspect suicide danger, and continue to be there for him. If you think there is an immediate danger, take him to the hospital emergency room. Create or revisit his safety plan, and watch him for changes.

Your client has attempted suicide
This is the time for practical action. Save the supportive exploration for later.

The first step is to take a deep breath, drop your jaw and stay calm. Everyone involved will need you to be an anchor for them. Not only does the victim who has attempted suicide need swift practicality and calmness, so do any witnesses or family members present.

Immediately call 911, if someone has not already done so. If there is need for immediate first aid to save his life, direct someone else to call 911 while you do whatever is needed to save the client. Cut down his rope, put pressure on his cuts, do whatever you need to do.

After the victim has been taken to the hospital or nursing station, assist family members to remove weapons and other means of self-harm, and clean up if needed.

Your main job now is likely to comfort and support distraught family members. Offer a shoulder to cry on, an opportunity to vent, company if they wish or safe solitude if that is what they ask for. If you will be there for a while, try to create a light and positive atmosphere for the family members. Cook a meal, help them clean up, whatever would make their lives easier.

If the client is discharged, stay with him if that seems appropriate, and watch for changes to his emotional state in the next few weeks, since he may decide to complete the job later.

Now go find some support for yourself. Recover in the arms of a loved one, take a hot bath, talk to a colleague. No one can be involved in responding to an attempted suicide without experiencing some distress themselves.

If you find yourself responding to several attempted suicides, and you are beginning to feel some mental health symptoms of your own, consider accessing post-trauma treatment. First responders are pretty much at the top of the list of people who develop Post Traumatic Stress Disorder, or PTSD.

Your client completes suicide
If you learn of a completed suicide from someone, call 911 and stay away unless family members need assistance and support. If you do not need to go the scene, don't. Too many people involved creates confusion for the police and muddies their investigation. And the sight of a dead body, especially one that bears obvious signs of violence, is **not** an image you want to have seared into your brain. That type of image can well lead to you developing PTSD, which you want to avoid at all costs. Even seasoned police offers and EMTs will say, "If you don't need to see it, don't look."

If you are the person who finds him, stay calm, call 911, and attempt to save him. However if it is clear that he is already dead, back away and secure the scene.

Do not allow anyone in and don't touch anything. The police will need to do an investigation to determine cause of death and you don't want to muddy the evidence any more than necessary.

If you did attempt to give first aid before the police arrive, make note of everything you did and everything you touched to help the police do a thorough job (and to prevent any suspicion of murder falling on you).

If possible, remove distraught family members from the scene and get them whatever support they need. Consider taking them to the hospital if they are very upset, or to the home of someone who can take care of them for a while in calm emotional safety.

Your main job when a suicide has been completed is to support family members, friends and any community members who are affected. Watch for distress in others, and be there to listen. In small communities, suicides often occur in batches, especially among young people. When one person suicides, others who are at risk may have a "copy cat" response.

Support family members for a while after the event. If it is appropriate, depending on your role, reach out in any way the family can accept. Drop in to visit, take them out for a coffee, spend time doing things together that you both enjoy, and in general try to provide stability, calmness and light ordinary, everyday companionship. Refer them to a pro therapist if they seem to be having difficulty recovering from their shock and loss.

Family members and close friends left behind may have to face guilt. ("Why did I not see the signs? How did I miss that he was suicidal? If only we had not had that argument…Why why why did he do that?") It is a myth that a suicidal person always leaves some hint or sign of their intent. Even when there are obvious risk factors, suicidal people often do not make their intentions known.

It is also a myth that only truly suicidal people give no hint of their plans, and that people who are not really committed to die are the ones who talk about it.

Do your best to comfort family members while not offering any possible reasons why their loved one chose to die. No one else can really understand what happens in the mind of a suicidal person, and it would be too easy to offer an explanation that might hurt the family in some way you cannot predict or understand, or minimize or trivialize the loss.

This is the tine to talk about not *why* did it happen but rather *how* do we move forward from here? How do we rebuild shattered lives?

Responding to suicide can be **very** stressful for a helper. Find someone to talk to yourself, and try to shed any left-over emotions you are carrying about the death. If you have a nasty image seared into your brain, consider seeking a trauma therapist to give you EMDR to reduce the impact of the image so that it does not trouble you.

The triage tool on page 153 can guide your responses.

To learn more
There are many internet sites with information about suicide and how to assess risk and respond. Start with those listed here:

> seawinds-education.mykajabi.com/o-pt-in-to-resources-for-the-non-therapist

Self-harm

What you need to know
The words "suicide" and "self harm" are sometimes used to mean the same thing, but in fact they are quite different. Suicide is usually about wanting to end the pain of life by dying. Self harm is about something different.

Young people often say they cut themselves in order to numb their pain, to escape their living for a while, or sometimes in order to feel anything at all. Whatever the intent of self harm, it is not death. It is possible to accidentally die from cutting, if a major blood vessel is pierced and bleeding cannot be stopped fast enough, but that was not the intention, although the authorities may label such a death to be suicide.

Self harm is usually done in secret: seeing the scars is usually what alerts parents or health care providers to the issue. It tends to be repeated, sometimes with accompanying rituals, often over years and sometimes well into adulthood, although it is usually a coping mechanism used by youth.

Those most at risk typically have experienced trauma, neglect, or abuse, but not always. In some youth social circles, scars may be worn as a fashionable badge of honour or membership in a group that celebrates negativity.

There is no direct causal link to suicidality, but a person who is feeling distressed enough to harm themselves may feel distressed enough at some future time to think about suicide.

Self harm often shows up as cutting or burning, but it may show up as pulling out hair, picking at wounds, putting one's self in the line of danger unnecessarily, or injuries leading to broken bones.

Many people feel shame afterwards and try to hide their scars, which may be permanent, with clothing such as long-sleeved shirts with high necklines or pants in hot weather.

Self harm is a sign of emotional distress that indicates a need for better coping skills. Mental health issues such as depression, eating disorders, anxiety, post traumatic stress disorder (PTSD) or personality disorder may be behind self harm, or may go along with it. These mental health issues are usually the focus of treatment.

How to respond effectively
There is not a big role for a helper, other than to listen well and refer the client to a pro therapist who has experience with self harm. Avoid trying to extract a promise not to harm again, because it usually takes more than self discipline to be able to stop. If the client harms themselves again, their shame at their "failure" to stop could drive them to even more of the harmful behaviour.

You might find yourself comforting the family and providing some information on the topic, rather than working with the person who is cutting.

To learn more
Start with the online resources listed here:

> seawinds-education.mykajabi.com/o-pt-in-to-resources-for-the-non-therapist

Trauma and past trauma

Trauma is an emotional response to a deeply-distressing event like an accident, an assault, rape, natural disaster, or military combat. Events are traumatic if they undermine a person's sense of safety in the world and create a feeling that catastrophe could strike at any time.

The emotional reaction to a distressing event overwhelms the person's ability to cope, causes feelings of helplessness, and diminishes their sense of self and their ability to feel a full range of emotions and experiences.

Immediately after the event, shock and denial are typical. Longer-term reactions include unpredictable emotions, disturbing memories and flashbacks, anxiety that won't go away, inability to trust people, strained relationships, and physical symptoms like headaches or nausea.

The body has amazing defence mechanisms that create a stress response, which may be flight, fight, freeze, or even more complicated responses. The chemicals that surge through the body after a trauma produce heightened blood pressure, increased heart rate, increased sweating, and loss of appetite. The body is getting ready to fight off that polar bear, or throw that spear, or run from that sabre toothed tiger.

Usually, action happens, we run or fight, and then the hormones disappear and so do the symptoms. We can usually function normally again within a few moments.

But that is not always what happens. Sometimes the stressors do not go away and become part of our everyday life. Sometimes the stress response has been so intense that it does not back off completely. When the body continues to pump out stress hormones, the long-term effects can become a big problem.

Every person responds to trauma differently. Some can throw off their experience easily. Others may suffer an immediate and acute effect. Still others may not show signs of stress until sometime after the event.

If the distressing symptoms go away after a few days or weeks, there is not a great deal to worry about. If the symptoms last for a month or more and get in the way of life, then we call it PTSD (Post Traumatic Stress Disorder). Stress responses escalate and may be seen as panic attacks, depression, suicidal thoughts, increased drug abuse, feelings of being isolated, inability to trust other people, not being able to complete daily tasks, exaggerated startle response, nightmares, insomnia, difficulties with relationships, irritability, and anger, and other inconvenient and distressing symptoms.

> Traumatic experiences often involve a threat to life or safety, but any situation that leaves you feeling overwhelmed and isolated can result in trauma, even if it doesn't involve physical harm. It's not the objective circumstances that determine whether an event is traumatic, but your subjective emotional experience of the event. The more frightened and helpless you feel, the more likely you are to be traumatized.
>
> -helpguide.org/articles/ptsd-trauma/coping-with-emotional-and-psychological-trauma.htm

Approximately 20% of people who experience a trauma develop long-term PTSD, but 80% do not. Why? While it is not clear why one person develops long term problems after a trauma and another person does not, recent research indicates that people whose childhood was happy, healthy, and safe are less likely to develop PTSD.

People who had safety issues as children or who lacked the security of a loving adult are more prone to develop PTSD after a trauma. So are those who have recently dealt with a heavy stress load, a series of recent losses or previous trauma, or who have experienced dissociation (zoning out of awareness of the present moment).

If there is a death or threat of death involved, the stakes are even higher. PTSD is more likely to develop and treatment takes longer. People who feel a sense of guilt following a death, whether or not that guilt is reasonable, have a greater challenge moving past PTSD.

I once helped two people who had been in a car accident. Both were sitting in the front seat, side by side, and experienced the same event. Neither was hurt physically, but they were both shaken up. One person was fine after a few weeks of support, and the other person needed long-term therapy for PTSD. The only difference between them was their childhoods: the one who developed more serious issues after the accident had had a frightening childhood, filled with repeated violence, insecurity, and fear. The other person's childhood, while not perfect, was safe and loving.

Some occupations expose people to PTSD-producing stressors more often than others. First responders are especially at risk: police, firefighters, and EMTs frequently develop PTSD; but for many of those people, there is a culture of denial which can get in the way of recognizing they are damaged and seeking help. "Suck it up, buttercup." Some are punished by their peers or even their organization for admitting they need professional help.

I often support first responders and hospital medical staff who have experienced something traumatic. I use a visual image which some find helpful: Imagine you are carrying a backpack. When you experience a particularly bad call, it is like you pick up a rock and stuff it into your backpack. You might not notice the first one, or the second or the third, but eventually the weight of those rocks becomes unbearable and you falter.

That is often when the first responders decide to reach out for help. Unfortunately, some never do.

I encourage first responders and medical people to talk about their experiences with their co-workers, who get it. In spite of protocols around confidentiality, it is essential to not stuff those feelings and memories into your backpack. Fortunately, many police forces and ambulance services now employ their own trauma therapists to support stressed-out responders.

You might hear pros or medical people talk about different types of trauma.

- *Acute trauma* results from a single incident such as a rape, a physical attack, an accident, a natural disaster, a plane crash, or a terrorist attack.
- *Chronic trauma* results from repeated and prolonged exposure to stressors, such as domestic violence, bullying, childhood neglect, living in a crime-ridden neighbourhood, experiencing prolonged racism, or battling a life-threatening illness.
- *Complex trauma* results from exposure to varied and multiple traumatic events, often of an invasive nature.
- *Secondary or vicarious trauma* is common among first responders, doctors and nurses who witness other's people traumatic events.

Even some commonly-overlooked events can cause a trauma reaction, for example, surgery, especially for a very young child, the breakup of a significant relationship, or a humiliating or deeply disappointing experience, especially if someone was deliberately cruel.

How to respond effectively
PTSD is definitely territory for a pro therapist with specialized training in trauma treatment. The role of a helper when PTSD is present is to listen well and refer your client to the right therapist.

However immediately following a traumatic event, the helper can assist in several ways:

- Assess the client's immediate state of being. Get your client to physical and emotional safety as quickly as possible following a traumatic experience. Look after her immediate needs, such as clean clothing, a safe place to stay, a toothbrush and cosmetics if she has come away from home quickly, someone to look after children or pets so that she can focus on her own wellbeing.

- If she is required to deal with emergency services or police or to go to the hospital, stay with her for emotional support. Drive her to wherever she needs to go.
- Help her calm down with a warm blanket, a cup of tea, relaxing music, whatever it takes to help her feel safe and calm and able to function.
- As soon as possible, get your client moving. As long as your client has not suffered physical injury in their traumatic event, movement works wonders. Movement restores the body's balance of hormones, burns off adrenaline, produces endorphins (the "feel good" hormone), and helps to repair the brain and nervous system recovering from the onslaught of stress hormones. Rhythmic movement that uses both arms and legs is best, so encourage your client to walk, run, swim, bicycle, or dance. Even simply a walk down the hospital hall can be restoring. Go with her to make sure she stays safe, since her attention and judgment may be temporarily impaired. Show your client how to focus on her body and how it feels as she moves it. Encourage her to notice the sensations of her feet hitting the ground, or the rhythm of her breathing, or the feeling of wind on her skin.
- Make sure your client has supportive company. Isolation only makes things worse, in spite of the survival instinct to crawl into a hole and be alone. If you are the only company available, then don't leave her alone. Stay with her for as long as you can manage. If she needs more company for longer than you are able to give, arrange for a friend or one of your helping colleagues to stay with her. Face-to-face contact will help her to heal.
- Protect her privacy by helping to screen visitors. She may not be ready yet to smile sweetly and pretend to enjoy even the company of a friend or well wisher. Let her decide when she is ready to see well-meaning friends and whom she wishes to see. Screen out the "looky-loos" and those parasites who want to capitalize on her distress for their own benefit.
- As soon as she can, encourage her to engage in her usual social activities, ones that have nothing to do with the traumatic event, and to connect with friends to do "normal" stuff. This is a perfect time to make new friends or maybe join a support group for trauma survivors.
- Demonstrate self-regulation skills, techniques for calming one's self down. Self regulation is covered in Chapter 5. Better have these skills under your belt yourself first!
- Help family members understand what the traumatized person is likely experiencing and encourage them to not take trauma and post trauma symptoms personally. Being angry, irritable, withdrawn, and emotionally distant is common and does not necessarily have anything to do with their relationships. Help them to be patient and to try not to judge their loved one's response or healing.
- Offer practical support for every-day tasks that may seem overwhelming to even contemplate, such as grocery shopping or housework. Gradually getting back into a routine can be quite helpful.
- Encourage the client to make a list of tasks she is comfortable having someone else do, and perhaps think about who would be the best person in her supporting circle to do each. Then when someone asks "What can I do?" they can be offered a menu of ideas to

be helpful.
- Continue to be available to talk. Remember that healing from a trauma takes time. Be patient and understanding. Be available to talk, but don't pressure the client into talking until she is ready.

> Avoid trite reassurance, such as 'God does not give you more than you can handle'. Nonsense. Individuals often feel totally overwhelmed. If you are overwhelmed, you are overwhelmed. Reassurance like that is more about the person saying it, the helper, than it is about the client.
>
> It is never easy to be in the presence of people who are grieving or traumatized. We want to do something, but are often unsure what that "something" should be. Too often we resort to repeating things we have heard others say in similar circumstances. Sadly, these sayings often do more harm than good. They are often trite and minimize and trivialize what the grief-stricken person is experiencing. A child who has just lost a beloved parent does not need to hear that 'God needed another angel in heaven'. Nor does a victim of violence need to hear that 'God never gives us more than we can handle'. All too often we are overwhelmed with 'more than we can handle'. We handle it because we have no other choice.
>
> Try instead to follow the grief stricken/traumatized person's lead. If they need to cry, just sit with them as they cry, quietly holding that time and space for them. Ask what they need or how you can help them. Perhaps remind them others will want to be of help and then offer to help them make a list of things that need to be done and select folks who would be good at the listed tasks. If they want to talk, let them talk. If they just want to sit with you without speaking, honour that, too.
>
> In the case of children, understand they grieve differently and their grief will be revisited over time as they mature and come to grips with the nature of their loss. Alan Wofelt has written a number of good books on children/teens and grief.
>
> Most hospitals have staff chaplains—try reaching out to them for suggestions.
>
> - The Rev. Christina Baxter, Chaplain

The triage guide on page 157 can guide your responses.

To learn more
Start with the online resources listed here:

> seawinds-education.mykajabi.com/o-pt-in-to-resources-for-the-non-therapist

Kate Tompkins

Emotional crisis

An "emotional crisis" refers to a state of distress resulting from being unable to make good use of usual coping mechanisms and problem-solving approaches, which causes a feeling of loss of balance. The person likely feels unable to deal with a situation and experiences a range of emotions, including hopelessness, panic, anxiety, tension, depression, confusion, sadness, chaos, and disorganization.

Anyone can experience an emotional crisis. There is no real way to prevent them; unpredictable life events and other stressors can overwhelm anyone. We can learn to recognize the signs and triggers and step up our healthy coping mechanisms when a crisis is looming to prevent it from being any more stressful than necessary.

Illustration: Gianna Pellerin

Crisis is generally short-lived; humans seem to have a built-in drive to resolve a crisis sooner rather than later. Generally, six weeks is about all we can tolerate of being in this distressing state. We try to return to old familiar coping mechanisms if we can or turn to new ones if that does not seem to work.

A crisis can be resolved in either a healthy direction or an unhealthy direction. Clearly, it is better to choose healthy approaches than harmful ones to reach a new steady state.

Everybody responds uniquely to the same type of event. One person may breeze on through with little distress while the next person is deeply affected.

It seems to have a lot to do with how we think about our lives and our circumstances. If a person can look at a problem situation and see it as an opportunity for change and growth rather than as potential danger and harm, the impact of that problem situation will greatly reduce.

It also seems that our pre-existing coping mechanisms determine to some extent how far an unexpected event knocks us off our comfortable perch. If a person is already taking good care of themselves before a crisis event occurs, they will probably weather the storm more easily than someone who is already in trouble thanks to drugs or alcohol.

If a person has never encountered an emotional crisis before, it can be distressing. A person who has successfully dealt with a crisis before and has learned how to manage their emotions may be in better shape when a new trigger comes along. If a person has unsuccessfully stumbled through a previous crisis but did not manage to resolve it in a healthy way, he will be more vulnerable to the next one.

When a person is in an emotional crisis, it usually impacts him in every possible way. His thinking processes may be a bit skewed, his emotions can be all over the map, he may develop mysterious physical ailments, and he may find himself doing impulsive or destructive things he would not attempt in a more balanced state of mind.

Emotional crisis is not the same as a mental imbalance or disorder, although a person who does suffer from a mental health issue may experience emotional imbalances more frequently and more strongly than others might.

An emotional crisis can be a sudden reaction to a traumatic event, such as an accident, a death in the family, an earthquake, or being fired; or it may seem to appear suddenly but in fact has been quietly building for some time, like feeling unable to cope with a mental health issue like PTSD or experiencing long-term, insurmountable financial pressures.

> I recall that, several years ago, before I realized that I had PTSD, I would periodically become an emotional mess, with no idea why or where my distress came from. I'm sure I drove my friends nuts at times, when I yet again dissolved into a mass of tears!

An emotional crisis can do a lot of damage. We may withdraw and hide, or turn to anger and aggression as a way to attempt rebalancing ourselves, which can damage relationships. We may choose to self-medicate with alcohol or drugs, which could lead to substance-abuse disorder. If we cannot find a way to resolve the crisis, we may turn to thoughts of suicide or self harm. If we deal only with the immediate crisis and ignore what prompted it, then return frequently to an emotional crisis state, that could lead to mental health issues.

What does an emotional crisis look like? The American Psychological Association lists these signs:[18]

- Neglect of personal hygiene.
- Dramatic change in sleep habits, such as sleeping more often or not sleeping well.
- Weight gain or loss.
- Decline in performance at work or school.
- Pronounced changes in mood, such as irritability, anger, anxiety or sadness.
- Withdrawal from routine activities and relationships.

The diagram on the next page[19] illustrates how a crisis develops and resolves.

---

18 apa.org/topics/mental-health/help-emotional-crisis
19 Inspired by Eugene Kennedy, *Crisis Counseling: the essential guide for nonprofessional counsellors*, Conrtinuum Publishing, 1981.

Kate Tompkins

Stages of a Crisis

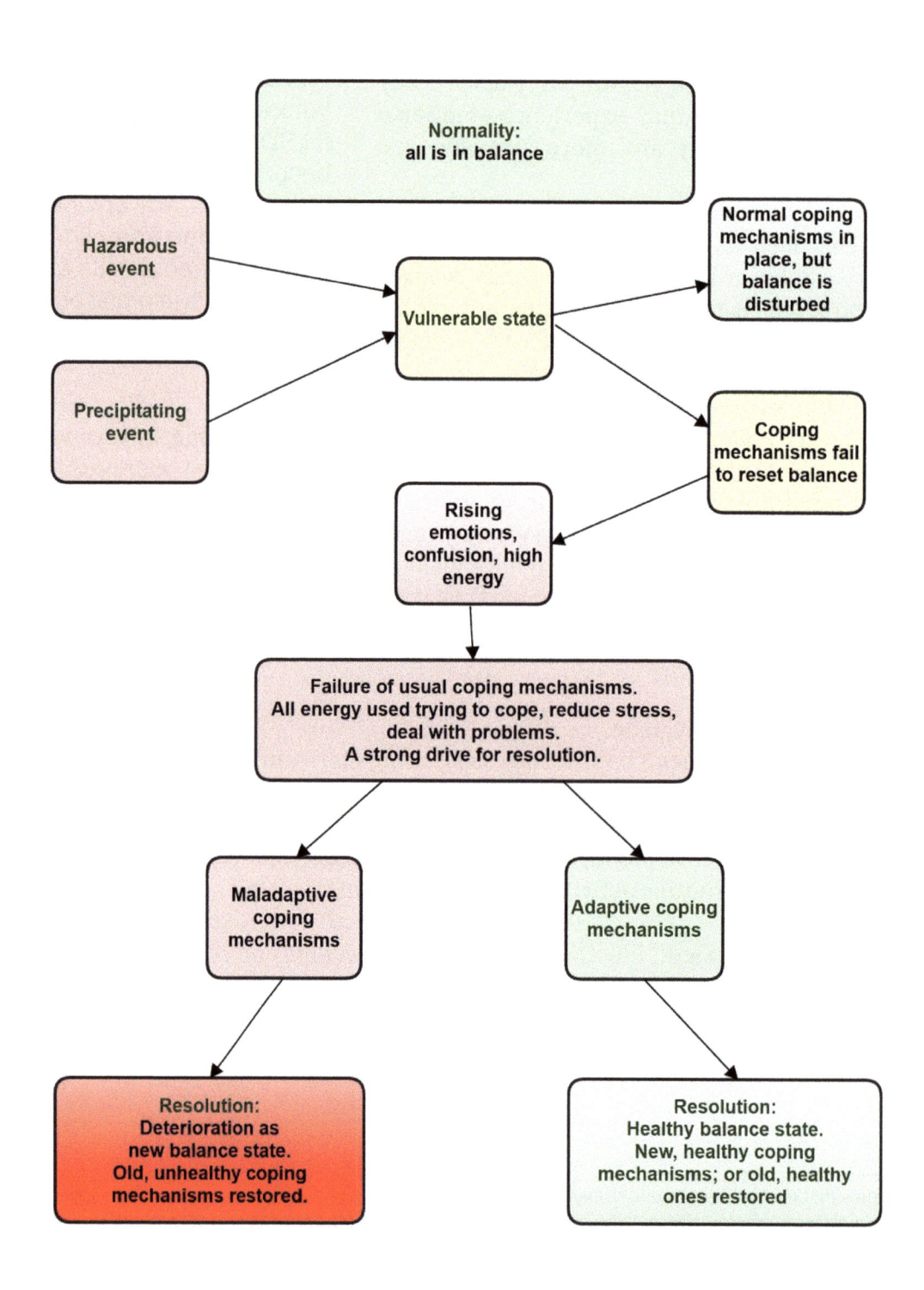

Normality: all is in balance

Hazardous event

Precipitating event

Vulnerable state

Normal coping mechanisms in place, but balance is disturbed

Coping mechanisms fail to reset balance

Rising emotions, confusion, high energy

Failure of usual coping mechanisms. All energy used trying to cope, reduce stress, deal with problems. A strong drive for resolution.

Maladaptive coping mechanisms

Adaptive coping mechanisms

Resolution: Deterioration as new balance state. Old, unhealthy coping mechanisms restored.

Resolution: Healthy balance state. New, healthy coping mechanisms; or old, healthy ones restored

Often the crisis situation begins some time earlier. A hazardous event that caused distress sometime in the past few months put the client in a vulnerable position, especially if it was not resolved completely or not in a positive way. Then along came another event, which we could call a "precipitating event" that pushed him over the edge. If there had been no older hazardous event, he might not have experienced the current event so intensely. Or if there had been no current precipitating event, he might have managed the aftermath of the older event without too much difficulty. It often takes both to create an emotional turning point.

Once he was emotionally vulnerable, he may have found that his usual coping mechanisms worked to give him back a sense of balance. However, if they failed to do so, then he likely found that his emotions began to rise, and he may have found himself agitated and confused. In a crisis situation, most people will sense that their coping mechanisms are not working, so then there is a drive to resolve the situation through other means.

This is usually the point at which a client seeks help, so helpers usually enter the crisis situation at a time when distress is at its highest.

Anyone in crisis can choose either healthy coping mechanisms which lead to a new steady state or unhealthy mechanisms which lead in a different direction. Our client may adopt new coping mechanisms, so now he has more tools in his toolbox. Or he can choose unhealthy coping mechanisms to reach a balance state, but this balance state is not all that steady. In fact, deterioration is the usual result. The next time there is a trigger, the client is likely to fall into a deeper state of emotional distress.

How to respond effectively

It is not always necessary to involve a pro therapist or a medical pro to help a person in emotional crisis. In fact, a friend may actually be a more effective support in times of emotional distress.

Speaking from my own experience, I can say that I would have shied away from a doctor or therapist when I was in trouble. "Love is a more powerful force and a stronger healing agent than professional credentials." [20]

What I wanted was someone to just sit with me and be gently supportive and not demanding. After one terrible life event, it was knowing that I had friends who were not afraid of what I was going through, and who would simply be with me, that got me through. I could talk when I needed to and I could sit quietly when I needed to. I was in the hospital, but the medical staff had no time for me. My friends and one sensitive pastor did.

The role of a helper in an emotional crisis is to—surprise!—listen well and get the client to professional or medial help ASAP if the emotional crisis lasts longer than a week or so, or if there is a significant risk involved. (Are you seeing a pattern here yet?)

On the next pages are some specific thoughts about responding to an emotional crisis:

---

[20] Deborah Trueheart, power2u.org/responding-to-emotional-crisis

- Listen well. You know how!
- Assess the immediacy of the situation.
  - Is there current risk of self harm or suicide? If yes, follow the suicide protocols. The most dangerous emotional crisis is a suicidal crisis or a desire to harm someone else. In this case, immediate referral to medical care is the best way to respond. Check out the section in this chapter about suicide and how to respond effectively. Don't wait!
  - Is your client threatening to hurt someone else? If yes, then call the police first, and remove yourself from danger if you think you might be a target. Tell the police your client is having a mental health crisis and ask for someone who has mental health training to respond to your call. Remember that once the police are involved, you will not be in control of the situation and the police may take your client to jail rather than to the hospital. You can advocate a little on your client's behalf but there is not much room for your agenda once the police arrive on the scene. Their job is to take over. While a hospital visit may in fact be the ideal situation, given the lack of medical and mental health care resources today, a temporary stay in jail might not be such a bad idea. At least your client and anyone your client wants to target with violence will be safe for the time being, although the underlying issue still needs to be resolved.
  - Is this a familiar type of feeling which the client knows how to manage? Your supportive presence may be enough. Call on the client's friends and family to help support him.
  - Is this the first episode? Some information might help, along with your support. Your client is probably frightened if this is a new feeling, so pointing out that this is a temporary situation and can be resolved might make the client feel less anxious about it and more able to take action for themselves.
  - Does the client have known underlying mental health issues? A referral to a pro therapist might be in order.
  - Is the client is coping relatively well, and choosing healthy coping mechanisms? If so, then your supportive presence is likely the best approach.
  - If the client is not coping well, does not seem to be getting any better, or is using risky coping strategies such as alcohol or drugs, and is open to discussing change, then a trip to the family physician may be the first place to start.
- Helping out with practical needs such as babysitting, housework, grocery shopping, or other errands can be helpful in a time of crisis.
- Encourage your friend to make use of or adopt new healthy coping mechanisms, such as exercise (the best stress buster!), yoga, tai chi, meditating, eating healthy foods, avoiding drugs and alcohol, getting enough sleep, or taking time off work to focus on rebalancing.
- Encourage your client to focus only on this moment and avoid stressing about the future. Meditation training can help with learning to be present.
- Encourage your client to make good use of their time. Focusing only on what actually

must be done can mean there is time to take whatever action is needed to resolve the emotional crisis. Stressing about unnecessary tasks or bogus worries will only make the situation worse.
- Keep your voice quiet and avoid over-reacting. Be a calm anchor for your client.
- If you take your client someplace to decompress, keep the atmosphere quiet, uplifting and private. Some light music might be helpful, if you know what type of music the client likes to hear and finds calming. (For example, no opera if the client prefers country and western.)
- If your client experiences emotional crises frequently, then encouraging him to build a network of supportive friends and family can help to reduce the impact of the next episode.
- If the situation seems too overwhelming for the client to manage, or if he has a pattern of emotional crises, encourage your client to find a pro therapist.
- Joining a support group of people who have the same issue might help.
- Taking some action can help to reduce stress during a crisis. Any task that can help to resolve the crisis in a good way is helpful. Even immersing oneself in physical activity such as housework, renovations, gardening, going for a walk—it all burns off adrenaline, which reduces the production of stress hormones.
- Ask what the client would like you to do and encourage her to do as much as she can herself.
- Give your client space, both physical and emotional. Don't make him feel trapped. Pacing is a common response to feelings of crisis.
- Be prepared to possibly support the client's family as well. It can be quite stressful to have a family member in crisis. The family may feel confused, disoriented, angry, exhausted, guilty, and afraid.
- Help your client to see his current emotional crisis as an opportunity, to change something that is not fantastic in his life, to reorganize, or to create some new sense of authenticity and wholeness. Trying to get out of his crisis too quickly might actually rob your client of an exciting transformation opportunity.
- Remind your client that this is only temporary. We are unable to sustain a real crisis for very long. We seem to have a built-in drive to resolve the crisis in some way. Humans are in fact quite resilient and creative. In spite of how upsetting the crisis may be for the client, we all contain within us the sense of wholeness. We all have the potential for transformation.
- Rather than trying to skate quickly through a crisis, encourage your client to be present with it, to engage with it, to honour the feelings he experiences to create the best possible outcome for himself. Sitting on the ground, or taking off his shoes and feeling the grass under his toes, can help to ground one when emotions seem too high for comfort.

Kate Tompkins

To learn more
Start with the online resources listed here:

> seawinds-education.mykajabi.com/o-pt-in-to-resources-for-the-non-therapist

Intimate partner violence

Abuse can take many forms—physical, emotional/psychological, sexual, or financial actions, or neglect. The goal of an abuser is to frighten and control their partner to meet some need of their own. If your client feels unsafe and is experiencing any of these forms of abuse, she lives with violence.

Intimate partner violence happens in all types of relationships, not just heterosexual unions, and men can be victims as well as women. Social service agencies are seeing more men who are targets than ever before. The issues men face are pretty much the same, although men who are targets seem to experience more shame about their situation. In North American society, there is still a macho sort of attitude that prevents men from admitting to or talking about anything that might be perceived as a weakness. It may also be much more challenging to find support services specific to intimate partner violence that will look after men, including shelters and transition homes.

I use the feminine pronouns in this section to discuss the issue, since there are many more women who find themselves the target of an aggressor than men do.

In the *United Nations Declaration on the Elimination of Violence Against Women*, the term violence against women refers to

> any act of gender-based violence that results in, or is likely to result in, physical, sexual or psychological harm or suffering to women, including threats of such acts, coercion or arbitrary deprivation of liberty, whether occurring in public or private life.

Violence against women is also a manifestation of the historically unequal power relations between men and women, which have led to domination over and discrimination against women by men and the prevention of women's full advancement.

Sometimes violence against a woman is a one-time event, sometimes even a random event, such as rape by a stranger on a dark street or violence accompanying a home invasion. Sometimes violence in its many forms is visited upon a woman for the purpose of controlling her in a long term relationship. This is "intimate partner violence."

Violence against women can take many forms. When it occurs repeatedly in a pattern, it can be called "abuse".

Intimate partner violence is most commonly divided into the following types:[21]

---

[21] With permission from the Centre for Research & Education on Violence against Women & Children at Western University.

Physical violence or abuse
> The most obvious ranges from pushing and shoving to hitting, beating, physical abuse with a weapon, torture, mutilation and murder.

Emotional/Psychological violence
> Encompasses various tactics to undermine an individual's self-confidence, such as yelling, not letting her see her friends or family, insults, mockery, threats, abusive language, humiliation, harassment, contempt, deliberate deprivation of emotional care or isolation.

Sexual violence or abuse
> Any form of non-consensual (forced on an individual) sexual activity ranging from harassment through unwanted sexual touching, to rape. This form of violence also includes incest.

Financial violence or abuse
> Encompasses various tactics for total or partial control of an individual's finances, inheritance or employment income. It may include denying access to money or one's own financial records and knowledge about personal investments, income or debt, preventing a partner from taking employment outside the home, or engaging in other activity that would lead to financial independence.

Neglect
> Includes failure to provide for an individual's basic needs and human rights, and the refusal or delay in the provision of food or medical care.

The **cycle of violence** theory looks at the repetitive nature of a perpetrator's actions that hinder a victim's ability to leave an abusive relationship. The cycle of violence theory illustrates how the behaviour of the perpetrator can change very dramatically, making it difficult for the target to leave. Those who have experienced violence may recognise this cycle.

Dr. Lenore Walker developed the cycle of violence theory in 1979. to describe the phases an abusive relationship moves through.

It is important to understand that intimate partner violence tends to be cyclic, in a fairly predictable pattern. The length of time it takes to work through a cycle can vary. As time goes by, the violence tends to get more severe and more frequent. These are the three stages:

Stage 1: Tension-building
> Tension between the people in the relationship starts to increase and verbal, emotional, psychological, or financial abuse occurs.

Stage 2: Acute explosion
> The peak of violence is reached in this stage. The perpetrator experiences a release of

tension by being violent and this behaviour may become habitual.

Stage 3: Honeymoon

At this point, the perpetrator may start to feel ashamed and may feel remorse for his actions. He may become withdrawn and try to justify his actions to himself and others, often by blaming the victim. For example, he may say, "You know it makes me angry when you say that."

Then comes a pursuit phase, when the perpetrator may promise to never be violent again. He may try to explain the violence by blaming other factors such as alcohol or stress at work. The perpetrator may be very attentive to the target, including buying gifts and helping around the house. It could seem as though the perpetrator has changed.

At this point, the person experiencing the violence can feel confused and hurt but also relieved that the violence is over.

Both people in the relationship may be in denial about the severity of the abuse and violence. Intimacy can increase during this phase. Both people may feel happy and want the relationship to continue, so they may not acknowledge the possibility that the violence could happen again.

Over time, this phase passes and the cycle begins again.

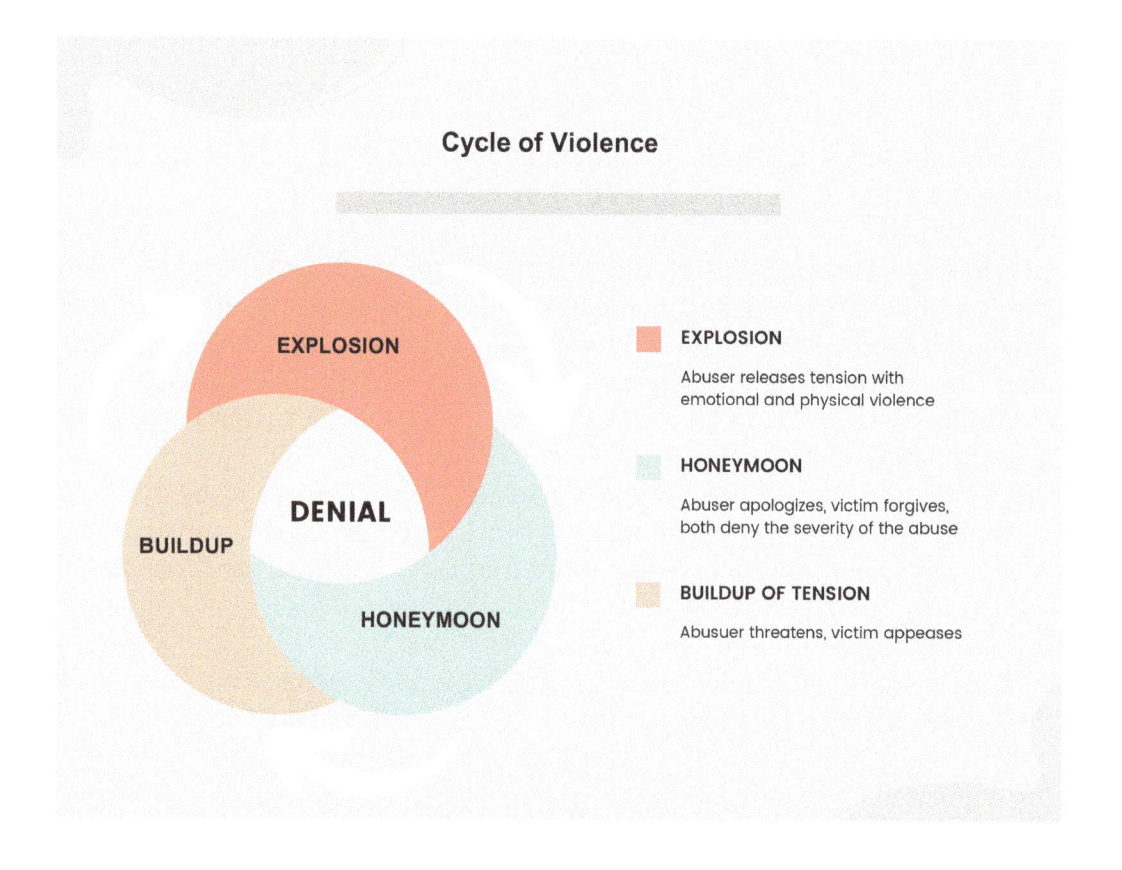

Cycle of Violence

- **EXPLOSION**
  Abuser releases tension with emotional and physical violence

- **HONEYMOON**
  Abuser apologizes, victim forgives, both deny the severity of the abuse

- **BUILDUP OF TENSION**
  Abusuer threatens, victim appeases

It is important to understand that violence against women, as well as violence from men to male partners, occurs in a broader social context. Violence is a choice. "Male privilege" as a justification for violating others is still very prominent in North American society, and even more so in countries where the "machismo" influence is strong.

Misogyny is frequently behind mass attacks. Three of the most violent mass killings in Canadian history (the 2018 Toronto van attack, the 1989 massacre at Montreal's École Polytechnique and the 2020 mass shooting in Nova Scotia) had their roots in misogyny, as do up to 50% of mass shootings in the USA. The fact is that violence against others continues in our society because our society allows it.

Another point you need to understand is that it is not easy for most targets, male or female, to actually leave their abusive partners. Well-meaning bystanders often advise the target to simply leave the abuser, but it is not that simple.

Here are a few of the many factors that make it tough to leave:

- Society normalizes unhealthy behaviour, so targets may not understand that their relationship is abusive.
- There might be an attempt to shift the blame to something else, such as substance abuse.
- Shame is a big hurdle for the victim, especially for professional women who find themselves in an abusive relationship.
- Often friends and professionals from whom targets of assault seek help don't believe them.
- Emotional abuse shatters a target's self esteem, making it tough to start fresh.
- During the "honeymoon" phase of the cycle, when everything feels so good, the target may want to try to stick it out with the hope things improve.
- The aggressor may threaten to kill her, or their children, or her family, pets or himself, if she tries to leave.
- Feeling like a victim may seem familiar to many targets, and the abuse may feel safer than the unknown.
- Escaping from patterns of control is very difficult and the target may have developed an actual addiction to the abuse and to the abuser.
- When a target is planning to leave is the most dangerous time. The abuse increases, the degree of violence ramps up. Most partner homicides occur as she is thinking about leaving.

For more on this topic, check out the video "Why Is It So Challenging to Leave?" The link is at this site:

    seawinds-education.mykajabi.com/o-pt-in-to-resources-for-the-non-therapist

How to respond effectively
The most important role for the helper is to be patient, and be there for her, regardless of whether she is ready to leave her abusive partner. She may leave her partner and seek help several times before she is ready to make her departure permanent. Try not to judge her if she does not make the choices you think she should make, and offer her unconditional support for as long as it takes.

Refer her to an agency or service that supports women in intimate partner violence in your region. Consider going with her when she researches her options with police, lawyers, social services, shelters, transition homes, financial management and rental options.

If she elects to stay with her abusive partner, teach her about how to set boundaries and how to stay safe. If she decides to leave, help her find a safe place to land and create a new, safe life. Help her to deal with any mental health issues she has developed dealing with the violence and support her as she deals with practical tasks and her kids.

One important issue to think about: how to stay safe yourself. Never enter the home of an aggressor if he is in a rage without the assistance of the police. If you assist her to pack up and move while he is out of the house, take along the police for backup. Keep your identity, phone number, home and location as confidential as possible, although that can be next to impossible in a small town. Take whatever precautions you can in your own unique circumstances.

The triage tool on page 155 may help guide your response.

To learn more
Start with the online resources listed here:

>   seawinds-education.mykajabi.com/o-pt-in-to-resources-for-the-non-therapist

In particular, for more information and skills for helpers supporting a target caught in an abusive relationship, consider the online course *The Breakout Pro for Frontline Workers*. The course includes handouts you can use with your clients and suggestions for helping your client at each step of the way:

>   seawinds-education.mykajabi.com/offers/zDtYCe6Y

There is also a course for your client with much of the same material, but aimed at the target of abuse:

>   seawinds-education.mykajabi.com/offers/tdZMMo2V

Both versions come with 28 CE credits from the Canadian Counselling and Psychotherapy Association.

Also take a look at the various documents in Chapter 5, which will be helpful.

Depression

Depression is as common as daisies in a field. Since approximately one in six people experience depression at some time in their lives, and at least 30% of all women find themselves depressed[22], you probably know at least a couple of people who are depressed, whether they realize it or not.

When men get depressed, they may show it as irritability, anger, or discouragement, so it is sometimes overlooked or misdiagnosed. Women are more likely to seek treatment for depression. Depressed men are more likely to complete suicide, mostly because they often choose more aggressive, lethal methods; however, depressed women are more likely to attempt suicide.

Depression needs to be taken seriously because it increases the risks for suicide. Depression can impact the person's home life, his relationships and his work.

Depression can come from several sources. Family history plays a role. If someone in your family has experienced depression, you may, too. Researchers are not sure yet whether family patterns of depression come from genes (none have been found yet that can be proven to cause depression) or whether the habits of depression are learned from other family members. In other words, if your mother's go-to mood was depression, you may have learned that is the "normal" way to see the world.

Some medical conditions can make depression more likely. Chronic health issues and injuries can mess up a person's mental health and lifestyles. Sleep problems, low blood sugar, menopause, and menstruation have all been linked to depression, too.

Some medications can create depression as a side effect, and some drugs and alcohol can lead to or worsen depression. Heavy use of marijuana over time, especially if one is using a high dosage of THC, can cause depression. High levels of CBD, another compound in marijuana, can help to treat depression.

How a person deals with stress and worries matters, too. If your client holds in those feelings, low self esteem is a likely result. Perfectionism, being overly sensitive to personal criticism, dependency on another person, or being self critical or pessimistic are also risk factors leading to depression.

When a person is diagnosed with depression, there has usually been more than one trigger. Depression develops and grows over time, taking us into a downward spiral, rather than pouncing on us suddenly.

Long-term stress punctuated with stressful life events takes its toll. Here are some examples:

---

22   American Psychiatric Association

- An unhealthy relationship
- A toxic workplace
- Being overworked and underpaid
- Losing your job
- Being unemployed for some time
- Being socially isolated
- Going through a breakup or divorce
- Being diagnosed with a serious illness
- Grieving a lost loved one
- Chronic financial issues
- A major move
- Traumatic events, such as physical or sexual abuse
- Being lesbian, gay, bisexual or transgender, or having variations in the development of genital organs that aren't clearly male or female (intersex) in an unsupportive situation
- Other mental health issues, such as PTSD, anxiety, or eating disorders
- Alcohol or drug abuse

Not everyone develops depression after one or more of these stressful life events. How we deal with them seems to be more important than the fact that they happened. For example, if I decide I am a victim because someone shouted at me at work, and I decide to cower in my office and not say anything to anyone because, of course, it **must** have been my fault, then I am more likely to develop depression. But if I take action, confront the shouter assertively, and ask for an apology and a different style of communication, then I am much less likely to develop depression as a result.

If I am unemployed and no new job is on the horizon, and I allow myself to sit on the couch and feel sorry for myself, isolate myself, and think dire thoughts, then I am a good candidate for becoming depressed. However, if I make lots of contacts, actively search for a new job, and use the time newly available to me to be creative and develop new hobbies, then I am much less likely to fall into that pit.

Now, I don't want to give the impression that taking action alone is enough to turn around depression, because it may not be. The situation is a bit more complex than that. The chemistry of depression takes over after a while, so simply wanting to feel better won't work.

I cannot think myself out of depression just because I want to. I will need to be more strategic about it. More about the treatment of depression in a bit.

Think of it this way: have you ever been in a car that was only running on three cylinders? It sputters and grinds away trying to get the car moving, but it's rough, the engine backfires and does not work properly. That is your brain when it is depressed. The chemicals in our brains need to be in perfect sync with each other and if, for any reason, those chemicals are out of balance, as the result, say, of long-term stress, then the electrical impulses find it challenging to travel properly from one neuron to the next. The result is like that car backfiring. The entire body is affected.

What does depression look like in a client? The following are common symptoms:

- Poor sleep or sleeping too much is often the first thing that a depressed person notices.
- Appetite changes often come next. Either wanting to eat everything in sight or not wanting to eat at all can occur.

- Difficulties focusing on everyday tasks, remembering, and making decisions are common.
- Feeling either agitated, restless, and unable to sit still, slowed movement or speech, or else feeling like you can't be bothered getting out of bed are frequent states.
- Feeling like you are trying to swim through mud and your muscles just won't work right, or perhaps physical pains that have no good explanation sometimes are experienced.
- Feelings of sadness, emptiness, or hopelessness can be expected.
- Feelings of dread, guilt or self blame for no good reason, feeling like life is not worth living, or perhaps even suicidal impulses are a risk.
- Feelings of uselessness, low self esteem, and worthlessness are often involved with depression, leading to suicidal thinking.
- Low energy and fatigue usually accompany other symptoms.
- Loss of interest in activities we used to enjoy often leaves us feeling empty.
- Loss of interest in sex is a relationship-damaging side effect of depression.
- Crying easily, or wanting to cry but not being able to are partners in depression.
- Angry outbursts, irritability, or frustration over small matters can be misdiagnosed, but are common symptoms of depression, especially in men.
- In extreme cases, losing touch with reality or having ideas other people think are strange have been noted and may indicate other mental health issues along with depression.
- For teens, poor performance or poor attendance at school, feeling misunderstood and very sensitive, using recreational drugs or alcohol, self harm, and avoidance of social interaction are sometimes what family and school see first. Misreading these symptoms as willful misbehaviour can lead to further depression, especially if punitive measures are forced on the teen.
- In children, sadness, irritability, clinginess, worry, aches and pains, refusing to go to school, or being underweight are indicators to look for.
- In older adults and seniors, memory difficulties or personality changes, physical aches and pains, fatigue, loss of appetite, sleep problems, or loss of interest in sex that is not caused by a medical condition or medication may be seen. Wanting to stay at home, rather than going out to socialize or do new things may be a sign of depression. Suicidal thinking or feelings, especially in older men are frequently hidden.

Notice how depression is a total-body experience? That is one of the reasons why it feels so bad. Depression, also known as clinical depression or "major depressive disorder", is not simple unhappiness. It is a complex mood disorder requiring specialized treatment.

There are several sub-types of depression, such as post-partum depression, seasonal depression, (SAD, or Seasonal Affective Disorder), and bipolar disorder. These all require the intervention of a doctor, and the helper's role is just referral to medical care.

When it comes to treating depression, I think of it in three levels, with different treatment suggestions for each:

Level of Depression	Treatment
Mild: has not lasted very long	The gold standard for treatment of mild to moderate depression is cognitive behavioural therapy, CBT. At this stage, no medication is needed. The depressed person can accomplish a lot by exercise, such as walking for at least 30 minutes daily, to produce endorphins.
Moderate	At this stage, there is room for negotiation between a patient and their doctor about whether to take an antidepressant. CBT is still the best treatment for long term stability.
Severe: depression which has lasted a long time, or when suicidal thoughts are present.	For severe depression, I recommend starting off with an antidepressant, followed with CBT.

It is important for your client to understand that taking an antidepressant alone will probably not be enough to turn the tide of their depression and maintain their happiness. In our medication-rich culture, some people assume that because they feel better when they take an antidepressant, they will continue feeling better when they stop taking it. "My depression is cured!"

Unfortunately, life does not work that way. Unless we change whatever triggered the depression in the first place, it will just come back after we wean off the medication.

It is better to take advantage of the fact that antidepressants give us hope to see life differently and energy to do things, in order to start a course of cognitive behavioural therapy. CBT helps us to think differently about our selves and our lives, train ourselves out of habitual thoughts that have been damaging or have prompted our depressed feelings, and thus create a new emotional state.

You can reassure your client that anti-depressants are not addictive and have few side effects, although some can produce issues for men's sexuality. If that is the case, a patient can simply ask their doctor to prescribe a different type of antidepressant. Every body is different, it sometimes takes a few tries to get the right antidepressant at the right dosage, so there may be some experimenting with medication at first to get it right. Sometimes it takes a few days or a few weeks for the medication to "kick in", so advise your client to be patient and report all changes or lack of change to their doctor.

The "bible" for CBT is this book: *Mind Over Mood, Change How You Feel by Changing The Way You Think,* which I highly recommend. The full reference is at the end of this section. Millions of copies are in print, in many languages. It is very popular, because it does the job! It is a workbook which your clients can read through at their own pace. It includes lots of hands-on activities and exercises to do. You can do the writing right there in the book or download just the exercise pages, if you want to keep your thoughts private. That way, more than one person can share the book.

Anyone with moderate or severe depression should also be in contact with their doctor to discuss using an antidepressant, and to monitor associated symptoms and their relationship with other medical conditions that may be present and potential drug interactions. Referral to a therapist is a must with severe depression and a good idea for moderate depression.

Most people do notice benefits from medication and CBT treatment and can return to their normal (or perhaps even better) lives soon.

There are other, more dramatic, approaches that have been used for treatment-resistant depression, such as the brutal but sometimes effective electroconvulsive therapy; however, these are way out of the scope of what a helper needs to think about.

Other therapies that work for some people include acupuncture, hypnosis, and biofeedback. However, these are not considered by most therapists to be the first line of defense against depression.

Other things a client can do to enhance their treatment are making sure to get lots of exercise, eat healthy foods, keep up with social networks, and continue with activities they enjoy. Avoiding alcohol, which is a depressant, and drugs, which can have many nasty side effects, is important when recovering from depression. A person who has other issues, such as drinking too much, may need to address those first before treatment for depression can be successful. Taking time off from work may be necessary, which usually requires a note from a doctor. Getting enough sleep is a must.

How to respond effectively

Listening well is the first and perhaps most important job for the helper. A depressed person needs to know they are not alone with their misery, there is someone they can talk to, and there is hope for them because there is effective treatment available. Providing your client with some information about depression and how it can be treated can be very helpful. Encouraging your client to accept that they are depressed is the first step for some people.

If you are not sure if your client is depressed, or your client *is* depressed and you are not sure how severely, then getting her to a doctor is an important step. Referring her to a therapist can also be very helpful.

You can recommend your client read *Mind Over Mood*. It can be purchased online or from most bookstores, and many libraries also have copies. If your client is not seeing a therapist, you can offer support as they work their way through the book.

To learn more

- The World Health Organization: who.int/news-room/fact-sheets/detail/depression
- *Mind Over Mood, Change How You Feel By Changing The Way You Think*, by Greenberger and Padesky, New York: Guilford Press, 2016. The website mindovermood.com also provides other resources.

Kate Tompkins

Grief

Grief—it's a natural, normal, and universal emotional response to loss, but it sure hurts like Hades. Grieving can follow any loss: the death of a loved one or a beloved pet, the ending of an important relationship, a job loss, a loss through theft or fire, the loss of independence through disability, or a diagnosis of serious illness.

Grief can last for weeks, months or years. Usually, grief lessens in time as we get on with the job of living and we adapt to the new life we have without what was lost.

Grieving is unique and personal. There is no "proper" way to grieve. There are no predictable stages to work through.[23] There is no "normal" amount of time to grieve. There is no specific time when someone can say "Enough! You have mourned long enough! Time to get on with life." A grieving person simply needs to work through whatever they need to work through, at their own pace. Any attempt to tell a grieving person what they should feel and how long they should feel that way can make it even harder to get past grief.

> Grief is the response to loss, particularly to the loss of someone or some living thing that has died, to which a bond or affection was formed. Although conventionally focused on the emotional response to loss, grief also has physical, cognitive, behavioral, social, cultural, spiritual and philosophical dimensions. - Wikipedia

You might hear people use the words "grief", "mourning" and "bereavement" to mean more or less the same thing, but there are some distinctions. Grief is a person's emotional response to the experience of loss. Mourning is the process of adapting to life after a loss. How a person mourns depends on the influences of their society, culture, and religion. Bereavement is the state of having experienced a loss.

Grief is also different from depression. Both a depressed person and a grieving person may feel sadness and may withdraw from their usual social circles and activities. Grief tends to come in waves, with extra sadness around anniversaries or holidays without the loved one. Depression tends to settle over a person like a dark blanket and stay there for some time. A grieving person may have happy memories of their lost loved one mixed in with the sadness, but a depressed person is likely to lose interest in whatever they used to like to do, and feel rotten most or all of the time. A grieving person normally keeps their self esteem intact, while a depressed person commonly feels self loathing and worthlessness. If thoughts of suicide arise, the grieving person talks about wanting to join the deceased loved one, but a depressed person talks about not being able to cope with the pain of their depression and feelings of not deserving to live any longer.

It is possible for someone to experience both grief and depression at the same time. In that case, the grief will be more severe, will last longer and will be harder to leave behind.

Grief can effect us in many ways. Our emotions when grieving might include shock, numbness, sadness, denial, despair, anxiety, anger, guilt, loneliness, depression, helplessness, relief,

---

23 In 1969, Elizabeth Kubler Ross postulated 5 stages of grief, which some later researchers extended to 7 stages, but more recent studies indicate that there is no predictability to what people experience or when.

and yearning. Tears and sadness are to be expected, even if the grieving person is not sure what triggered them. If the grieving person's relationship with the deceased was difficult, feelings of guilt may arise, making it even tougher to adjust to the loss. This is in part because of the lost opportunity to repair the relationship.

Our thoughts can be confused, and staying focused can be challenging. We can experience physical symptoms, such as back and joint pain, stiffness, digestive issues, binge eating, or loss of appetite, irritable bowel syndrome, headaches, dizziness, sleep problems, and fatigue. Our immune systems take a hit under high stress or grieving, as our bodies fail to balance the stress hormones, so we may land in bed with a bad flu or cold. Heart problems often surface after a loss or extreme stress, including chest pain, shortness of breath, and heart attacks.

These physical symptoms are caused by the stress hormones that flow though our bodies during grief, which effectively stun our muscles. Grief is a full body experience.

It is not surprising that a grieving person may want to isolate and sleep a lot, forget to eat, and feel restless, irritable, or aggressive. Some people will dive into their work or some other activity in a vain attempt to forget, or maybe to outrun, the emotions of grief.

Grief and loss may also cause a person to question his or her faith or view of the world. Or it may strengthen the person's faith by providing a new understanding of the meaning of life.

Sliding into unhealthy coping mechanisms, such as alcohol, drugs, self harm, or overworking does more harm than good. They can mask or dampen grief, making it even harder to move past it. They can also lead to more serious issues such as addictions, depression and suicidal thinking.

> After my house burned down, I was of course shocked and stressed. I stayed with friends for months. Not only was I incapable of doing much for myself in the first days, I soon developed the worst flu I have ever had. I was worried that I might actually die from it. I passed out in the shower one morning, hit my head on the floor, narrowly missing the hard edges of the toilet, and scaring the stuffing out of me.
>
> It was a huge relief when I started to feel better physically, and when I was able to put one foot in front of the other and get on with some form of life, without any possessions or a home. It was a full year before I felt "normal" again, physically, emotionally and intellectually. My grieving for my lost home and security took a long time.

Usually, these symptoms are short lived. Sometimes, though, grief becomes habitual. In fact, grieving can light up the reward centres of the brain, making it challenging to move on. The memories and the grieving can feed into addictive feelings. If this happens, the symptoms of grief can cause long-term problems, requiring medical treatment and professional therapy.

How we experience grief, and how we move on from it, depend largely on our cultural traditions. To understand more about cultural traditions of grief, consult *Handbook Patients' Spiritual and Cultural Values for Health Care Professionals* here:

spiritualcareassociation.org/wp-content/uploads/2016/03/
patients_spiritual_and_cultural_values_for_health_care_professionals-bf8.pdf

Kate Tompkins

How does a person get past grief? Certainly they cannot escape the pain of grief. Any attempt to do so will create more problems. Anyone who is in denial about the loss will need to face it head on, accept that the loved one is gone, and accept that the loss is real. The grieving person will need to find a way to adjust to the new reality and find new ways to stay connected to the lost person, while also moving on with life.

How to respond effectively

- Ensure that the grieving person knows they are not alone. Plan to spend time with them, arrange for company so they are not physically alone in the first few days after a serious loss. And be prepared to be in supportive contact with him for as long as it takes. Do not disappear after the initial dramatic response dies down.
- Follow the grieving person's lead. Don't push for closure or for faster resolution of the grief. Just accept whatever pace the person can manage.
- Remind him that it will take time and that whatever he is feeling is both temporary and normal. Taking one day at a time and not obsessing about an empty tomorrow will help reduce the weight of the burden of sadness.
- Resist judging how your client is grieving. Accept whatever feelings, thoughts or symptoms the person may have. If the grieving person seems stuck or overwhelmed, cannot stop criticizing themselves or feeling guilty, or is thinking suicidal thoughts, then refer him to a pro therapist to get back on track.
- Offer practical support—meals, babysitting, a drive to the doctor, whatever is needed.
- Allow your client to talk about whatever she needs to talk about. Acknowledge the loss, share memories, stories, photos, or music, ask questions. Confirm that whatever the grieving person is feeling is probably normal and healthy. Don't shy away from messy or gruesome details; just be there and listen. Adjust your Teflon cape if you need to.
- Encourage the grieving person to take care of herself, eat healthy foods, get enough exercise and sleep, and stay in touch with social networks. Self care may include activities that feed her soul, such as reading, walks in the woods, visiting with family and friends.
- Encourage the grieving person to return to hobbies and recreational activities and consider joining a support group, if there is one in your area.
- Encourage the grieving person to celebrate the anniversary of their loss with remembrance and honouring the lost loved one, and perhaps by creating something lasting to remember them, such as a special garden, collecting donations for a favourite charity, passing a name on to a new baby in the family, setting up a scholarship in their name, or creating a scrapbook or memoire.
- Assist the grieving person to return to their normal routine as soon as they can.
- Once the person has moved on from their grief, offer the opportunity to help someone else who is grieving. There is nothing like being a helper to get past one's own issues!
- Grieving is an acknowledgement of all we shared with the one we have lost, including dreams for a shared future. Encourage your client to look at the memories of the good times when she is able to.

Children grieve differently than adults do, and their responses to loss differ as they mature. The following chart [24] provides some pointers for supporting children of differing ages.

Children and grief

Ages 2-5	Ages 6-8
Understanding of death	
• Extremely egocentric and concrete, see death as loss of love and protection, as abandonment. • See death as a temporary departure or separation; find it difficult to understand the concept of finality. • May forget the person has died. • Connect death with the events that precede it, in a cause-and-effect way. • See some distinction between life and death; associate life with movement and death with lack of movement; may confuse death with sleep. • May attribute life to inanimate moving objects.	• Conflicting beliefs about death. • Confusion and misunderstanding. • Both concrete and magical thinking: • Language is used and understood literally. • Engage in wishful thinking ("If only…"). • Think of life as being linear, with a beginning and an end. • See death as being external and therefore avoidable (won't happen to them or their loved ones). • May see death as a punishment (for the dead person or themselves). • May see death as a result of old age. • May personify death as monsters or the bogey man. • The concept of life after death is a contradiction of terms as death is seen as the end of life functions.
Common reactions	
• Feeling abandoned, overwhelmed and lonely. • Denial, repression of facts. • Regression in behaviours. • Confusion about the circumstances of the death and a need to review it frequently.	• Ask a lot of questions, do research into the disease and death, focus on gory details. • Have fears of being abandoned, of changes in their world, or more family deaths. • Feel responsible for the death, for the family's future, for making family members happy.

---

[24] With permission from "Medical Care of the Dying", 2nd Edition, Victoria, BC: Victoria Hospice Society, 1993.

Ages 2-5	Ages 6-8
	• Experience nightmares, restlessness, diarrhea. • Show regressions in behaviours and emotions (eg bedwetting, thumb sucking, fears).
What helps	
• Consistent repetition of the facts. • Simple explanations about whatever happens (eg funeral, rituals, burial, the death). • Someone to support them and answer questions at high stress times (eg following the death, funeral, visits to the cemetery). • Accurate honest information at their level of understanding. • Discussing what the person who dies can no longer do (move, breathe, eat...). • Physical contact, calm soothing tones, quiet times. • Continued reassurances (about their future, events prior to the death). • Consistent maintenance of usual routines and discipline.	• Information and explanations should be accurate and literal. • Explain death in terms of body function (breathing, heart, brain). • Grant permission to decide their own level of involvement in rituals, funerals and gatherings. • Provide a support person and models for appropriate grieving. • Provide information and reassurances about their grief reactions and feelings, their responsibility for the death and their future. • Encourage child to engage in concrete survival activities (chores, play, exercise). • Provide opportunities to share their experiences with other grieving children.

Ages 9-12	Ages 13-17
Understanding of death	
• Become less egocentric and develop social concerns. • Make transition from concrete to more abstract thinking. ○ Understand the universality of death; see death as removed in time from themselves.	• Intellectually able to understand the implications of death as an adult would. • Feel shock that it could happen to their family and confused about how to react. • Feel overwhelmed by the intensity of

Ages 9-12	Ages 13-17
<ul><li>○ Can generalize about death, understand its magnitude.</li><li>○ Begin to believe that it can happen to anyone and struggle with this.</li><li>See death clinically; fear that it may be painful and scary.</li><li>See death as a part of life—natural, universal and permanent.</li><li>Express interest in what happens to person's body and spirit after death; fear non-existence and separation.</li></ul>	the emotions.<ul><li>Feel a sense of isolation and loneliness, even among friends and family; feel different.</li><li>Vacillate between acting like an adult and a child.</li></ul>
Common reactions	
<ul><li>Anxiety and general fearfulness.</li><li>Covering up emotions and trying to appear normal.</li><li>Concern about other survivors.</li><li>Concern about personal future and security.</li><li>Regressive behaviours (bed wetting, nightmares, acting out).</li><li>Withdrawal or endless questions about the death.</li></ul>	<ul><li>Withdrawal, difficulty finding a balance.</li><li>Guilt about things said or not said, done or not done.</li><li>Fear or disgust of the body.</li><li>Tendency to remember only good things about the person.</li><li>Tendency to blame others for the death and how it affects their life.</li><li>Totally empty feeling and exhaustion; may not be able to cry.</li><li>Difficulty with eating or sleeping.</li></ul>
What helps	
<ul><li>Honest and accurate information about the death.</li><li>Opportunities to ask questions.</li><li>Reassurances about their future (eg, if the other parent died, who would care for them and how?).</li><li>Adults to model appropriate grieving.</li><li>Respect for the privacy of their thoughts, feelings and writings.</li><li>Inclusion, as wished, in adult activities associated with the death (funeral, discussions, plans).</li></ul>	<ul><li>Honest and accurate information about the death and its circumstances.</li><li>Support from friends and teachers, as well as family.</li><li>Inclusion in discussions and decision making, as wished.</li><li>Opportunities to spend more time alone.</li><li>Balance between having time to be a child and time to take on some adult responsibilities.</li><li>Keeping a journal or diary.</li></ul>

Kate Tompkins

To learn more
Start with the online resources listed here:

>   seawinds-education.mykajabi.com/o-pt-in-to-resources-for-the-non-therapist

Anxiety

If depression is as common as daisies in a field, then anxiety is as common as blades of grass. Approximately 30% of people feel anxiety at some point in their lives. Anxiety is your body's natural response to stress. It's a feeling of fear or apprehension about what's to come.

Ordinary anxiety comes and goes and does not interfere with everyday life. For example, anxiety about writing an exam can motivate us to work hard and do well. As soon as the exam is over, the anxiety disappears.

Anxiety is vital for survival—if our ancestors did not feel some anxiety when they encountered a predator, we might never have evolved into modern humans. Now, our stressors are more likely to be pollution, overcrowding, climate change, financial pressures, and work issues. The problem is that, while the sabre-toothed tiger will give up and retreat once he has you treed and you are safe, modern day stressors are more persistent.

Only when anxiety gets out of hand does it actually cause a problem. Like a run-away freight train, anxiety can last a long time, it can get worse over time, and can disrupt our lives significantly by stopping us from engaging in things we want to do and by messing up relationships and careers.

When an anxiety disorder develops, the feeling of fear or dread may stay attached to us like Peter Pan's shadow, and it feels like it has a mind of its own. It can become extreme and debilitating.

Like depression, there may be a genetic component. Anxiety tends to run in families, but is that because some mysterious genes are passed along to our kids, or did we teach them anxiety as a response to stress? I have seen small communities in which every man, woman and child exhibits anxiety—it has become normalized.

There is probably a combination of factors, including brain chemistry, lifestyle, genes, and learned behaviour patterns.

Anxiety knows no age borders—it can effect people of all ages, from kids to grannies. More women than men are diagnosed with anxiety. There are many types of anxiety, including panic attacks, phobias, anxiety about social situations, obsessive compulsive disorder, separation anxiety, fear of illness, fear of places that might cause you panic, anxiety caused by a medical problem, and PTSD.

Anxiety can feel like some (or all!) of the entries in the list on the next page:

- Butterflies in the stomach
- Racing heart, rapid breathing, sweating, chills
- Headache, stomach ache
- Feeling faint or dizzy
- Shortness of breath
- Dry mouth
- Feeling out of control
- Feeling like your mind and your body are not communicating well
- Nightmares
- Panic attacks
- Intrusive thoughts or memories that you cannot control
- General feelings of fear and worry
- Restlessness
- Trouble concentrating
- Trouble falling asleep
- Numbness or tingling
- Nervousness
- Shyness
- Wanting to isolate from others
- Poor performance in school
- Skipping social events
- Substance abuse
- Irritability, short temper
- Feeling wound up, on edge or tense
- A sense of impending danger or doom
- Worry that is out of proportion to the actual future event
- Anxiety caused by misusing some street drugs, withdrawal from street drugs, taking some medications, or being exposed to a toxic substance.

Some people experience many of these symptoms, others only a few. You may feel some symptoms and your neighbour may experience others.

Depression and anxiety sometimes go hand in hand. It is possible to feel anxious and depressed simultaneously. Anxiety is not the opposite of depression; it is a close sister. Anxiety can be a symptom of depression and depression can be a symptom of anxiety; depression can be made worse by extreme anxiety.

People are more at risk for developing problem anxiety if they have experienced trauma, especially early in life, have a serious illness, have some other mental health issue, have close family members with anxiety, or use drugs or alcohol.

How to respond effectively
Ordinary anxiety is not a medical condition and does not require treatment, although lifestyle changes might help. It's time to refer your client to a doctor if any of these conditions develop:

- Anxiety is interfering too much with life.
- Anxiety feels uncontrollable and is causing your client to be frightened or upset.
- Depression or other mental health issues are also present.
- Your client's drug or alcohol use to try to dampen anxiety are getting out of hand.
- Your client thinks a medical problem might be involved.
- Your client is thinking about suicide.

Some people will try to dampen anxiety with a sedative such as alcohol or street drugs, which might work well for a very short time. It does not take long for this coping mechanism to became substance abuse disorder.

The best treatments for anxiety are medications (the client needs to see a doctor) and cognitive behavioural therapy (CBT). A person can work through CBT on their own, although getting involved with a pro therapist or a support group is a good idea.

Medications for anxiety may be antidepressants or sedatives, usually benzodiazepines such as Valium and Ativan. This class of drugs is highly addictive and so can cause some troubling side effects, such as building up a tolerance (the medication does not work anymore unless the patient increases their dosage again and again), becoming dependent on the medication to sleep, get through the day and feel relatively okay; and withdrawal symptoms when the patient stops taking them. However, for someone with severe anxiety, these medications can be lifesavers, if used with supervision and medical monitoring.

> Once I suffered a major life trauma (an arsonist burned my house down). I was admitted to the hospital (there was a heavy locked door which made me feel safe) where I was fed Ativan to knock me out and keep me quiet. I took only three pills and I was hooked.
>
> It took another two weeks or so of sleepless nights before I cleared the Ativan out of my system and could sleep normally. Then I could use more healthy ways to cope, such as exercise and visiting with friends.

These tips may help you support an anxious client:

- Encourage your client to see a doctor if her anxiety is creating serious problems in her life.
- Encourage your client to get adequate exercise to burn off adrenaline, the hormone that produces all those anxiety symptoms, and produce endorphins, the "feel good" hormone.
- Encourage your client to avoid unhealthy coping mechanisms such as alcohol and drugs, which do a lot more harm than good in the long run.
- Encourage your client to adopt or maintain healthy lifestyle choices, such as getting enough sleep, eating healthy foods, relaxing with yoga or meditation, and avoiding caffeine and tobacco.
- Introduce your client to *Mind Over Mood*, the CBT "bible".
- Introduce your client to foods that help to beat anxiety, such as salmon, chamomile, turmeric, dark chocolate, yoghurt, and green tea. Caffeine should be avoided.
- Encourage your client to stay socially active, and to avoid isolating. (If this feels impossible, then it is time for medical intervention.)
- Suggest that your client get on the internet and research chat rooms, online support groups, and apps to help with anxiety.
- Assist your client to select and use stress management and relaxation techniques that can help to reduce the overall stress which can trigger anxiety.

To learn more
Start with the online resources listed here:

> seawinds-education.mykajabi.com/o-pt-in-to-resources-for-the-non-therapist

This book may be useful: Mind Over Mood, Change How You Feel By Changing The Way You Think, Greenberger and Padesky, Guilford Press, 2016.

Loneliness

We have all felt lonely at some point. Short-term loneliness, that we know will end because our situation is going to change, is not much of a problem. However, chronic loneliness is a big problem with medical, emotional and social complications. The way we experience loneliness varies from person to person and the solutions are unique too.

Loneliness is the distress we feel when we see a gap between the social connections we feel the need for, and what we actually experience in our lives. Loneliness is an emotional condition that differs from solitude. We think of loneliness, which usually is not our choice, as being a painful, bad thing to be avoided, but voluntary solitude is a chosen state that many people find has benefits, such as being able to focus and recharge. We can feel lonely in a crowd and we can feel the joys of delicious solitude living alone in the bush many miles away from civilization. Our thoughts about being alone are what make us feel lonely or not.

Loneliness can warp our thinking, make people feel unworthy, rejected, unwanted, abandoned, empty, cynical, and suspicious, which makes it even more difficult to form connections with other people. Loneliness then can become chronic.

Loneliness can be a signal of mental health issues, such as low self esteem or depression, which causes people to withdraw socially, leading to isolation, and feelings of loneliness. Loneliness can result from the loss of a loved one, small social networks, poor quality relationships with people who are actually close by, lack of authenticity in relationships, moving to a new location, divorce, or a habit of negative thinking.

About 1/3 of North Americans feel lonely. Who is most at risk to become lonely? Various studies have pointed to the following groups of people:

- Immigrants who are missing their home culture and have not yet had time to build new social networks.
- Members of the 2SLGBTQ community who feel left out of or ostracized by mainstream society.
- Students from countries where collectivism is the norm who move to a country where individualism is the primary social style in order to study often feel isolated.
- Adolescents, especially if they do not feel a strong healthy bond to family members.
- The elderly, especially if they are living alone, have disabilities or limiting medical conditions.

- Victims of elder abuse.
- Having a small circle of meaningful relationships.
- People who have experienced a significant loss – the death of a loved one, death of a beloved pet, breakdown of a romantic relationship, disruption of social circles, or home-sickness.
- People who rely on social media for their connections with people.
- People who grew up in a family that was not healthy, where they did not learn how to connect or build trusting relationships. In time, these people may become discouraged or apathetic from trying and failing to make friends.
- People who are normally outgoing and extroverted but find themselves living in an area of low social density with fewer people to interact with.
- People with pre-existing mental health conditions, such as anxiety or depression.
- People who regularly have long commutes to get to work.
- People who lack a romantic partner or are in an unstable or dangerous relationship, or whose romantic partner is emotionally cold.
- People who are in medical lockdown and cannot see friends and family.
- Youth in detention centers who have experienced solitary confinement.

Loneliness may be disguised: for some people there is a stigma to feeling lonely, as if there must be something wrong with them to feel that way. Your client may signal loneliness by saying something like these comments:

- "I need a companion."
- "I feel left out."
- "I just don't feel like I am 'in tune' with the people around me."
- "It's just me!"
- "I don't feel friendly or outgoing right now."
- "I don't have anyone I would feel comfortable talking to about my life."

Loneliness has a bad influence on our medical and mental health. Studies have shown the following effects resulting from loneliness:

- Substance abuse.
- Increased (as much as double) risk of developing Alzheimer's disease, and speeding up its progress.
- In children especially, antisocial and self-destructive behaviour, and hostile behaviour towards others.
- Higher risk of cardiovascular disease, stroke, high blood pressure, high cholesterol, Type 2 diabetes, arthritis.
- Depression and suicidal thoughts.
- Increased stress hormone levels, leading to weakening of the immune system, obesity, poor sleep, anxiety, depression, digestive problems, and increase in inflammation which

is a precursor to several serious medical issues.
- Self harm is directly related to lack of close ties with family members.
- Weakening of willpower and the ability to make good decisions, learn and remember.
- Decrease in healthy exercise.
- Poor sleep.
- A diet with a high level of fat, leading to obesity.
- Daytime fatigue.
- Higher rates of mortality in general. The risk of mortality from loneliness equals that of smoking 15 cigarettes daily or being an alcoholic and exceeds the health risks of obesity.

How to respond effectively
Since loneliness is the perceived lack of social connection, then the best cure for loneliness is connecting in a meaningful way with other human beings. If your client has forgotten how to do that, you might need to support him to recall how and to find the courage to put himself out there. Reaching out can be the hardest thing to do when a person is lonely, especially if depression is in the picture as well, but it is the best cure for the unhappy feelings.

You can help by doing the following:

- Remind him to spend more energy on being kind to others and putting more emphasis on building relationships with others.
- Reaching out to family members and existing friends to strengthen those relationships may be a great place to start re-connecting, if those are healthy, supportive relationships. Any form of communication that works, including phone, emails, texts, and social media, can help him stay in touch.
- Joining in group activities is a great way to connect and make new friends. If he can't find a group that suits him, he could start his own by inviting people with similar interests to gather. He might also join a class or a book club.
- Reengage with old friends by reaching out in whatever way your client can manage, by social media if that is all he is up for, but better yet by Zoom or—the very best way to connect—in person.
- Become more connected to the community, perhaps by volunteering to help out some worthy cause or activity locally. Your client will meet others who share the same interests and values.
- Your client would do well to realize that loneliness is a sign that something in his life needs to change. Sometimes a lonely person's thinking has become warped, so a course of CBT to address irrational automatic thoughts about people and relationships would be very helpful. A 2019 study suggests that this is the most effective way to combat loneliness. Your client can go a long way in learning about modifying his thinking by working through *Mind Over Mood*. Some people will also need to work with a pro therapist. Almost every formally-trained therapist will have expertise in helping clients using CBT.
- Loving a pet can help a lot. If your client already has a pet, then spending quality time in

outdoor activities can light a spark for your client. If he does not already have a pet, try borrowing a puppy or a willing, affectionate pooch to visit or take on walks.
- Remind your client that loneliness is just a feeling, and one that can be changed.
- Its important for your client to take a look at why he feels lonely, so that he can take action where it might help the most. This is another possible role for a pro therapist.
- Being strategic helps. Encourage your client to seek out people who have healthy relationships with others and who seem to be good communicators, and people who share similar attitudes, interests, and values. Your client will need to learn to communicate well (you can teach him what you have learned from this book!) and to be assertive to ensure that his needs are met in any relationship. He will also need to accept that not everyone will be his best friend, and that that's okay. It is not an indication of his value or worth, just a sign that he has not yet found the right people to connect with.
- Expecting the best when cultivating a new relationship is a good attitude to nurture. Lonely people often expect rejection, so learning to focus on positive thoughts in social relationships can go a long way.
- Help your client brainstorm ways to overcome any barriers to connecting, such as child care, mobility, or transportation. This may require the assistance of other people, such as helping organizations in your area.
- Remind your client not to compare himself or his life to other people's lives. For example, if he sees only smiling, manicured faces on his Facebook feed, he might easily feel left out because he does not have a legion of close affectionate friends or a stunning knockout romantic partner to post photos of, and feel that there must be something wrong with him, that he is unlikable and so why not just give up and settle into depression. Remind him that most of what is posted on Facebook is nonsense anyway. Remind him that his feeling is only a feeling and is not reality.
- If your client has recently experienced some big transition, such as moving to a new place or starting a new job, it can take a while to settle in, find his place and make new friends. This is the time to be patient while still making the effort to make new connections, and to not expect magic to happen quickly. Loneliness may be only a temporary stop along the way.
- You might need to help your client consider what else is going on in his life to fuel or add to his feelings of loneliness, such as anxiety or depression that bring up difficult thoughts that make it easier to avoid social situations. Managing challenges in other parts of his life can reduce feelings of loneliness.
- Encourage your client to look at time spent alone as a gift: time to pursue a hobby, to recharge and get rest, to learn something new, read a good book, listen to music or connect with nature.
- It sometimes helps to be accountable to someone. If someone calls you to ask, "What did you do today?" it might be motivating. The lonely person might take a walk just to have something positive to report, but at least he was out and about, so some benefit might come from that action.
- Face-to-face contact is always the best, but for some people, that might be too daunting.

There is a role for technology to play to combat loneliness. There are apps that warn users they are spending too much time online. There are apps that encourage mindfulness to develop more fruitful alone time. There are digital dating services. There are always robot companions too, although being old school, that idea creeps me out.

If none of these ideas work, then it is probably time for your client to see a pro therapist.

To learn more
Start with the online resources listed here:

> seawinds-education.mykajabi.com/o-pt-in-to-resources-for-the-non-therapist

Sexual assault

Sexual assault is an act in which one person intentionally sexually touches another person without that person's consent, or coerces or physically forces a person to engage in a sexual act against their will. It is a form of violence, and includes child sexual abuse, groping, rape and attempted rape (forced vaginal, anal, or oral penetration or a drug facilitated sexual assault), the torture of the person in a sexual manner, or the threat of unwanted sexual contact.

Removal of a condom during intercourse without the consent of the sex partner, known as stealthing, may be treated as a sexual assault or rape in some jurisdictions.

> Sexual assault is about power and control.

Definitions vary somewhat from place to place, but lack of consent is usually at the heart of the matter.[25]

"Child sexual abuse" is a form of child abuse in which an adult or older adolescent abuses a child for sexual stimulation. Forms of child sexual abuse include asking or pressuring a child to engage in sexual activities (regardless of the outcome), indecent exposure of the genitals to a child, displaying pornography to a child, actual sexual contact with a child, physical contact with the child's genitals, viewing the child's genitalia without physical contact, or using a child to produce child pornography, including live streaming sexual abuse.[26]

"Sexual harassment" is intimidation, bullying, or coercion of a sexual nature, when either submission or rejection of the perpetrator's advances might affect her employment, unreasonably interfere with work performance, or create an intimidating, hostile, or offensive work environment. The definition of what constitutes sexual harassment and the punishments for those who do it differs from culture to culture and may include a wide range of behaviours, some of which overlap with sexual assault.

The most important thing to understand is that sexual assault is not about sexual desire. It is about power and control.

---

[25] Wikipedia
[26] Wikipedia

Sexual assault is a gender-based crime, with 93% of victims being women and 99% of perpetrators being men.[27]

Sexual assault is more common than most people realize. The United States Department of Justice estimates that every 107 seconds, someone in the USA is sexually assaulted.[28] Most victims are between 12 – 34 years of age. Girls aged 16 – 19 are 4 times more likely than the general population to be victims of sexual assault. Close to 30% of women have experienced rape or attempted rape during their lifetime, as compared to just over 1% of men. So when you are gathering with your women friends, look around: one third of your group has been assaulted at some point. When men are victims, they are more frequently gang raped, more likely to have been held captive for longer, and more likely than women to experience physical injury.[29]

2sLGBTQ, bisexual men and women, transgender people, people with disabilities and indigenous women are much more vulnerable than others.

Sexual assaulters tend to be mostly white men in their 30s, half of whom are married or in long-term relationships.[30] Only a few rapes involve a weapon and, in Canada, up to 80% of rapes are committed by someone known to the victim.[31] In fact, 80% of sexual assaults happen in the home.[32]

Most sexual assaults are never reported. In Canada, of every 100 incidents of sexual assault, only 6 are reported. In only a few cases are charges laid and very few result in a conviction.[33]

In the USA, 98% of rapists do not spend time in jail. Reasons why victims choose not to report the assault to the police include the following:

- They are so traumatized, they cannot handle that step, fearing it will bring more trauma for them or it will lengthen the time they have to live with the pain and shame of assault before they can bathe, change their clothes and feel safe again.
- They may be physically damaged and cannot bear the thought of being touched again.
- They may fear that that no-one will believe them, or may think it was their fault, that they in some way contributed to the attack, or that they did not fight back hard enough, so that they will be judged harshly.
- They may fear reprisals from the attacker if they report him, or from relatives, especially if the assault comes from a family member. This is even more so for women who are in an abusive relationship and the sexual assault was another form of domination.
- They may fear that the trial itself will be traumatizing, as the defence lawyer attempts to discredit the victim's reputation and credibility.
- They may not trust the legal system to follow through for them in a satisfying way, so decide that the lengthy and often re-traumatizing process is not worth it.

---

27 uottawa.ca/sexual-violence-support-and-prevention/quick-facts
28 Wikipedia
29 Wikipedia
30 Wikipedia
31 https://www.rainn.org/articles/sexual-assault
32 sexassault.ca/statistics.htm
33 uottawa.ca/sexual-violence-support-and-prevention/quick-facts

- Children who are victims of sexual assault may be confused because the attacker was someone who is supposed to love them. Or the perpetrator may have bribed, or threatened to hurt, them or some other family member or a pet if they tell. The child may be too young to understand what has happened to them or may not be able to put it into words, or may believe that the abuse is a form of punishment. If the parent to whom they disclose their experience does not believe them, the child may never report the abuse.
- Childhood sexual assault often goes on for years, so it may seem somewhat normal until the victim is older and understands things more clearly. Victims may fear they waited too long to report the assaults, or that someone will accuse them of liking the activity or even of instigating it, or that the attacker is a prominent community person and they would be causing that person to lose face in his community.

Sexual abuse can have serious impacts for victims. Psychological damage is particularly severe when children are sexually assaulted by a parent. Many of those children will grow up to become assaulters themselves. The following issues have been reported as resulting from sexual assault:[34]

- Denial
- Learned helplessness
- Anger, aggression, anxiety, fear
- Self-blame, shame, guilt
- Mood swings
- Flashbacks, nightmares
- Emotional numbness
- Promiscuity
- Difficulty trusting oneself or others
- Loneliness, being withdrawn
- Mental health disorders, such as PTSD, obsessive compulsive disorder, bipolar disorder, depression, eating disorders, substance abuse disorders
- Headaches, chronic pain, sleeping issues
- Suicidal thinking

Any and all of these responses to the shock of a sexual assault are "normal" and predictable. After the assault, victims may be shamed, blamed, bullied, isolated, and their credibility questioned. It is a sad commentary on our society that victims would be seen as being responsible for their own fate. Her clothing, her hair, her choices, rather than the behaviour of the assaulter, may be presented as being the "cause" of the assault. Our justice system still takes this view in some cases.

Given the response women know they are likely to face if they report a sexual assault, it is not surprising that confidence in the legal system is poor and so few women bother to report.

---

34 Wikipedia

Kate Tompkins

How to respond effectively
The main roles for a helper when a sexual assault has occurred may be any of the following:

- Get the victim to a safe place. Provide something she can cover herself with and keep warm if her clothing is missing or torn, but do not throw away or wash her soiled clothing.
- After a violent assault, it is a good idea for her to go the hospital or nursing station to be examined. However, many women will refuse. She may be unable to tolerate the idea of having her private parts exposed, again, with likely several people in the room, or to be touched intimately on her private parts, which may be damaged after a rape, in order to collect evidence to hand over to the police. If she is brave enough to report and go to the hospital, advise her not to change her clothes, shower or bathe, or comb or brush her hair, clean her fingernails, change her clothes or disturb the 'scene of the crime' in any way. If she can manage it, avoiding urinating might be helpful also. Tell her not to consume any drugs or alcohol, so as to present an accurate picture of how the assault happened. Physical evidence can still be collected several days after a sexual assault, but the sooner the better to retain as much DNA evidence as possible.
- Not washing or cleaning up may be a challenge for her, because the first impulse for many is to wash away the taint, to be clean and free from anything left behind by the rapist. The police or a special medical team will want to observe the collection of evidence using what is known as a "rape kit" before the evidence becomes too old to be useful. If the victim is not yet able to speak coherently for herself, you might ask for a female police officer to be present in the room rather than a man. Most police forces already have protocols for this situation, and some have female officers specially trained to respond to a violent sexual assault, but it doesn't hurt to ask. Have her bring clean clothes to change into after the examination. The hospital can store evidence gathered using a rape kit for some time if the victim is not yet ready to report to the police.
- If she does not feel up to a hospital visit or a visit to a rape crisis center, then take any clothing that has semen, hair or blood on it, seal it in a plastic bag and store it in the freezer until she is ready to report. Do not wash the clothing.
- Call the police if she is willing to report. For a look at what happens when a victim reports a sexual assault, read this article:
edmontonpolice.ca/CrimePrevention/PersonalFamilySafety/SexualAssault/ReportingSexualAssault
- If you are a woman, stay with her during conversations with the police and at the hospital. If she wants your company and if you are allowed to, stay with her in the examining room as well so she knows she has an ally who is safe and who cares while she is being examined and evidence gathered.
- Take her home, help her with practical things like finding clean clothes, a cup of tea, a warm blanket. If the assault occurred at her home, then she may want to be someplace else for a while. If she lives alone, consider finding someone to stay with her for a few days until she feels safe again.

- Ensure that she has female company she trusts. The comforting presence of women friends and relatives can go a long way to re-establishing a feeling of safety.
- Refer her to a sexual assault support center if there is one in the area. Call the service for her if needed, and drive her there. Some have 24-hour access.
- Reassure her that any emotion she experiences in the aftermath of a sexual assault is normal and that she will in time get past those feelings. If they persist for several weeks after the assault, then refer her to a pro therapist.
- If the assault happened some time ago, then your role may be just to listen, and to refer her to a pro therapist if she still has troubles as a result of the abuse.
- Men, we know you care. But this is a time for you to call in a female helper. If a woman or child has just been physically violated by a man, she most likely does **not** want to be anywhere near a man right now, no matter how well-meaning you are. You might be more useful by supporting the female helper, who may be affected herself by the stresses of responding to this type of trauma.
- Do not touch the victim, unless she initiates it. She has just been violated in a way so profound that she cannot escape yet from her fear and shock. Let her decide when she wants a hug or even a gently-supportive touch. Ask her permission first before even helping her into a vehicle or into a chair. Her consent and the ability to control what happens to her body has been annihilated by a steam roller. Something as mundane as, "May I help you into this chair?" can help her to restore her sense of control and safety.
- Keep in mind that many victims of sexual assault never report to the police, for a variety of reasons, so don't push her to do so. Just be there and support her in whatever her decision may be.
- There are many places where sexual assault support centers provide counselling; a supportive nurse to look after physical injuries, test for pregnancy and STIs; administer emergency contraception and gather evidence; provide information about how to use the legal system to their advantage, and support as they progress through charges and court proceedings. Why not take the time to research what is available in your region before you need it!
- Your client may want to speak with a lawyer. Some Canadian provinces provide free legal aid to victims of sexual assaults. Check with your regional legal aid society, law information line, Department of Justice, or sexual assault information center. Unlike the USA, in Canada, there is no "statute of limitations". A victim may report a sexual assault many years after it happened. She may choose to have evidence handed over to the police and lay charges, or not.

To learn more
Start with the online resources listed here:

> seawinds-education.mykajabi.com/o-pt-in-to-resources-for-the-non-therapist

Kate Tompkins

Substance abuse

What is "substance abuse"? Or "dependency" Or "addiction"? And when does using a substance turn into "abuse"?

In common usage, "substance use" simply means that a person consumes alcohol or a drug, legal or not. A glass of wine at dinner, a cigarette at coffee break time, a puff of a joint at a party are examples of simple use. From the medical perspective, "using" in this way is not considered to be a problem.

When a pattern develops of using for the purpose of changing a mood, or becomes a problem in some way for the user, it is called "substance abuse disorder". Substance abuse disorder also includes using something in a way that is not intended, such as sniffing gasoline, or using too much of a prescribed drug, or taking a prescription medication intended for someone else. "Harmful use" is another way to think of substance abuse disorder. For example, repeated use causing significant problems in a person's life or some type of impairment, such as making risky choices in order to continue using, developing or worsening physical and mental health issues resulting from use, failing to look after the necessities of life, or failing to meet responsibilities to family or work describe this type of pattern.

> A substance use disorder... is a mental disorder that affects a person's brain and behavior, leading to a person's inability to control their use of substances such as legal or illegal drugs, alcohol, or medications. Symptoms can range from moderate to severe, with addiction being the most severe form.

A person who has frequent hangovers, misses work or school to use, finds themselves using more than they had intended, or uses to cope with unpleasant memories or an intense mood, to face frightening situations, to stay focused, or to alleviate a hangover has probably crossed the line from "use" to "abuse".

That distinction is not clear, though. Perhaps the only person who can really say where use ends and abuse starts is the user himself. The questions a user needs to ask are "Does using this substance cause me harm? Is it causing problems in my life?" If the answer is yes, then your client has a problem to be addressed.

The term "substance use disorder" has replaced the older and confusing terms "addiction", "dependence", and "substance abuse".

About half of people who have a substance use disorder also have some other mental health issue, such as anxiety, depression, ADHD, or bipolar disorder. The substance abuse may make the mental issue worse, or the other way around: the mental health issue may lead to substance abuse as people "self medicate" to temporarily relieve their symptoms. There may even be a genetic factor, since both substance abuse disorder and other mental health issues tend to run in families.

Almost any substance can be abused, including:

- Prescription drugs, especially opioid painkillers (such as heroin, fentanyl, morphine, oxycodone), sleep medications, sedatives ("downers" such as Valium, or Ativan), stimulants ("uppers", such as amphetamines, "speed"), cocaine and cough and cold medications are frequently abused. Opioid abuse and its resulting deaths are a painful epidemic right now in North America.
- Inhalants and solvents such as nail polish remover, gasoline, glue and aerosols.
- Hallucinogens, such as LSD ("acid"), mushrooms ("shrooms"), peyote. Many of these substances are considered sacred to some aboriginal peoples, are used for spiritual purposes, and are being investigated now by mainstream medical researchers as potential medications, especially for mental health concerns.
- Mood changers, such as marijuana, when used in large quantities, and when the THC content is high. Marijuana is also used as a medication in Canada and some American states where it is now legal. The issue occurs with the use of large amounts of "weed" with high THC content frequently over a long period of time.
- Synthetic drugs, also known as "designer drugs", such as ecstasy ("molly").
- Performance enhancing substances, such as anabolic steroids.
- Products such as nicotine, caffeine and sugar, which are the most commonly-used substances in the world.
- Alcohol.
- Even supposedly-innocuous substances can be abused, such as the ink in some coloured drawing pens, which have been treated to make them appealing to children. These are outlawed now in North America but did their damage for some years before they were banned.

How can a friend or loved one identify signs of a substance use problem? Here are some common signals:

- A significant change in routine or habits, such as eating more or less than usual, mixed-up sleeping hours, losing interest in personal grooming and self care.
- Losing interest in people, places, and activities that used to be prominent in the user's life.
- A disruption in relationships, wanting to spend more time alone than usual, dropping friends, or taking up with new friends whose lifestyles appear risky.
- A significant change in attitudes to family members, such as becoming aggressive or secretive.
- Mood changes, especially going rapidly from feeling okay to depression or anxiety.
- More problems at work or school than usual, including falling grades, behaviour problems, making mistakes, anger, missing school or work.
- Recurring financial problems, such as missing money, or incurring large debts to pay for substances, causing problems for family financial obligations such as mortgage payments.
- Drug paraphernalia, such as rolling papers, small pieces of cling film, small plastic bags,

pipes, bongs, pierced plastic bottles or cans, burnt aluminum foil, burnt spoons or knives, syringes, bottles of medications intended for someone else, frequent renewal of prescriptions that may be harmful in large quantities.
- Strong desires to use, cravings for particular substances.
- Loss of control of the amount used or the frequency of use.
- Continuing to use, despite the negative consequences.
- Needing increased amounts of the drug of choice to get the same effects.
- Withdrawal symptoms when the user tries to quit or cut down.
- Spending a lot of time planning to use, obtaining the substance of choice, using or recovering from using.
- New health issues.

Some of these signs may indicate something other than substance use, such as normal teen-aged development stuff, or the advent of a mental health issue, so look for other evidence before jumping to conclusions.

Not everyone who uses a substance will develop a problem with using it. Think of substance use on a spectrum. At one end, there is use than can be helpful, offering social or even spiritual effects. Then, moving along the spectrum, casual recreational use that is not a problem. Marching on down the line, we might see problematic use that begins to have negative impacts on health, relationships, and legal consequences. At the far right, we see use that has become habitual and compulsive, even though there are negative consequences for the user.

For a graphic that illustrates this continuum, check out this site: ontario.cmha.ca/addiction-and-substance-use-and-addiction.

The good news is that substance abuse disorder is treatable, even when combined with other mental heath issues. Treatment might take several forms, such as a stay in a residential detox or withdrawal program to get cleaned out under medical supervision, medication, counselling; peer support and recovery groups such as Alcoholics Anonymous (AA) and Narcotics Anonymous (NA), apps, and on-line assessment tools.

People with additional mental health issues seem to do best if their treatment addresses both issues at the same time. Follow-up care after the treatment program ends is key to long-term success. Programs that help a user find employment can help.

An important feature of treatment should be learning healthier coping mechanisms to manage stress, deal with unpleasant feelings, recognize triggers, and make plans for responding in a way that does not include using any substance.

For people who are not yet ready to stop using totally, a harm-reduction program may be useful. Harm reduction offers strategies to reduce the risks while using, such as a needle exchange, educational programs, overdose prevention education, and access to naloxone to reverse a dangerous opioid overdose. If a user can begin by engaging in harm reduction services, it may be easier to transition later to treatment aimed at sobriety.

It is not easy to break a substance abuse disorder, so anything that can help is a good thing, even if the result is not total sobriety right away.

Culturally-sensitive treatment works well for specific groups of people. For example those who identify as being 2sLGBTQ, aboriginal, or immigrant may find programs that speak to them more than the mainstream programs do. Some treatment programs specialize in helping people who have been using a specific substance, such as cocaine, and some treat both substance-abuse disorder and mental health issues, so some research to find the right program for a user can go a long way.

Treatment may be provided in a residential centre, a hospital outpatient program, day programs, or drop-in counselling services. AA and NA are always good supplements to treatment; many people attain sobriety and stay that way with only participation in AA or NA and no additional treatment.

It is a good idea for a user who is ready to change their patterns to start off with a visit to his family physician to assess medical concerns and treatments needed, and to an addictions counsellor, who can provide information and support. Both will be knowledgeable about treatment options in your area and can refer the user to the most suitable program for his needs.

The user has a much better chance of success in beating his disorder when it is recognized early, before it can develop into a serious issue. Watch out especially for the following people, who have special issues making them more vulnerable to overdosing or developing a more serious problem:

- Combat veterans, many of whom have PTSD.
- Women veterans who may have experienced sexual harassment or sexual assault from their own comrades in arms while serving, as well as developing PTSD.
- People who binge drink.
- People who use while driving.
- Pregnant women who are using.
- People who mix opioids with alcohol or other drugs.
- Children and adolescents.
- 2sLGBTQ community members who are also facing discrimination.
- Aboriginal users who are also facing racism wounds.

It is important to note that relapses are par for the course. A man I used to know was an addictions counsellor at a treatment centre. He confided to me that he went to treatment for his alcohol addiction five times before the treatment "stuck" and he was able to remain sober. When I asked what made the difference the fifth time, he said it was the support of one person who believed he could do it, his parole officer, as I recall. His office was adorned with his mug shots from arrests over the many years before he attained his sobriety, which he kept in plain view to remind him what his life used to be like. This, he said, helped him recommit to sobriety every day.

There are lots of reasons why people might avoid substance abuse treatment. A user may think he does not have a problem, or underestimates his problem and overestimates his ability to control it, even when others around him think he has a serious issue; he might realize he has a problem, but not yet be ready to stop using; he does not have health coverage; he fears that if knowledge of his disorder were public, it would affect his friendships or his job; he does not know how or where to find treatment; the location or hours of the treatment available may be inconvenient.

How to respond effectively
The guidelines following are not only useful for you as a helper when someone comes to you for help with a substance use problem; they are also tips you can give to a family concerned about a loved one who is abusing a substance.

The first thing to remember is that the only person you really have any influence over is—you! You can adjust your own expectations and strategies, but you cannot really do a great deal to influence or force a user to change his ways. The old adage that "you can lead a horse to water but you cannot force him to drink" is really true when it comes to substance use issues. The user will need to come to his own conclusions about how using is impacting his life, make his own decisions about what to do about it, and make his own arrangements to get help. Or not to.

Fortunately, there are things that you, the helper, or the loved ones of a user can do to increase the odds that a user will think though his status and come to the conclusions you want him to. At least you can avoid getting in the way and making things worse, possibly damaging yourself in the process. Consistent support, done properly, can play a very important role in the user's recovery.

- Start with your expectations. Be realistic about what you can and cannot control, and about what "success" may look like. It's different for everyone. One user may be content to cut down the amount he uses while another will need total abstinence in order to stay healthy. If the user is able to find peace and stability in his life, then expressing disappointment that he is not entirely sober is likely to produce feelings of failure and stress. Since stress is one of the forces driving a user to overuse, that would not be helpful at all.
- Accept that relapse is common, even expected, and try to be patient. Think of any relapse as an opportunity to push the reset button and start again.
- Avoid enabling, which means shielding the user from the consequences of their use. For example, calling in sick for the user when he has a killer hangover, booking medical appointments for him, or picking up a bottle from the liquor store for him, lending him money, paying his rent or his bills, or paying for his rehab program. It may seem that actions like this are compassionate and supportive, but in fact they simply make it easier for the user to continue using. What reason would a user have to change his ways if his partner or friend or helper continues to mop up after him? Setting boundaries about the way the user treats you not only encourages the user to take responsibility for his own choices and learn from experiencing the consequences, it also protects you or the family member from burning out, being unable to provide any more support, and damaging your own mental and physical health and family relationships. Saying "no" to someone you care about can be gut-wrenching but it is a key factor in ensuring the user's "success". For a refresher on how to set limits on the user's behaviour, return to the section on boundaries in Chapter 5 of this book. For examples of things you or the family might

like to set boundaries about, check out this article:
helpguide.org/?s=Helping+someone+with+addictions

- Watching someone you love destroy themselves is extremely stressful and can take a toll on your own mental and emotional wellbeing. The loved ones of a user should be encouraged to seek support for themselves, such as counselling, on-line support chat rooms, or joining Alanon or Alateen, which are 12 Step support groups for loved ones of a user.
- Encourage family members to look after themselves first. Managing stress is critical for supporting loved ones, including the standard stress busters—exercising regularly, getting enough rest, eating healthy foods, and practicing relaxation techniques such as meditation or yoga.
- Encourage loved ones to keep up their friendship networks, hobbies, and social activities, or to develop new interests and relationships. This is good advice also for a user who has stopped using and is now in recovery. It is important for the newly-minted sober dude who wants to stay that way to develop new healthy relationships with people who were not part of his using activities before he quit.
- Encourage family members to be patient. It may take a long time for their support to bear fruit with the user. Consistent support with specific boundaries about what behaviour is acceptable and what is not can make the difference for the user. Understanding that relapses are to be expected is important, too. Lecturing, emotional appeals, threats, or bribery are more harmful than useful and may drive the user back into their self-destructive patterns.
- Encourage family members to educate themselves about the substances their loved one is using, their effects, the laws surrounding their use, and the realities of substance abuse disorders, so they know what to expect and can support the user appropriately. The internet has many useful sites, some of which are noted on our website. It would be helpful for the family to consult with an addictions counsellor as well for advice on how to best support the user in a helpful way. Having information about treatment options to provide to the user may be useful at some point too.
- Be prepared for denial. Users may feel shame and anger and refuse to discuss the problem. Warn the family supporting the user to not force the issue; just leave it be for now and try again when the user seems more calm. Coming from a place of understanding and compassion has a better chance of winning the user's trust and motivation to change than shaming, demeaning, or criticizing, which are more likely to drive the user to self-comfort with their substance of choice.
- It might be useful for you the helper to teach the family members how to listen well, using the techniques we looked at in earlier chapters of this book. Offering help without judgement is what the family should aim for. If they can listen well, be honest about their own feelings and their concern for the user, without arguing or contradicting what the user has to say, they might be able to build a road into his inner conflict and help to create a new path that leads towards a healthier lifestyle.
- Encourage the family of a loved one to speak up with their concerns earlier rather than

later. The longer the problem usage goes on, the worse it is likely to become. The earlier a substance abuse disorder is treated, the easier it is to treat.
- It is a good idea for the family to encourage the user to address any other mental health issues such as depression or anxiety that accompany the harmful using. Researching treatment programs that address both using and other mental health issues is a good first step, so that the family can present the information on what is available to the user. After that, leaving the user to make his own decisions about treatment and making his own arrangements to attend is an important step in his recovery, because he is then taking responsibility for his own sobriety. If the family members are not sure how to do this, having them research the idea of "tough love" may be helpful. Check it out yourself, so that you can support the family as they learn to support the user appropriately. Tough love is not universally supported; some researchers think it is authoritative and controlling and may do more harm than good. However the idea of establishing boundaries with loving attention to the long-term welfare of the recipient is not at issue. As with most things in life, how you do it is key!
- Help the family of the user to prepare for the future after their loved one completes treatment by making a plan to help the user respond to cravings and triggers in a healthy way. An addictions counsellor can help with this task.
- At some point, family members may decide they cannot survive the process of living with their loved one with a substance abuse disorder any longer. Love has its limits. After family members have done all they can to support the user without substantial change and find themselves in danger of burnout, the time may arrive for the hard decision. The role for the helper may be to support the family to do what they need to do for themselves, or it may be to support the family in their decision afterwards. If things have gotten to this point, it is unlikely there is more you can do to support the user, but if you have the moxie and the support to do so, continue to let the user know you are available to talk when needed. You never know, it might be what makes the difference sometime in the future. Remember my friend, and his one believer who allowed him to achieve sobriety?

To learn more

- For information on the most commonly abused substances and their effects, check out this resource: webmd.com/mental-health/addiction/substance-abuse#1
- "Get Your Loved One Sober, Alternatives to Nagging, Pleading, and Threatening", Robt. J. Meyers PhD, Brenda L. Wolfe PhD, Hazelden Publishing, Minnesota, 2004. A good resource for the family members of a loved one with a substance abuse problem, and for you to support the family.

Also review the online resources listed here:

    seawinds-education.mykajabi.com/o-pt-in-to-resources-for-the-non-therapist

Child protection concerns

In every province and territory in Canada, and every part of the United Kingdom, the law requires that anyone who suspects that a child is in danger from abandonment, physical assault, neglect, sexual assault, or exploitation **must** report that to whatever branch of the provincial government concerns itself with child protection matters. The same is true in many other countries as well.

In the USA, each state has its own requirements. For example, California has mandated several professions to report, but the general public does not have the same obligations.

Some jurisdictions add emotional or psychological harm and serious behavioural disturbances to that list of reportable circumstances. There are stiff penalties for professionals who become aware of such risks and do not report them.

How to respond effectively
There is no leeway here: if you have reasonable grounds to suspect that a child is at risk, you are expected to report that. Don't worry about causing trouble for a family where children are at risk—the children's welfare trumps any other issues.

They are your friends? So what? Protect those kids. (By the way, why would you want to be friends with people who abuse their children?) You are afraid of the parents? Call the police and call the child protection authorities to report the parents.

To learn more
Why not research the phone number of your local child protection authorities now and keep it close by? Ask a child protection officer to explain any parts of the legal requirements that you are unsure of.

What does the legislation say in your area? What resources exist for families in your area?

Also review the online resources listed here:

> seawinds-education.mykajabi.com/o-pt-in-to-resources-for-the-non-therapist

Social justice issues

Social justice refers to the idea that all people should have equal access to wealth, health, well-being, justice, privileges, and opportunity regardless of their legal, political, economic, or other circumstances, and that governments, organizations and individuals have a moral responsibility to redress any circumstances that do not respect and promote this premise. Equality, equity, rights, and participation are some of the principles of social justice.

Social justice usually looks at balances between large groups and society; however, the welfare of the individual affected by society's imbalances is where the rubber hits the road.

The basic ideas behind social justice have their roots in ancient Greek philosophy (Plato, Aristotle, and Socrates) and informed the American and French Revolutions, but came into their own during the industrial revolution, when individuals, even young children, were exploited by industrialists for profit.

Martin Luther King's civil rights movement for African Americans, the Black Lives Matter movement, the "Me Too" movement, Human Rights advocates, and the work of labour unions are some modern examples of social justice activism. Social justice is key to socialist economies and to some religious philosophies.

Social justice initiatives tend to respond to issues such as the following:

- Accessibility to affordable health care for all.
- Humane immigration policies.
- Eliminating potential biases towards certain demographic groups engaged with the criminal justice system.
- Breaking barriers for social mobility and class.
- Creating social safety nets.
- Equal pay for equal work, regardless of who the worker is.
- Removal of barriers of all types for the differently abled.
- Workplace safety.
- Freedom of thought, freedom of speech, and the right of assembly to use these freedoms.
- Trafficking of people and weapons.
- Modern day slavery.
- Rights for children to be protected from physical and mental violence, injury or abuse, neglect, maltreatment, and exploitation, including sexual abuse.
- Food security for all.
- Discrimination based on sexual orientation and gender identity.
- Aboriginal rights to land, clean water, education, healthcare, and decision making.
- Violence against women and children.
- Ageism, sexism.
- Freedom of religious choice.
- Poverty and access to the essentials of life.
- Developing an "inclusivity" mindset.
- Addressing vulnerability for seniors, the homeless, veterans, refugees, 2sLGBTQ individuals.
- Freedom from sexual harassment at work.
- Dignity and worth of the person.
- Meaningful employment opportunities.
- Access to food, clean water and shelter.
- Discrimination based on religion.
- Discrimination based on race.

Yeshiva University listed the top nine social justice issues of 2020:

- Voting rights and the barriers to voting that hold back low-income voters, seniors, and others.
- Climate justice and strengthening social responses to environmental changes, as they impact the wellbeing of entire communities and put a strain on resources.
- Quality healthcare coverage, especially concerning mental health care resources, which

affects the struggles of individuals and of entire communities.
- The crisis of refugees across the world trying to access education, healthcare, job opportunities, and other resources while trying to escape conflict and natural disasters.
- The devastating and long-term consequences of racial injustice on the mental and physical health of individuals.
- Income gaps, and pay equity based on race, gender, or sexuality.
- Gun violence, which impacts many people, both mentally and physically, including not only those who are injured or killed, but also their families and those who witness violence.
- Hunger and food insecurity remains a stubborn issue to solve. During the COVID pandemic, even food banks and free school lunches became unavailable or difficult to access.
- Equality pervades all of the other issues listed above. This is a Big Picture issue that helpers will continue to address.

Yes, acting on social justice issues is political and requires that its proponents take a public stand against injustice and inequities. After all, why are you a helper? It is more than just supporting individuals whose welfare or happiness has been affected by some injustice in society, it is also acting to make a difference for that individual and for others.

As helpers, we need to pay attention to the social factors that affect our clients' lives and struggles. Depression, anxiety, intimate partner violence, substance abuse, and health concerns often have their roots in poverty, unemployment, lack of affordable housing, the economy, and environmental worries. Helpers worldwide advocate for the big and the small issues effecting their communities.

In North America, unions play a major role in addressing social justice issues. Union reps routinely deal with questions concerning health changes and disability, on-the-job safety, career changes, interpersonal conflicts, discrimination, and oppression, harassment and bullying. While these may present to a helper as being of importance mostly to the individual employee seeking assistance, resolving them may involve wider initiatives that impact the workplace as a whole or even the entire community.

How to respond effectively

- As with most other issues, start by listening well, allowing the client to make their own conclusions and decisions, respecting their choices, even if they are not the same as yours would be, being available to support, avoiding making promises about the outcomes of your help or the client's actions, and referring on to someone else if more help is needed.
- Research the social justice issues your clients bring to you to learn about all their dimensions. Connect with other helpers and groups that have experience advocating and acting to improve the issues to solicit their expertise and their help. Mutual support and action can move mountains, making changes in society that have important and long-

lasting impacts.
- Now add in this step, essential to social justice issues: take whatever action is required and is within your group or organization's mandate to address any circumstances that are causing problems for your client. Think both of your individual client's needs and the needs of your community. Think globally, act locally.

To learn more

Michael Novak, Paul Adams, Elizabeth Shaw, *Social Justice Isn't What You Think*, Encounter Books, 2015.

Also review the online resources listed here:

> seawinds-education.mykajabi.com/o-pt-in-to-resources-for-the-non-therapist

Multiple issues

What if you recognize that your client has more than one issue? Life is always more complicated for someone with more than one situation to manage.

As we have seen, some common mental health issues such as depression and anxiety can complicate other situations, or even lead to problems such as substance abuse disorder. Struggles with other issues can also lead to mental health issues.

A woman stuck in an abusive relationship likely is experiencing some anxiety. The dude who feels his struggle with cocaine is hopeless may be depressed and may be considering suicide. The older worker struggling with social justice concerns may be under-producing at work and may be in danger of being fired. The single parent who is struggling to feed her children may be enveloped in grief for the life she has lost and may not be taking adequate care of her kids. The teen who has been sexually assaulted is traumatized and later begins to cut herself. The older gentleman who is alone and lonely and struggling to have enough healthy food to eat might become overly fond of his favourite whiskey.

Confusing, right? Where do you start?

How to respond effectively

- As with all helping encounters, begin by listening well. The client needs to feel seen and heard in her struggles and to know she has not bowled you, the helper, over with the intensity of her need. Adjust your Teflon cape if you need to. Ask what the client needs to deal with first and what type of help she wants from you.
- Address first the situations that are potentially life-threatening, such as suicidal thinking. The rest can wait.

- Next, look at the safety and well-being of others around your client. Do the children need care? Is there a child protection issue you need to report? Do the kids or a dependent adult need to be looked after while your client is dealing with his issues?
- Next, move to the circumstances which are contributing to other problems, such as depression, housing, finances, food security, intimate partner violence, or substance abuse disorder.
- Next, address the issues which are uncomfortable for the client but not an immediate threat to his wellbeing, such as grief, loneliness, or job insecurity.
- It is very likely that a referral to a helping agency or a pro therapist will be required. If you have done your homework and know what services are available in your area, you can choose the best resource for your client and his problems.

To learn more
Start with the online resources listed here:

> seawinds-education.mykajabi.com/o-pt-in-to-resources-for-the-non-therapist

Key take-away points

- Listening well is the recommended first step in any situation in which a helper is engaged.
- Looking after practical matters is a key role for a helper.
- Don't be afraid to take whatever action is required to support your client, friend, or community.

Activities to consolidate your learning

1. Research the agencies and services in your area to learn what is available for you and for your clients. Consider asking questions such as these:

- What is your organization's area of specialty? What services do you provide?
- Is your service based on some set of values or faith? Do clients need to share your values to receive service?
- Who can you accept as clients?
- What is the referral procedure you prefer?
- Is there any fee for your service?
- Do you have resources such as information pamphlets, videos?
- Do you have easy access to other professionals your client might need?
- Are you accessible 24/7? If not, how can your client reach help after hours?
- How do you safeguard your client's confidentiality?
- How do you work with other organizations and with the police?
- Who else do you recommend that I talk to?

2. If you work in a group or organization, consider assigning one issue or area of service to each person to research in more detail. Then each person can report back their findings to the group. You can develop a binder or electronic collection of notes about all the services and resources in your area for quick reference.

3. If you have a client with an issue, research that issue and how to respond to it. Develop a plan of action:

- What can I do to support this client's journey to wellness?
- What activities and tools would be useful to help this client?
- What services or agencies can I refer this client to when more help is needed?
- What do I need to learn to feel comfortable working with this client?
- What response can I expect from the client?

- What pitfalls or risks can I predict? What can I do to lessen the risks?

Don't forget to review the online resources listed here:

    seawinds-education.mykajabi.com/o-pt-in-to-resources-for-the-non-therapist

7: Plan and structure for a helping encounter

Now it's time to put it all together! Where do you put all the skills, the tools and the knowledge? It helps to have a bit of structure in mind.

When helping encounters occur, they will often not be planned ahead of time. They just happen, willy nilly, and you will need to respond as best you can under the circumstances. For example:

- A friend or neighbour drops in for coffee and you gab across the kitchen table, then she opens up about her relationship, which is a bit shaky.
- A community member calls and asks for advice with his teenaged son who is in distress, since he knows that you have the willingness to listen.
- You are a hairdresser and your client starts babbling about her messed-up job.
- You are a cabbie and the customer you are driving home from the bar starts crying.

In this type of situation, just dive in with some reflections and paraphrases and open-ended questions and trust your instincts, and your new knowledge and skills to lead you in a good direction.

Sometimes a helper has the luxury of being able to plan an encounter. You agree to meet with the community member or the neighbour or your friend, or you make an appointment to meet your parishioner in your parish office, or when you have a break from your nursing duties you plan to visit with a patient. You find a place that will be private and quiet, or perhaps you have an office where you can meet with your client. Lucky you! You have the time to think through how you will approach the encounter.

Even if the encounter is spontaneous, you can still have a bit of structure in mind.

Things will not always go the way you plan. You will frequently find yourself responding to the moment, maybe jumping about from one phase of the encounter to another and back again. Being flexible and open to unpredictability is helpful.

The basic structure that seems to work most of the time goes like this:

Phase 1: Contact
Use the skills of attending, empathy, respect, and reading body language to accomplish these groundwork steps:

- Set an atmosphere of trust and permission.
- Let the client know they are seen, heard and safe.

- Begin to assess the client's emotional state by their body language and voice.

Phase 2: Exploration
Use open-ended questions, paraphrasing, reflection of feeling, and clarification to find answers to these questions:

- What is happening in the client's life?
- What is the most important and immediate problem that needs to be addressed today?
- How does the client feel?
- Have there been any recent stresses, losses, changes, or challenges in the client's life?
- What else may have contributed to the problem?
- What coping mechanisms are working for the client?
- What is not working for the client?
- What supportive ties does the client have with other people?
- What is the client's goal? What does she want to get from your encounter?

Phase 3: Integration
Use open ended questions, scaling questions, miracle questions, clarification, paraphrasing, reflections, reframing, summarizing, supportive confrontation, and probing to learn the answers to these questions:

- What solutions are open to the client?
- What assistance does the client already have and what help will the client need?
- What outside resources would be available and appropriate for helping the client to deal with the issue?
- What does the client want to do? What can the client do?
- What does the client want you to do?
- What are the pros and cons of solutions the client comes up with?
- Is there need for immediate intervention from the counsellor, or can the client handle the situation on her own?

Phase 4: Action
Use assertive communication "I statements" to come to an agreement on who will do what to follow up on the conversation.

- I will do.....
- You will do...

What does all this look like in practice? Review the following abbreviated transcripts (the entire conversations would most likely take much longer). As you read, try to imagine what you would say before reading the Helper's lines. How close would your choice of words come to these? Would they accomplish the same thing?

Kate Tompkins

The first is a conversation between a member of the clergy and a parishioner and his teenaged son, which takes place in the church office. This example more or less follows the usual structure for a helping encounter.

~

Clergy:	Come in, come in! Nice to see you. May I take your coat? There's tea on the stove, can I get you some? The green chair is comfortable.	Making contact, establishing comfort

Aligns his own chair to be at an angle to those of his visitors.
        How can I help today?

Parishioner:	This is sort of awkward. I'm not sure where to start.	
Teenager:	Yeah right, of course you don't know. You don't know anything about me.	
Clergy:	Well I can see there is some tension between you two, can we start there?	Reflection to respond to the obvious emotion
Teenager:	Tension? You can say that again.	
Parishioner:	Eric, calm down. That won't help.	

The teenager fumes in his chair.

Clergy:	Eric, I can see that you have something important on your mind.	Observation of body language to begin exploration
Teenager:	He made me come here. I tell him about the most important thing I have ever told him, and he gets all weird and tells me we have to go see you. What the hell can you do?	
Clergy:	I'm not sure, but I can at least try.	
Parishioner:	Yes I did want you to come here today. Maybe together we can talk some sense into you.	
Teenager:	I'm not going to change! Can't you see that? Getting all holier than thou won't change who I am, you asshole!	
Clergy:	Let's all take a deep breath.	Model self-regulation

He breathes obviously, deeply and slowly, in an exaggerated way, and the parishioner and son both breathe with him and calm a little.

	Now, I gather that some important conversation has taken place that was upsetting for both of you. I'd love to hear about it.	Offer support and assistance, but don't make promises about outcomes
Parishioner:	Eric told me last night that he is gay. I'm sure he doesn't really mean it, it's just a phase. He'll get over it.	
Teenager:	No I wont! Can't you see? This is ME! This always has been me. You just don't want to know about it.	

The Non-Therapist

Parishioner: Your mother is devastated. How could you do this to her? You are selfish and rude. What will our friends say?

Clergy: Eric, I can hear that you are very distressed about this conversation. And Tom, you seem concerned, too. I can assure you that anything said in this office, stays in this office. I can see that both of you feel hurt. Eric, let's start with you. I'd love to know if you can tell me what your father is feeling. Can you put yourself in his shoes?

> Reframe away from blame, toward healthy expressions of emotions

Teenager: I guess he just doesn't understand. He thought he was bringing up a good Christian boy who is just like himself. But I'm not!

Clergy: Tom, can you tell me what your son is feeling?

Parishioner takes a deep breath.

Parishioner: I expect he feels hurt. I guess I did not respond very well last night, son, I'm sorry. I just don't get it.

Clergy: Eric, I notice that you seem a bit more comfortable. How are you feeling right now?

> Asking each to imagine what the other is feeling helps build empathy between the father and son and helps both feel heard so they can calm down and be able to listen

Teenager: I guess I did fly off the handle myself. Sorry, dad. I wish you could understand.

Clergy: I am curious to know what set off the difficult conversation you had last night.

> Invitation, prompting both to look deeper

Parishioner: I guess it started when I criticized Eric's choice of clothing. It seems too wild to me. And that hair! Too flamboyant. Why would you want to dress that way? You will just draw attention to yourself. What were you thinking?

Teenager: I *want* to draw attention to myself. I want the world to know who I really am. I don't want to hide anymore. I am gay! Please accept that, dad.

Parishioner: *(to the clergy.)* What do you think? Is this real? What Eric is doing? What he says he is going through?

Clergy: It's not for me to say what is in Eric's head; that is for Eric to say. But I do see from his body language, and I hear in his voice, how important it is for him that you accept who he is right now.

> Observation of body language. Put the issue back into the client's hands.

Teenager starts to cry.

Teenager: Yeah, dad. I just want you to love me, no matter what clothes I wear, or how I wear my hair, or who I want to hang out with. Can't you see that?

Parishioner: Yes I guess I can see that. I guess I need to learn

	more.	
Clergy:	How is everything else going in your family right now?	Exploring other factors that may contribute to the issue
Parishioner:	Well, there are some problems at work that are stressing me out. I guess that has made me more anxious than usual. I suppose I jumped too easily.	
Teenager:	I was afraid to tell you this, dad, but I failed my math midterm last week. My teacher says I need to pull up my socks to make it through the semester. I need help, a tutor or something.	
Parishioner:	You got it, Eric. I always had trouble with math in school when I was your age. We'll work that out.	
Clergy:	If I were to wave my magic wand and tell you that a miracle happened overnight tonight, and both of you woke up the next morning and found that everything was fantastic, how would it look to you? How would you act yourself? What would you feel?	A miracle question to create a vision of what could be
Parishioner:	Eric would be happy and successful. He would be a grade A student. His mother would be happy and I would have my son back.	
Teenager:	A grade A student. Yeah! And dad would play hockey with me again. And I could dress like I want.	
Clergy:	What needs to happen for you to both get there? To that great vision you both have?	Integration. Client comes up with the possible solutions.
Parishioner:	I need to spend more quality time with Eric. I guess I have been too busy lately to pay attention like I should.	
Teenager:	I need for someone else to write my math exams for me!	
Everyone laughs.		
Clergy:	Where would you like to go from here? How can I help? What would be of most use to your family right now?	Begin to create an action plan
Parishioner:	I think mom and I need to learn more about what this is all about. And I should talk to someone about what is happening at work so I can de-stress some. Maybe then it will be easier for me to listen.	
Clergy:	That is something I might be able to help with. I know a therapist in town here who you could talk to, to help you explore this new reality in your family's life. And I can direct you to an agency that can provide information. Eric, what do you need?	

The Non-Therapist

Teenager:	I'd like to meet some other gay guys. I want to know what its like. Being gay. Surviving at school, I mean, I don't want to be bullied.
Clergy:	Give me some time to do some research, I think I know someone you can talk to, but I'll need to check it with him first. I'll get back to you in a week or so, is that okay?
Teenager:	Thanks! Sick.
Parishioner:	What? Sick?
Teenager:	It means great, dad. Jeesh.
Parishioner:	Oh. Okay, then.
Clergy:	Is there anything else that needs to get talked about today?
Parishioner:	I feel better. Thanks.
Clergy:	I'm here if you want to talk more, anytime. Just give me a call.

(margin note: Externalizing the problem)

The second transcript is a coffee meeting over the dining room table that becomes a helping encounter.

~

Neighbour:	Knock knock? You home?
Helper:	Come on in! Coffee?
Neighbour:	Yeah, thanks, I could use a pick-me-up.
Helper:	A "pick-me-up?" What's up? You look worried.
Neighbour:	Oh, it's nothing, just, well, life, I guess. You know.
Helper:	Life? Hmmm. Well, what is going on in yours today?
Neighbour:	Not much. Nothing new, anyway. God, my head hurts. The 24-ounce flu! There seem to be more and more mornings when I wake up this way.
Helper:	I'll bet that's rough. Do you want some Tylenol?
Neighbour:	Now, don't get all moral with me.
Helper:	No worries. You know that when you want to talk, I am here.
Neighbour:	Yeah, I know. Sorry I went off on you like that. I guess I'm a bit twitchy today. I will take a Tylenol, thanks.
Helper:	There's more on your mind, I can see it written all over you.
Neighbour:	You always could see right through me. Yeah, it's Glenn again.

(margin notes: Indicates helper heard the underlying thought; Exploration, picks up on what is not said; Offers understanding, unconditional support and practical help, but not judgement.)

227

Kate Tompkins

She pulls up the sleeve of her sweater, where a recent bruise in the shape of three fingers can be seen on her arm.

        He threw me against the wall last night. That was a new one. Usually it's just a twisted arm or a foul look and an insult. If it weren't for Shadow barking like an insane animal I don't know if he would have stopped at that. He was like someone I have never seen before. His eyes were like ice and kinda bulging outta his face. *(She shivers.)*

Helper: It's getting worse, isn't it?

The neighbour nods silently, her eyes cast down.

Helper: There is a phone number I'd like you to have. Here, it's on this card. This is the Women's Centre in town. They have counsellors there who understand. I went to check them out last week, to see what they can offer. The women I spoke with were really friendly and kind, and knowledgeable.   *[Offers a helpful resource, no judgment]*   *[Helper is prepared]*

Neighbour: Well, maybe. It's hard to talk about. I trust you, but how can I face anyone else? I'm supposed to be a leader in this community. What if word gets out?

Helper: I understand your concern, but think about it this way. Confidentiality is a big part of what the Women's Centre offers. Your secrets would be safe with them. What is more important is keeping you safe.   *[Reframing to highlight what is most important]*

Neighbour: Yeah, well. Maybe. If I'm still here by then.

Helper: If you are still here? What do you mean?

Neighbour mumbles something, shifts in her chair. She is looking anywhere except at her friend.   *[Picking up on what is hinted at]*

Helper: Janice, what's wrong?

Tears are forming, but she is silent.

Helper: I can see that this is really bothering you. I need to ask a nosy question. Janice, are you thinking about hurting yourself?   *[Responding to the obvious emotion with a direct]*

Neighbour turns away, then starts to cry.

Neighbour: I can't stand it anymore. I think about it all the time. I married Glenn for ever, for better or for worse. I just never thought it would get this bad. I pick up that damn bottle—God, I hate that stuff!—so I can sleep after he does something to me. It's the only way I can escape for a while. I don't know which will happen first. Will he get really bad one night and kill me? Will I just end up sick and die of alcohol poisoning?

The Non-Therapist

	Or maybe I should just drive off the bridge and get it over with myself. God, I'm a mess. How can you stand to sit here with me?	
Helper:	Janice, I can tell that you are really upset. It must be terrible to feel that way. I'm not going anywhere, old friend. I'm afraid you are stuck with me!	Helper lets her know she is okay to hear whatever the neighbour has to say

Neighbour looks at the Helper with gratitude, sniffles some more, and blows her nose. She throws a look at her friend that says 'Thank God for you!'

Helper:	First I want you to know that there is hope, and there is help. Now, let's talk about this some more. When was the last time you felt like hurting yourself?	As soon as suicide is hinted at, dive in to assess her current risk.
Neighbour:	This morning. On the way here. I even thought about it as I drove past the bridge down the road. But I kept on going. And now, here I am.	Her risk is immediate. Respond to her suicidal thinking. All else can wait.

Helper takes a deep breath, drops her jaw, and adjusts her Teflon Cape.

Helper:	I'm glad you kept on going. Okay, so it's on your mind right now. And you are quite agitated about what happened last night. I'd like to take you to the hospital, to talk with the nurse practitioner. She should be able to give you a room for a few nights, so that she can keep an eye on you, and she can refer you to the Mental Health team so you can talk to a pro.	Client has shown manner, motive, a viable plan and the means to do it, so immediate care is called for. Don't waste time. Take charge.

Neighbour nods, sniffles some more.

Helper:	Then sometime later, if you like, I can go with you to talk to the Women's Centre.	

Neighbour sits up a tiny bit straighter.

Neighbour	Okay. I guess that would be good.	Action plan. For the issues with less immediate risk, the onus is on the client to act or not when she is ready to.
Helper:	But let's get you to the hospital first, okay? Then sometime later, if you like, I can go to an AA meeting with you. I think they meet on Thursdays.	
Neighbour:	*(Weakly.)* Thanks	

Here the helper adapted the usual structure to respond to the immediate risk. As soon as suicide is in the air, that should be the focus. Using your judgement and responding to whatever is right in front of you is more important than adhering to any plan.

The third example follows a social worker (SW) and a client and illustrates the typical structure for a helping encounter.

~

Kate Tompkins

SW:	Welcome, come on in! Have a seat.	
Client:	Thanks.	
SW:	How can I help today?	Begin with an open-ended question
Client:	I'm not sure. I need to talk, I guess.	
SW:	You are certainly welcome to talk here. What is on your mind today?	
Client:	It's my job. I've been working at the same place now for nine years. I have really liked my job; that is, up until now.	
SW:	Up until now? I gather something has changed for you.	Pick up on what is not said with a paraphrase
Client:	Well, not, really. Little piddly things, I guess. Nothing really horrible.	
SW:	Such as?	
Client:	Well, the locks have changed; security issues, they say. It's annoying but not really major.	

SW nods; waits quietly.

Client:	And our shift scheduling is kinda confusing. I guess it's hard to balance when we are so short-staffed.	
SW:	I would imagine it is. How do the changes impact you?	Acknowledge the issues described, open the door for more information with an open-ended question
Client:	I just need to adapt to working on Monday mornings again! No biggie.	
SW:	Ah, I see.	
Client:	Even the toilet paper is different. I know that sounds petty, but, you know, comfort and all that.	
SW:	So there have been some minor changes that you tell me are no big deal. Yet you started by saying you were happy until now. So I'm confused. What has caused you to be less than super happy with your job?	Paraphrase to highlight the discrepancies: a supportive confrontation
Client:	(*Thinks a bit, bites her lip*). You know, now that I think about it, nothing, really! (*They both laugh*).	
SW:	Okay, so now I'm really curious, what else is going on in your life?	Dig deeper to search for the real issue with an open-ended question
Client:	Well you know, I think it's just that my dream job may be opening up in June. I'd love to get that job! I think I'll quit my current job so I'll be free to take that new job when it comes up. That's it! I'll quit tomorrow!	
SW:	Let's think this out some more. You seem to be mov-	Paraphrase for clarity

	ing really quickly to leave a job you already have, that is secure and that you really love, to wait for another job that may or may not be available, sometime, and which maybe you could win if you apply, or maybe not. Is that about the size of it?	
Client:	(*Sheepishly*). Yeah, I guess so.	
SW:	How do you feel about that plan?	Open-ended question to promote reflection
Client:	Confused. It seemed like such a good idea for a moment there! I don't want to miss out on the potential new dream job.	
SW:	Yeah, I could see that. What if the new job does not open up? Or what if you don't win it?	Probing to encourage analysis
Client:	Oh, good point. I could end up high and dry with no job. I think I was so excited when I heard about that new job, I may have actually invented issues with my current job. That's it. I think I have been looking for excuses to focus on the dream job. But you are right. It would be risky.	
SW:	Ah yes, I understand.	Validation of client's ideas
Client:	So what should I do?	
SW:	What do you want to do? What would be the best choice for you?	Put problem solving into the client's hands
Client:	(*Thinks*). What I want to do is to jump right into my dream job this afternoon. But I realize now that would not be wise. So what I should do is just stick it out in this job to see what happens.	
SW:	That sounds like a good plan. But I can see in your face that there is more on your mind.	Validate client's plan. Point out incongruence in body language
Client:	Yeah. It's my hubby. He is being downsized at his work. He may have only another month. Then what happens? Maybe that is why I was so anxious to start that new job. It pays more, you see.	
SW:	I do see. What type of help would you like from me?	Again putting solutions in the client's hands
Client:	Nothing, thanks. I see now what I need to do. My hubby needs career advice and I need to relax about all this. Thanks for listening.	
SW:	You are welcome. Any time.	

Here, the best help was simply to let the client figure out the issues and the solutions on her own. She needed a place to reflect, to be heard, and validated. Then she was able to look after the rest without any further assistance.

Kate Tompkins

So now you are ready! You have learned the basics. You know how to craft your own role. You know about the foundations of helping and you can use paraphrases, reflection, open-ended questions, and the other basic listening skills in a helping context. You can plan a helping encounter and you have at least some idea what to expect and how to respond.

What's next? Get out there and use your skills! Anywhere, any time. With anyone. In any circumstance.

Why not be part of changing the world?

To learn more
Start with the online resources listed here:

>seawinds-education.mykajabi.com/o-pt-in-to-resources-for-the-non-therapist

Key take-away points

- Plan a helping encounter when you can, and just dive in when helping is spontaneous.
- Be flexible and open to the unexpected.

Activities to consolidate your learning

1. Ask a friend to help you with some role-playing. Your friend can use a real situation, which is best, or make up something feasible. Pretend that the two of you are in a helping encounter, with your friend as the client, and respond as if the scenario were real. Ask your friend to give you feedback on how she felt in response to your words and make note of any techniques or approaches that worked especially well; and those which did not advance the conversation in a healthy or useful way, or which caused an issue.
2. After a helping encounter, debrief by talking with a colleague or supervisor about the conversation. Review your approach and its results and seek feedback from your colleague about your part in the encounter.
3. If you are working with a group of people to provide a helping service, the group can role play and provide feedback together so that all may learn from each other. Take turns being the client and the helper. Make note of what approaches you liked as a client and which you did not, and notice their impact on you. The group should probably agree on a way to safeguard any confidential information that was revealed, since role playing often has elements of truth, as people usually bring in their own life experience to the exercises.

> In my clergy days, I found it important to note down things I might not just remember (name of parishioner's aunt's nasty boyfriend) as soon after the counseling meeting as possible, (And keep them in a secure place, of course.)
>
> I also found this useful on occasions when the person in need went away having heard something I did not say.
>
> - Andrew Wetmore, editor

8: Wrap-up

This chapter offers you a chance to assess your skills, and provides links to resources to help you to learn more.

How can I assess my skills?

You may already have some useful skills in your tool box. If you are a person with compassion and interest in other people, you may already have some understanding of what to do and say to be helpful. You may even feel that helping comes naturally to you. Maybe you have attended some training to enhance your natural abilities. Maybe your initial professional preparation included basic counselling skills, even though you might feel somewhat rusty now if you have not used them often.

Here are some suggestions for assessing what you already know how to do and where you need to refresh your knowledge.

- Ask your friends who they might go to if they had a problem. If it's you, that's a good sign! If not, (and if the friend is a **good** friend!), ask why not you? You might learn something that will guide you in your journey to becoming a more effective helper.
- While watching TV or a movie, or reading a book, see if you can come up with appropriate and useful comments to help a character resolve their problem.
- Ask a professional therapist to share their #1 secret for success with a client. If the suggestion is new to you, maybe it's time to learn about the new skill.
- After you have helped someone, and the need for intense intervention has past and the person has calmed down, ask them what helped them the most. If it was something you did, great! If it was something that someone else did, then it's time to learn about what the other person did that was helpful.
- Ask yourself tough questions, and be honest with yourself. Is there anything you are uncertain about, or a skill you wish you had, or a skill you think you have that does not seem to be working too well? Is there any aspect of your helping activity that you feel uncomfortable with? Or that you find yourself BSing about? If so, it's time to plan a way to learn what you need to know.
- Ask your colleagues for feedback. What have they seen you do in a helping context that was actually helpful? Is there anything they saw that was unhelpful, and why? This can help you pinpoint knowledge and skills that will enhance your ability to help.
- Take the skills self-assessment quiz that follows. (Be honest, now!)

Self-Assessment Quiz

You might be able to come up with lots of helpful responses, other than these. But of those offered below, which do you think would be the most helpful?

1. A 23-year-old man says, "I see no future. I'm a waste of skin."
   Which of the following responses would be most helpful, and why?
   a) Well, I like your skin.
   b) I hear desperation in your voice. I'm here to listen, if you want to talk about it some more.
   c) You are scaring me. Let's talk about yesterday's game.

2. A woman says, "I just can't forget about what he did to me. I think about it all the time, I can't sleep, I'm making mistakes at work, and I snap at my kids. I think I'm going crazy."
   Which of the following responses would be most helpful, and why?
   a) A good night's sleep will help. Have you taken some sleeping pills?
   b) I can babysit, if that would help.
   c) It sounds like you have lots going on right now. How can I help?

3. A neighbour child comes to play with your child. Normally, your child's friend is happy, bubbly, full of fun and energy. However, today she is quiet, withdrawn, close to tears. You notice a bruise on her arm that looks like finger marks.
   Which of the following responses would be most helpful, and why?
   a) You seem sad today. Is everything okay? Is there anything you'd like to talk about?
   b) Tell me everything. I'm a counsellor, you know.
   c) That's a bruise. Were you a bad girl at home? Do you really expect me to believe that you fell off your bike?

4. A man in your community suicides. His widow is distraught.
   Which of the following responses would be most helpful, and why?
   a) He's gone to a better place. Just trust that he will be fine.
   b) You are welcome to stay as long as you need to. Don't worry about anything, we will look after all the details.
   c) Here is a tuna casserole. Get better, okay?

5. A woman tells you that she is pretty messed up, her life is in a shambles, she gets angry far too often, she has nightmares, she startles much more easily than her friends, and she is often very emotional over nothing much. You ask her a few well-crafted, open-ended questions, and eventually she admits that she was sexually assaulted as a child and the memory still haunts her.
Which of the following responses would be most helpful, and why?
a) No problem, I can fix that for you. Just tell me all about it.
b) Get a grip, girl! That was ages ago, no need for you to be crying about it now. It's done.
c) That sounds rough. I can continue to meet with you anytime to chat, but it sounds like you may have PTSD. That is above my pay grade, but I can put you in touch with a therapist who can treat you for PTSD. Would that interest you?

6. A man seems disoriented, is talking to himself, and says he sees things that should not be there, and hears voices that only he can hear. He is walking down the street waving a gun. You were called to intervene by the local municipal bylaw officer who found him and is trailing him with his car.
Which of the following responses would be most helpful, and why?
a) This man needs to go to the hospital (or the nursing station). This is not the time for me to help him; he needs psychiatric help. Since he has a weapon, I suggest that you call the police and have them escort him to the hospital. Maybe you could continue to follow him in your car to monitor him and tell the police where he is.
b) No bloody way! I'm not getting involved in that mess!
c) Ah, ummm, sure...I guess I can see what I can do.

Self-Assessment Quiz discussion

1. A 23-year-old man says "I see no future. I'm a waste of skin."

Responses	Discussion
a. Well, I like your skin.	Does not acknowledge client's distress. Makes a joke of his deep feelings, minimizes and trivializes his experience. By not acknowledging his desperation and likely suicidal thoughts, you are signalling that it is not okay to talk about suicide. Check out the sections in this book "Be a mirror for your client" (Ch 4), "Empathy" (Ch 3) and "Suicidal thinking" (Ch 6).
b. I hear your desperate feelings in your voice I'm here to listen, if you want to talk about it some more.	**Best response** Opens the door for the client to say more if he wishes to, which gives him permission to talk about uncomfortable feelings.
c. You are scaring me. Let's talk about yesterday's game.	An honest description of your own feelings, but as in the first response, you are saying outright that your client is not supposed to tell the truth about how he feels. Check out the section "Empathy" (Ch 3).

2. A woman says, "I just can't forget about what he did to me. I think about it all the time, I can't sleep, I'm making mistakes at work, and I snap at my kids. I think I'm going crazy."

Responses	Discussion
a. A good night's sleep will help. Have you taken some sleeping pills?	Ignores the main issues. Jumps to advice given in a way that might make her feel wrong if she had not taken pills. Also prescribes without a medical licence. Check out the sections "Empathy" (Ch 3), "Ask helpful questions" (Ch 4) and "Intimate partner violence" (Ch 6).
b. I can babysit, if that would help.	It might be helpful to babysit, it's good to know that someone is there to support; but it fails to acknowledge the main issues.

Responses	Discussion
	Check out the section "Be a mirror for your client" (Ch 4).
c. It sounds like you have lots going on right now. How can I help?	**Best response** Acknowledges that the client has multiple concerns, and opens the door for her to say more. By putting the control of whether and how she speaks about her issues into the client's hands, not only gives her space to talk freely, it also helps to empower her, which she may need in order to take action to improve her life.

3. A neighbour child comes to play with your child. Normally, your child's friend is happy, bubbly, full of fun and energy. However, today she is quiet, withdrawn, close to tears. You notice a bruise on her arm that looks like finger marks.

Responses	Discussion
a. You seem sad today. Is everything okay? Is there anything you'd like to talk about?	**Best response** Acknowledges the child's mood, and gives her the option to talk about what is really going on, or not. With that permission, the child is more likely to be open and honest. But be prepared for the child to hide the truth if it was a parent who hurt her. What would you do next?
b. Tell me everything. I'm a counsellor you know.	Big deal. Why would she care? Heavy handed and arrogant, which kids do understand. Expect her to disappear without talking much. Check out the sections "Ask helpful questions" (Ch 4) and "Child Protection" (Ch 6).
c. That's a bruise. Were you a bad girl at home? Do you really expect me to believe that you fell off your bike?	Really? By suggesting that she has been bad, is lying, or is to blame for being injured will send her running. She is more likely to respond well to gentleness. Check out the sections "Ask helpful questions", "The body cannot lie" (Ch 3) and "Clarify and confront therapeutically" (Ch 4).

4. A man in your community suicides. His widow is distraught.

Responses	Discussion
a. He's gone to a better place. Just trust that he will be fine.	Platitudes are the last thing she needs to hear right now. Fails to acknowledge her shock and her likely mixed emotions at this terrible time. Check out the sections "Empathy" (Ch 3) and "Be a mirror for your client" (Ch 4).
b. You are welcome to stay as long as you need to. Don't worry about anything, we will look after all the details.	**Best response** When a person is in shock after a crisis, she needs a safe supportive place to spend time in, and safe, supportive, gentle people to look after her and all the practical details that always accompany a tragedy of this type. She may want to talk at some point, but just being there is probably the most immediate need for her right now.
c. Here is a tuna casserole. Get better, okay?	Well maybe she will appreciate the food as it's one less detail to have to worry about. But it fails to acknowledge the widow's feelings and her immediate emotional needs. Check out the sections "Be a mirror for your client" and "Empathy" (Ch 3), and "Suicidal thinking" (Ch 6).

5. A woman tells you that she is pretty messed up, her life is in a shambles, she gets angry far too often, she has nightmares, she startles much more easily than her friends, and she is often very emotional over nothing much. You ask her a few well-crafted open-ended questions, and eventually she admits that she was sexually assaulted as a child and the memory still haunts her.

Responses	Discussion
a. No problem, I can fix that for you. Just tell me all about it.	Enthusiasm is great, and your confidence may give her hope, but you are making promises you don't know how to keep, you are BSing, and you are taking away from her the opportunity to learn for herself, which is an important part of the healing process. Check out "Be a mirror" (Ch 3).
b. Get a grip, girl! That was ages ago, no need for you to	Minimizes the woman's distress, implies that she should not be hurting, and that she is unacceptable if she has PTSD

Responses	Discussion
be crying about it now. It's done.	symptoms. Totally disrespectful. This client will evaporate.
c. That sounds rough. I can continue to meet with you anytime to chat, but it sounds like you may have PTSD. That is above my pay grade, but I can put you in touch with a therapist who can treat you for PTSD. Would that interest you?	**Best response** It acknowledges her distress, but does not promise miracle cures you cannot provide. Providing a referral to a trauma therapist is the best option for this client.

6. A man seems disoriented, is talking to himself, and says he sees things that should not be there, and hears voices that only he can hear. He is walking down the street waving a gun. You were called to intervene by the local municipal bylaw officer who found him and is trailing him with his car.

Responses	Discussion
a. This man needs to go to the hospital (or the nursing station). This is not the time for me to help him; he needs psychiatric help. Since he has a weapon, I suggest that you call the police and have them escort him to the hospital. Maybe you could continue to follow him in your car to monitor him and tell the police where he is.	**Best response** The man needs psychiatric assessment and there is no role for a helper to play at this point. Since he has a weapon, stay away from the situation, for now. After he has received psychiatric help, there may be a role for ordinary support.
b. No bloody way! I'm not getting involved in that mess!	The instinct to stay away is a good one, but does not offer the bylaw officer any support or guidance about how to proceed.
c. Ah, ummm, sure…I guess I can see what I can do.	Dangerous, because the client is incapable of rational thinking at the moment, so there is no advantage to anyone in

Responses	Discussion
	agreeing to try to help. There is no value in meekly accepting this request and its associated risk. Be assertive and do what you know is right, even if it is not what the caller asked of you. Check out the section on "When should I call in the big guns" (Ch 3).

If you got most of these right and can explain why, then congratulations! You are on your way to being an effective helper.

If you missed some, go back and review your choices and assess which skills you need to brush up on.

How can I learn new skills?

Online courses

- The Canadian Mental Health Association offers many on-line courses in various mental health issues. This link will get you to CMHA's main page where you can view courses available in your region. cmha.ca/what-we-do/national-programs/recovery-colleges
- Mental Health First Aid is the help provided to a person developing a mental health problem, experiencing a mental health crisis, or a worsening of their mental health. They have trained more than 500,000 Canadians since 2007. This link will take you to the Canadian site where you can enrol in a course: mentalhealthcommission.ca/what-we-do/mental-health-first-aid/ .
    - This link takes you to a US site: mentalhealthfirstaid.org/.
    - This is a site in the UK: mhfaengland.org/
- *The Non-Therapist* is available as an on-line course with offerings tailored to specific occupations. Check here for current course dates: seawinds-education.mykajabi.com. Lots of hands-on practice to consolidate your skills and a community of like-minded folks to network with. A great follow-up after reading this book!
- Readers of *The Non-Therapist* are invited to join me in a monthly get-together to network, discuss ideas, ask questions, and share stories and strategies. No charge to join this group. Register here:
    seawinds-education.mykajabi.com/opt-in-to-the-non-therapist-discussion-group
- The Breakout Pro is an online course aimed at women who are in abusive relationships. The Breakout Pro for Frontline Workers is aimed at helpers who want to be effective supporting women in abusive relationships. Lots of hands-on exercises and a community of supportive people.
    - Both can be accessed at seawinds-education.mykajabi.com.
- Visit the seawinds-education link, below, for a link to an online course for trauma

victims by Peter Levine PhD, one of the world's leading authorities on trauma.
- nicabm.com. This site offers on-line courses aimed at therapists, but non-therapists are welcome, too. The focus is treatment for post-trauma issues, but there are other courses and infographics as well that you can download.
- pesi.com/ and psychotherapy.com.au/ offer online courses aimed at therapists and counsellors that anyone may access. A variety of topics.
- tarabrach.com/ Tara Brach is a well-respected teacher of mindfulness. Her site provides courses, guided meditations, and other resources for dealing with a wide variety of issues using mindfulness techniques.

In-person resources

- Visit your local Canadian Mental Health office for pamphlets, information, and friendly folks to chat with.
- In the USA, visit the American Mental Health Association offices.
- Visit any of the agencies in your area that provide mental health services.

Books and magazines

- *Mind Over Mood, Change How You Feel By Changing the Way You Think,* Christine Padesky, Richard Greenberger, Guilford Press, 2016. The website mindovermood.com also provides other resources for readers. This is the "bible" for do-it-yourself Cognitive Behavioural Therapy.
- *The Body Keeps the Score,* Bessel Van Der Kolk, Viking Press, 2014. About PTSD, what it is, how it works and how to treat it. Bessel Van Der Kolk is the worlds leading expert on trauma treatment.
- *Waking the Tiger: Healing Trauma*, Peter Levine, PhD, North Atlantic Books, 1997. Peter Levine is also a world class expert on Trauma Treatment.
- *Getting Past Your Past, Take Control of Your Life with Self-Help Techniques from EMDR Therapy*, Francine Shapiro, Rodale Press, 2013. A do-it-yourself treatment for PTSD from the grandmother of EMDR, the go-to treatment for PTSD.
- *Psychotherapy Networker* Magazine and its website, psychotherapynetworker.org. Published every two months with articles of interest to therapists and other helpers.
- *Psychology Today* Magazine, and its website, psychologytoday.com/ca. A monthly magazine for the general public with the latest research presented in readable form.
- *Handbook Patients' Spiritual and Cultural Values for Health Care Professionals*, spiritualcareassociation.org/resources.html. A desk guide to the cultural dimensions of helping.

Even more!

This web page has links to many, many online resources:

>seawinds-education.mykajabi.com/o-pt-in-to-resources-for-the-non-therapist

Key take-away points

- Learning can be a life-long adventure. An effective helper is always on the look-out for new ideas, new research, new tools, and new skills to add to their toolbox.
- Focus your research on trusted websites.

The final words

Here is my final thought to guide your day: Learn the techniques, then forget them and just focus on the human being in front of you. When you have a good connection with people, something transformative can happen.

Go out and change the world, helpers. We can make a difference!

The Non-Therapist

Kate Tompkins

Acknowledgements

Kate:

Thanks to the police officers, social workers, child protection workers, nurses, union reps, firefighters, HR people, chaplains, community advocates, clergy, teenaged school peer listeners, mental health workers, sport coaches, and neighbours who shared their thoughts on what to include in *The Non-Therapist*. I won't name all these people who allowed me to pick their brains in preparation for writing this book, to safeguard their confidentiality, but you know who you are!

Thanks to Christina Baxter, my friend, colleague and partner in crime as we explore the Cape Breton back roads searching for epic views, tasty treats and incredible crafts. Christina slogged through every word of the manuscript, torturing those excess commas, tactfully asking, "What the heck does this mean?" and adding some examples and words of wisdom to the text.

Thanks to my old friend Liz who does not yet know that thoughts of her, talking with a friend over a coffee at her kitchen table, helped me keep my target audience in mind as I wrote.

And thanks to my fur-faced kids, Charlie and Sammy, who kept me real.

Christina:

First, I want to thank my flying partners. You taught me many useful skills, like how to ask for the bathroom and how much something costs in the language *du jour* of each lay over, how to keep passengers happy when a flight is dispatched 50 meals short, and how to stay calm in the face of whatever madness was happening in the moment. You are an amazing, interesting, and compassionate group. Never let anyone tell you differently.

Gerald, Lynne, David, and Ben, thank you for allowing me to learn from you as we accompanied those in need of spiritual care. Any mistakes in what is offered in this book are mine.

To my friends and family in the US, thank you for hanging in there with me even though you thought I was crazy to move from Sunny California to Snowy Nova Scotia. To the new friends I have made here, thank you for making me feel at home. Kate, thank you for inviting me to accompany you on the journey that is this book. And, it involved no time on the water! Now that the "Battle of the Commas" is over, I look forward to more Cape Breton road trips.

Finally to Olivia, my fur person: you are a little Buddha teaching me mindfulness daily.

Kate Tompkins

About the authors

Kate Tompkins is a rather white-haired curmudgeon who has been around the block several times. In her 50 years as a therapist and adult educator, she has worked with many small communities in crisis, and helped create community support groups, peer counselling groups, local shelters and crisis support phone lines. She has taught counselling skills to frontline workers, such as nurses, social workers, addictions counsellors, supervisors and union reps; and runs on-line in-service courses for therapists.

Kate is currently a Registered Counselling Therapist with a private practice in Nova Scotia, Canada; and an adult educator. She lives in a sleepy town with her two dogs, a sailboat and a penchant for musical theatre.

Photo by Brian Collins, Landwash Studios

Christina Baxter spent decades as a flight attendant, seeing the world one layover at a time. When not exploring the world on lay overs, she volunteered at a wildlife hospital cleaning dirty cages, scraping disgusting sheets and towels prior to laundering them, and eventually learning how to handle wildlife during exams. She managed to survived being bitten by a turkey vulture and not being bitten by the squirrel that got loose during an exam.

She then made the seemingly-weird transition to becoming a Board Certified Chaplain. Surprisingly, there was a lot of overlap in the two careers—gulping meals on the go, dealing with the diverse cultures of those she served, and never knowing what to expect when a code is called, or the "all call" from the flight deck.

Although retired, Christina keeps busy exploring The Bay of Fundy beaches, attending local craft shows, and keeping in touch with friends old and new. She lives with her fur person in a small village in the Annapolis Valley.

Milton Keynes UK
Ingram Content Group UK Ltd.
UKHW052006011224
451694UK00002B/13

9 781998 149681